WITHDRAWN

INSIDE PITCH

Life in

Professional

Baseball

George Gmelch

With a new chapter by the author

UNIVERSITY OF NEBRASKA PRESS
LINCOLN AND LONDON

First Nebraska paperback printing: 2006

Library of Congress Cataloging-in-Publication Data
Gmelch, George.
Inside pitch: life in professional baseball / George Gmelch with a new chapter by the author.
p.   cm.
Originally published: Washington, D.C.: Smithsonian Institution Press, 2001.
Includes bibliographical references and index.
ISBN-13: 978-0-8032-7128-9 (pbk.: alk. paper)
ISBN-10: 0-8032-7128-X (pbk.: alk. paper)
1. Baseball players—United States—Social conditions.   2. Baseball players—United States—Attitudes.   3. Baseball players—Professional relationships—United States.   I. Title.
GV867.64.G64   2006
796.357′640973—dc22   2006014981

For my father, George Sr., who introduced me to baseball;

my mother, Edna, who watched me play; my wife, Sharon,

who encouraged me to study the game; and my son, Morgan,

who made me a fan again.

Contents

Preface and Acknowledgments

For fans, baseball is entertainment, a diversion from the tedium of everyday life. For players, baseball, though a game, is a demanding occupation so encompassing that it becomes a way of life. For those who make it to the big leagues it is also the fulfillment of boyhood dreams, and the savings from even a short career in the majors can set a man up for life. Behind the fame and fortune, however, is the daily grind with few days off, half of each season spent on the road, frequent separations from wives and children, unrelenting pressure to perform, and the trauma and uncertainties of inevitable slumps and injuries.

My anthropological interest in baseball, the most cerebral of the team games, began in the 1960s when I was a minor leaguer in the Detroit Tigers farm system and attended college in the off-season. Returning to campus after my fourth season, I took an anthropology course called "Magic, Religion, and Witchcraft" in which my professor described the rituals of the Trobriand Islanders. I was struck by the similarities between what these so-called primitive peoples did to ensure their safety and success with what my teammates and I did to bring ourselves luck. I wrote a paper about it ("Baseball Magic"), and my professor encouraged me to examine other aspects of the game. But at the time I was too young and inexperienced as a fieldworker and too immersed in baseball to see it clearly.

Once in graduate school, and out of baseball, I turned to more traditional topics—development in Mexico and urbanization in Ireland—and put baseball out of mind. For the next two decades I scarcely noticed the game; I did not even watch the World Series. I was still fond of baseball, but I was often abroad in summer, and following baseball was too painful a reminder of failing to achieve my boyhood dream of playing in the big leagues. But as the popularity of baseball boomed in the 1980s and a few academics began to study sports, my wife—also an anthropologist—urged me to go back and look at the culture of baseball. At the same time my son became a Little Leaguer. Sharing this rite of passage with him rekindled my interest. My decision was sealed when I walked past a televised game just as the camera zoomed in on a familiar face—Pittsburgh Pirates' manager Jim Leyland. The man who was twice my teammate in the minor leagues was still in baseball. Another ex-teammate, Gene Lamont, was in the coaching box at third base. I sat down and watched the entire game. Before long, I was planning my return, this time as a researcher.

Like most anthropologists, I was trained to do fieldwork by taking up residence with the groups I studied and immersing myself in their lives. The closest I could come to this was to accompany teams on road trips. I began by traveling with the Birmingham Barons:

Hoover Met Stadium, Birmingham, Alabama. It's my first road trip in twenty-four years. As the Birmingham Barons' bus pulls out of the stadium parking lot—destination Jacksonville then on to Orlando, Florida, for eight road games—manager Tony Franklin stands up to introduce me. "I'd like you to meet George Gmelch. He's an anthropologist studying your lives as ballplayers. I don't know why anyone would find what you do interesting, but that's his business, and he's a whole lot smarter than me (laughter). Anyway, he was a player in the Tigers' organization in the '60s, so he knows his way around. I want you to help him anyway you can. . . ." The players turn in their seats, craning their necks to get a good look at me. I smile a lot, trying not to show my nervousness. I appreciate Tony's remarks, but I don't really know my way around. I'm not even sure I can talk baseball anymore. The jargon has changed—terms like "the show" are alien to me. I've been away from baseball for so long that I seriously wonder if I can relate to these guys. Will they allow me—a bearded, graying professor—to hang out with them?

It isn't long before I realize how different the world of pro ball in the 1990s is from my day. We've only gotten a mile from the ballpark when the team bus pulled up alongside a Blockbuster store. Half a dozen players pile off and return with an armful of videos. That night, during the thirteen-hour ride to Jacksonville, *Die Hard, Lethal Weapon, Road Warrior, Robo Cop 2,* and *The Abyss* are shown. Around 4 A.M., during *Robo Cop 2,* I wadded bits of paper napkin and stuffed them into my ears. Players who aren't watching movies listen to music on their walkmans and intermittently sleep. In the '60s road trips were like the popular image of them—long and uncomfortable. Buses were often old and cramped. There was no air-conditioning, or it was so weak you weren't sure if it'd be cooler to have the window open or closed. Players passed the time playing cards and trivia games, looking out the window, and talking. Someone usually had a guitar, and a few would join in singing. On the Barons' bus, the banter and fellowship I so fondly remembered are missing. In exchange, like the other team buses I was later to ride, there was comfort—leg room, bigger seats, large clean windows, a toilet in the rear, reliable AC, and TV, and VCR. When one player's walkman breaks, he tells me he doesn't know how he is going to survive the trip. When I comment on the contrast to manager Tony Franklin, who like me had grown up in the prepersonal-electronic era, he says, "Those damn things have ruined road trips. They've taken all the fun out of them."

After a few summers observing the minor leagues, I shifted to the majors. There I paid daily visits to the ballpark, arriving with the players in the early afternoon and staying through the evening, hanging out, observing, and talking informally in the clubhouse, dugout, and on the field during the long pregame preparations. Usually I stayed in a town for a few days interviewing both visiting and home teams. Then I would return to upstate New York to transcribe my interviews and fieldnotes and review my progress before going out again. In the first few years I was fortunate to have a Double-A team, the Albany-Colonie Yankees, in my hometown. It was a great loss when they moved to Norwich, Connecticut, after Albany failed to upgrade its ballpark.

By the time I finally sat down to write, I'd spent five seasons in the "field," twice the time I had planned. I was sorry to see the research end. While the bus trips were sometimes an ordeal, the ballparks were always exciting. There was always something happening—hitters taking batting practice, fielders taking ground balls or shagging flies, reporters and broadcasters doing interviews, fans at the railing trying to entice players to sign autographs, groundskeepers raking and watering, and then the game itself.

Inside Pitch follows the life cycle of professional baseball players, starting with their earliest ambitions and ending with their efforts to reinvent life after their baseball careers. It begins by looking at how players acquire the ambition to play professional baseball and how amateur players are scouted and drafted. The next chapter goes inside the rookies' first year of pro ball—the difficulties of adjusting to playing everyday, switching to wood bats, and the like—the intense competition, the small towns, and the new social milieu. Chapter 3 looks at how players are socialized into the culture of baseball—its beliefs and practices. It also deals with how players develop an identity as professionals. Chapter 4 follows a player's movement through the five levels of the minor league farm system. Getting the call to the majors and everyday life at the highest level of the sport are discussed in Chapter 5. Succeeding in pro ball is as much mental as having the physical tools. How players prepare to play and how they deal with failure and slumps is the subject of Chapter 6. More of the psychological dimensions of baseball are taken up in Chapter 7, with a look at the role chance plays in pitching and hitting and at the routines and rituals players develop to control some of this uncertainty. Chapters 8 and 9 deal with the place women occupy in the lives of ballplayers, specifically with wives and groupies. Finally, Chapter 10 looks at the end of a ballplayer's career, which happens earlier than in other professions, and how players cope with life outside of the game, when the glory and adulation, the camaraderie of the clubhouse, and the daily excitement of competition all come to an end.

A list of the players and coaches I interviewed for the book can be found in the Appendix. In the text I note the team individuals were with at the time of the interviews, rather than their current affiliations.

Acknowledgments

I began research for this book in 1991, and along the way many people helped. Marty Kuehnert got me started with the Birmingham Barons; Ed Creech and QV Lowe with the Jamestown Expos. The media relations directors of the Atlanta Braves, Baltimore Orioles, Boston Red Sox, New York Yankees, Pittsburgh Pirates, San Francisco Giants, and many minor league teams kindly gave me access. Librarians Tim Wiles, Bill Francis, and Bill Burdick at the Baseball Hall of Fame and Donna Burton, Mary Cahill, Bruce Connolly, and Dave Gerhan at Union College were an immense help. At the Smithsonian Insitution Press, Mark Hirsch gave wise counsel from start to finish and urged me to "exorcise the didactic" and reach out to a broader audience; Robert A. Poarch adeptly copyedited the manuscript. Patricia San Antonio helped analyze data on baseball wives and groupies through our collaboration on two papers about the women of baseball. I am also indebted to those who read drafts of chapters of the manuscript, including coaches Dave Dagostino, QV Lowe, Mike Lynch, John Noce; scouts Jim Howard, Scott Jaster, and John Stokoe; media relations specialist Sally O'Leary; ex-players Glen Kinns, Sam McDowell, and Nick Testa, and baseball pundits Michael DeLucca, George Gmelch Sr., Dan Gordon, Naomi Krupa, Lee Lowenfish, Joe Messina, Meredith

Melzer, Judy O'Dell, Frank Otto, Russ Parker, Bob Padgett, Bill Schwarz, Bill Tierney, Jennifer Unterberg, and Bob Wheelock. Their comments and suggestions have made this a better book. I am particularly indebted to Jean Ardell, Sharon Gmelch, and Bill Kirwin, writers themselves, for their in-depth criticism and editorial advice; their help was invaluable.

I also learned much from my students Ryan Almstead, Dan Gordon, Biju Salgunan, and J. J. Weiner, whose own research on baseball I supervised. Bill Kirwin, Tim Wiles, and Richard Nelson were brilliant in helping with titles. I am also grateful to Union College for supporting my research, to Janet McQuade for assisting in myriad ways, and to student aides Hannah Gaw, Cari Hepner, Mary McKay, Erin Rosenberg, and Justine Willey for transcribing interviews, and critiqueing drafts. The biggest thanks goes to Sharon Bohn Gmelch, for convincing me that the research was worthwhile, and to all the players and other baseball people who trusted me and graciously gave me their time.

1. Talent for the Game

I vividly remember deciding to become a baseball player. I was in the eighth grade and had gone by myself on a gray November day to Fitzgerald Field in my hometown of San Mateo, California, to watch the Baltimore Orioles play. They were not the real Baltimore Orioles; rather they, like other teams of the Peninsula Winter League, took the name and uniforms of the major league clubs that sponsored them. But some of the players were minor leaguers.

Memory is selective, and when it recalls distant events it provides little more than a few snapshots. Two images stand out from that day at Fitzgerald Field. One is the setting. The grass was lush, thanks to the start of the rainy season, and tall redwood trees grew in deep right field. The trees were in play, forcing outfielders to run around and between them to chase down extra-base hits. The other is the players: strong young men, resplendent in their Orioles uniforms, with its black and orange piping. Oddly, I have only one memory of the game itself. It was neither a spectacular base hit nor a terrific catch, but a tall man standing in the batter's box, firmly dug in, crowding the plate, his gaze fixed on the pitcher. A fastball whisked by, an inch from his chest, and he did not flinch. I wondered how he could be so sure the ball was not going to hit him. He seemed awfully brave to me then. My last memory is of the bus trip home, as the idea formed in my head that I, too, wanted to be a professional ballplayer.

My ambition must have appeared foolish at the time. Although I was a fair athlete, I was not a particularly good baseball player. I played on the school softball team, not the baseball team, and my talent was in pitching. Yet, on the heels of that life-altering game, I wanted to become a great hitter. Perhaps it is the vividness of this memory that prompted me to ask the professional players I interviewed how they had acquired their passion for baseball.

Beginnings

Most players decided at a young age, usually before high school, that they wanted to become pro ballplayers. Their ambition usually followed early success at the game.[1] John White, an outfielder for the Jamestown Expos, remembered the birth of his dream this way:

> I think I was thirteen. I just got done playing a Little League game, which my parents had attended, and I played fairly well that day, and I was feeling really good about baseball in general. I made a comment to my father—I still remember this vividly—I said, "Dad, I am going to play professional baseball!" I said it with a lot of confidence, I was pretty sure of myself, as most thirteen-year-olds are. He seemed to take it with a grain of salt. So I said, "No, Dad, I'm really going to play." He said, "Okay, your first major league game, tell ya what, I'll come out on to the field, and I'll take my clothes off." When I got drafted by the Expos, I asked him if the offer still stood, and he said something along the lines of "Well, I'll have to lose a few pounds, but. . . ."

Nick Sproviero grew up in a first-generation Italian-American household in Stamford, Connecticut. His father wanted his son to play soccer, as he had done in Italy, but Nick had more success in baseball:

> My first memory of wanting to be a baseball player was as an eight year old in Little League, when I made the all-star team. It was easy to dream about being a ballplayer then because it was so far off. But when I was eleven I really began to think about it. That year we went to the Little League World Series in Williamsport [Pennsylvania]. . . . It was unreal. I remember getting off the bus in Williamsport and seeing the field and thinking, "Wow, we've made it." And then the next day we were playing in front of 12,000 people. We were playing a team from Tampa, Florida, a thousand miles away from my home. Before that summer we were just playing in front of moms and dads, and now this. All those people. I think that was when I realized I really wanted to make something out of baseball. There was an aura about the whole thing, and I wanted to be part of it.

Not all professional players were Little League stars, and some were not even regulars. James Bishop, a ten-year-veteran minor leaguer with four different organizations, did not play baseball while growing up in the Los Angeles neighborhood of Watts until he was thirteen. A neighborhood coach looking for players knocked on his parents' door and asked if they had any kids who might like to come out for his baseball team. They introduced James to the coach, and that was the beginning. An old-timer in

Keeping score. Young fan at a Pirates' game, Three Rivers Stadium. (Photo by Dan Levine)

his neighborhood, Ray McNeil, who had played in the Negro Leagues, took James under his wing and taught him how to play. Pat Listach, the American League Rookie of the Year in 1992, had played from an early age but did not become a standout until much later: "It wasn't until my second year in college that things really started to turn around. I started to fill out, and I spent a lot of time in the weight room. I had some pretty good coaches in college who taught me the fundamentals of the game, things that I really didn't know coming out of a small high school."

Fathers, older brothers, and occasionally mothers figure prominently in many players' accounts of how they acquired their yearning for baseball. Many had fathers and brothers who played catch with them in the yard or street. "My dad would always find the time to play with me," recalled Randy St. Claire, a five-year major league veteran. "He'd come home from work, and he'd go get his glove. He'd make the time to do that kind of stuff. A lot of kids didn't have dads who could or wanted to take the time to play ball with them." Some fathers coached their sons in Little League. Scott Tedder, an outfielder for the Birmingham Barons, credits his early interest in baseball to the involvement of both his parents in Little League in Columbus, Ohio. "My dad would always take us to his softball games," he said. "And he was my coach in T-ball and Little League, and my mom was the scorekeeper. It was always a family thing."

Some scholars argue that much of baseball's appeal stems from the bonding that forms between boys and their fathers in playing ball or going to ball games together.[2] The ballpark is one of the few places where American fathers give their sons (and sometimes daughters) undivided attention. In interviews with professional athletes, sports sociologist Michael Messner found that many had startlingly clear memories of their trips with dad to major and minor league ball games. Often there was a dreamlike quality to their descriptions of these events.[3] Messner argued that such experiences are especially poignant for boys, because many fathers have never learned to express love openly. Instead, they show their love "indirectly and symbolically" by taking their sons to ball games or teaching them athletic skills.[4] About his youth, journalist Robert Morris recalled, "As I grew older and more distant (the way sons too often become with their fathers), playing catch was sometimes the only way we could talk."[5] While in the Baseball Hall of Fame library, I have on several occasions overheard middle-aged and older men asking a reference librarian how they might find a box score or article about a game their father had taken them to years before. The research librarian, Tim Wiles, later confirmed that such requests are common and that these men are interested in reliving a day at the ballpark with their fathers.

A surprising number of the players I interviewed had fathers who had not only taken them to baseball games, but had actually played professional baseball themselves. The frequency of second-generation pro players did not really strike me until I watched a game one evening between the Birmingham Barons and the Jacksonville Suns of the Double-A Southern League. Three of the players on the field—Scott Jaster, Bret Boone, and Jim Campanis—and one of the coaches, Rick Peterson, were the sons or grandsons of major league players from my generation. Another coach and former player, Jim Nettles, was the younger brother of a big leaguer.

Social scientists Savannah Williams and Wayne Patterson have studied "footstepping," the tendency of sons to pursue their father's occupations. Using genealogical information from *The Baseball Encyclopedia* and *The Sporting News Baseball Register,* they found that 10 percent of all professional baseball players have fathers who played pro ball, and half of these fathers had made it to the major leagues.[6] In contrast to these sixty-four baseball players, only four professional basketball players in the NBA were sons of former players. This lower incidence is at least partially due to success in basketball being more dependent upon sheer physical characteristics, particularly height.[7] No matter how well a father instructs his son in the fine points of the game, unless the boy is very tall, he will not have much chance of a career in the NBA.

With 750 openings on major league baseball rosters and about 20 million American men of the right age, the chances of finding even one big leaguer whose father had also played in the major leagues is about one in thirty thousand. The amount of footstepping in baseball, Williams and Patterson explained, is due to children enjoying the benefit of good and frequent early training—both skills and attitude—from their fathers. Randy St. Claire, most recently of the Atlanta Braves and the son of former big leaguer Ebba St. Claire, described the influence of his father:

> If it weren't for him, I wouldn't have become a major league ballplayer. I mean that without a doubt. Since I can remember, he was always teaching me the right way to play the game, how to do the right things—field a ground ball, hit, throw, everything. He would talk about situations that would come up in a game, so when they did come up you'd know what to do and you wouldn't defeat yourself. It's like an involuntary muscle reaction, you just do it automatically, from all those years of hearing about it. Dad never pressured me, never yelled at me, he never said, "That was terrible, you've got to do better," the way some fathers do. He would say, "In this situation you do . . . and this is why."

Looking back at my own teammates of a generation ago, it becomes clear that those whose fathers had been ballplayers were better prepared to play pro ball—to handle the daily grind of the long season, to pace themselves, and to stay positive when they were not performing well.

Sons of players can also hang out at the ballpark and watch their fathers at work. Unlike other professional sports, baseball is played daily. Before each game there are nearly three hours of warm-up, batting, and infield/outfield practice, during which it is possible for a player's son to be on the field—shagging fly balls, watching batting practice, or just hanging around the batting cage or dugout. During the great home-run race of 1998, fans saw a lot of Mark McGwire's son on the field. Few other occupations provide workplaces and routines in which sons can be present. (Farming is one exception, and it too has a high frequency of footstepping.) Scott Jaster, a Triple-A outfielder, began going to Atlanta's Fulton County Stadium with his father, Larry Jaster, when he was just five years old:

By the time I was eight or nine my father was finishing up in Triple A with the Richmond Braves. By then I was old enough to go out on the field and actually shag fly balls. I would go over to the ballpark early with my dad and hit on the field. That's when things started rolling, . . . that's what I lived for, when my dad went to the park. It was exciting, . . . you are driving to the park and you'd get closer and closer and you'd get more and more excited. I'd get into the locker room and wait for my dad to change, and I'd be itching to get out on the field. I'd be down there out on the field watching the crowds.

Everyone knew who I was at the ballpark, because I lived there. I would just go to the concession stand and get free hot dogs and free cokes. I can still remember the way other kids looked at me, "Wow, why is he out there on the field?" I remember those feelings inside me, but I also kept my distance [from the other kids] because I felt a little uncomfortable about it, about these kids wanting to be where I was and they couldn't.

I've heard people talk about drug addicts and how they get that high. But as a kid it was a high just being down there on the field. And I always knew that tomorrow I could get up and do it all over again.

From the way players talk about their fathers, there is no doubt that the attention their fathers received from the media and fans also made a big impression on them as kids. Not surprisingly, it inspired some to want a career in baseball.[8] It is not until they attracted the attention of a professional baseball scout, however, that their hopes turned into possibilities.

Scouting the Talent

Scouts are employed by major league organizations to find baseball talent. They locate, observe, evaluate, and report on all players who have the potential to play in the big leagues. Their task is uncommonly difficult since it requires much more than just being able to accurately assess a player's current physical skills. The scout must project how each prospect will develop. Major league clubs care little that a teenager can hit .400 in the local high school league; they want to know what kind of hitter he promises to be in five or six years against pitchers who throw 90 mph, have an assortment of pitches, and hit the corners of the plate.

Those who scout today's amateurs, or free agents, and decide who tomorrow's professional players will be are often former pro ballplayers themselves. Consequently, most scouts are men, although the Kansas City Royals and the Milwaukee Brewers have employed several women. Some former players go straight into scouting, but many first work outside of baseball in other occupations. Among the scouts that I know are a former school teacher, a former policeman, and a former insurance salesman. Each had played pro ball. Hep Cronin, who now scouts for the Atlanta Braves, taught high school biology:

> It's hard to compare work in the real world with being in baseball. Teaching, I had a six o'clock wake-up and had to be at school by seven. First class was at 7:30, and it was the same thing every day. Tomorrow was always the same as today, and after a while I didn't want that anymore. Now, if I want to wake up at 8:00 tomorrow, I'll wake up at 8:00. If I want to wake up at 9:00, I'll wake up at 9:00. If I want to have breakfast here [Birmingham, Alabama], I'll have it here, and if I want to have it up the road, I'll have it there. It's my decision. Tomorrow I'll decide if I'm going to Knoxville [to watch the Double-A Knoxville Blue Jays] or go straight on to Youngstown.
>
> I have a territory of two-and-a-half states, and it's basically my baby, my responsibility. Sure, if I have a first-rounder [a potential first-round draft pick], I'm going to call in the boss and have him and the national cross-checker [a sort of superscout] come take a look. But basically, whoever the Braves take or don't take from these two-and-a-half states is totally on my shoulders, and I will live and die with it. In other avenues of life you don't get that.

Every major league organization has between twenty and thirty full-time scouts. Not all are scouting high school or college players, however. Scouting is specialized. Some, like the "advance scout," travel ahead of the major league club to watch the team the club will play next; others scout major league players who might be offered to the club in a trade.[9] On the face of it, scouting in the big leagues, going to work in the best stadiums, and watching the world's top players seem preferable to scouting from hard wooden bleachers at high school and American Legion games. But many scouts, like the Braves' Hep Cronin, disagree:

> There's not much challenge to pro scouting. I've got the [Cincinnati] Reds in September, and I've got to see them five straight games. I'm not too excited about it, because, let's face it, they have three guys that I would like to have on our team, but there is no way that we are ever going to get them. The Reds are in our own division, so they are especially not going to deal them to us. The guys they might be willing to give us, we don't want. For me, writing up reports on all those players, all twenty-five of them, is a whole lot of paperwork that's never going to amount to anything. All you're doing is paperwork. With free-agent

scouting, when you walk into the park there is a chance of getting the player you want. And you are only going to write up the paperwork on the players that are prospects.

Those who scout free agents—the nation's best prospects from high schools, colleges, and summer leagues—are known as "territorial scouts." Their task of projecting the development of school boys is the most difficult job of all. The younger the player, the greater the difficulty. Judging the college player is slightly easier than the high school player, because he is several years older and closer to achieving his potential. Each territorial scout, as the title suggests, is responsible for a geographic area. In the Baltimore Orioles' organization at the time of writing, for example, Lamar North was responsible for all the amateur players in Georgia and South Carolina; Marc Tramuta had North Carolina, Delaware, and Maryland; Jim Howard had Pennsylvania, New Jersey, upstate New York, New England, and the Cape Cod League; and so on.

Below the area scouts are "associate scouts" or "bird dogs." They are often umpires, high school coaches, or others with a deep involvement in amateur baseball. When they see a prospect, they report him to the area scout they work with. Associate scouts are usually paid expenses, plus a commission when one of the players they recommend gets drafted. The Baltimore Orioles, for example, pay their associate scouts $100 when their player is signed and is kept on a roster for ninety days, another $100 if he advances to Double A, $200 if he reaches Triple A, and $500 if he makes it to the big leagues.

In ballparks across the country, scouts are easily identified. They usually sit behind home plate—the vantage point that provides the best view of both pitcher and batter—with their radar guns and notebooks. From almost anywhere in the ballpark, fans can observe scouts aiming their "guns" at the pitcher as he enters his wind-up, and then noting the digital readout of the ball's velocity. Scouts also tend to dress alike—knit shirts, windbreakers, and cross-trainers. An embroidered logo on a shirt or cap, or a sticker on a briefcase, often reveals the baseball organization they work for.

At the start of my research I assumed that a scout's status among his peers was probably determined by how far he had gotten in pro ball. Someone who had played in the major leagues, for example, would have higher status than someone who had played Double A, and so on down the line. But as I got to know scouts better, I discovered that what counted most was

Scouts with radar guns clocking pitchers in Albany, New York.
(Photo by Darren Mrak)

how good they were, not what they had achieved as players in the past. In the words of the Orioles' John Stokoe, "You don't have to have played to be a good scout. Just as you don't have to have played in the major leagues to be a good major league manager. I don't care about a man's background, it's what he does now that matters." Scouts often acquire their reputations from the players they sign who become major league stars. During my first spring training, I was introduced to the Detroit Tigers' scout Ed Katalinas, whom I knew as "the scout who signed Al Kaline." Similarly, when I was first told that Baltimore scout John Stokoe lived in my town, it was "John Stokoe, the man who signed Mike Flannagan." Many scouts, though, squirm at such attributions. Hep Cronin of the Braves:

> I've had scouts introduce me, "Oh, this is Hep Cronin. He signed Dave Justice." It makes me feel a little goofy when I hear that. It's amazing the respect you get once some of your players begin to perform. But it doesn't take a genius to see that a player like Dave Justice has great potential. Like when I saw Chipper Jones play, I knew he was going to be a top pick and that he had a good chance of making it. It was the same with guys like Dwight Gooden. To me the scout should get more credit when lower picks, guys that other organizations missed or underrated but he found, make it to the big leagues. Like our guy in New Jersey who recommended Mark Lemke. We got him in the twenty-seventh round; nobody else seemed to have him on their list, and he made it to the big leagues and did well.

For most scouts, the search for prospects entails spending about half of every year on the road, traveling from town to town, ballpark to ballpark. The scout's objective is not simply to watch as many ball games as possible, but to selectively watch those games in which the most talented players are performing. Rarely do scouts turn up at a game merely on the off-chance that they might spot a prospect. Rather they choose games based on recommendations they have received about particular players.

The Right Piece of Carbon

What exactly do scouts look for? At the most basic level, scouts talk in terms of five fundamental talents, or "tools": running, throwing, fielding, hitting, and hitting with power. Each talent encompasses several attributes or dimensions. The assessment of a player's throwing, or "arm," for example, includes both arm strength and accuracy. Fielding is divided into "softness of the hands" (the smooth fielding of the ball and its transfer from the glove to throwing hand) and "range" (the amount of ground a player can cover, such as the second baseman being able to get to ground balls that have been hit in the hole). Hitting is especially difficult to scout. For example, here is what scout John Stokoe observed in the hitters at an Eastern League game that we watched:

> You look at his stance and balance in the batter's box. Does he have good weight shift from his back to front foot when he strides? You look at his stroke. Is it

short and compact? You look at his bat speed. Does he have a quick bat? You notice if he has any bad habits, such as hitching, lunging, or bailing out. Does he have any fear? All that goes into what we call "pure hitting."

And then you have the power factor. And that's divided into raw power and the frequency of power. If in batting practice you see the kid driving the ball well out of the ballpark, you figure he has raw power. But there are some great six o'clock hitters who perform well during batting practice and then, when it comes to nut cracking time [the game], can't hit the ball because they are easily pitched to. You need to know the frequency at which he is going to hit the long ball in a game. That's a big intangible. You know that he can do it in batting practice, but can he do it when a guy is throwing some mustard or a good curve ball?

To assess what kind of potential power the kid has, you have got to figure out how much bigger or stronger he's going to get. Maybe you look at the size of his father. And then you have to factor in the effect of the kid using an aluminum bat. You gotta think about how much power he'll retain in the pros with a wood bat. All that goes into how you are going to rate the kid on hitting.

Scouts like to arrive at the ballpark early in order to watch players during batting practice and infield and outfield drills. As with hitting, however, players often do not show their true throwing arms in practice, so the scout must hope that a situation comes up in the game that will force the player to make his best throw. Scouts keep notes on their observations, which are more opinion than fact. Much like the notes that anthropologists jot down while observing behavior and later write up as full field notes, the scout uses his "game notes" to later write up a complete report on each player he likes. Jim Howard's scouting report on Nomar Garciaparra (see page 12), when he was an amateur player, assessed his strengths, weaknesses, and signability.

For every hitter, the scout charts the location of the pitches (in, middle, middle out), what pitch the batter hit, and to what part of the field the ball went. After observing a player over a series of at bats, a scout discerns patterns: which pitches the player handles well, and which ones he has difficulty with. These observations form the basis of the generalizations he will make in his reports, such as John Stokoe's notation on one hitter: "big, strong with power, chases high fastball, has to learn to lay off that pitch." And about a pitcher "short and quick [arm speed], little below average velocity (84–81), will come inside a lot with nothing on it, has to have good control to get by, should use change-up more."

While judging talent is highly subjective, scouts do have some tools that

Scouting report of Nomar Garciaparra.

enable them to collect "hard" data. The technology that gets the most attention is the radar gun. Radar guns were first introduced into baseball in 1975, after a Michigan State University baseball coach wondered if the radar guns campus police were using might work for clocking his pitchers.[10] Radar guns operate on the Doppler effect, in which a microwave beam bounces off the baseball and returns at a higher frequency depending on the speed of the pitch. The gun translates the difference into miles per hour.[11] (A new generation of radar guns employs a laser to measure maximum velocity.)

Before radar guns, scouts judged velocity visually. "You could tell a lot about how fast a guy was throwing by the hitter," recalled one veteran scout. "If the hitter would be swinging late or fouling the ball off, you knew the guy has a pretty good heater. Today we look at the gun, and we know exactly how fast he is throwing." Critics claim that scouts have become too dependent on radar guns, and that as a result some talented pitchers have been ignored because they do not have great velocity.[12] Velocity is only one dimension of pitching. Equally important is the amount of movement the ball has, whether the pitch has action—does it sink, tail, or rise?[13] A pitcher who throws at 85 mph with action, or "life," on the ball will have more success than a pitcher with a 90 mph fastball that is as straight as an arrow. Yet practically every schoolboy who can throw 90 mph is considered a prospect and is scouted.

Radar guns are especially useful at night, when it is more difficult to eyeball velocity. They also enable scouts to measure a pitcher's stamina by taking readings over the course of a game. How much does his velocity drop between the first inning and the sixth and the ninth?[14] The downside of radar guns is that they can spook young pitchers. Top high school and college pitching prospects often see a half dozen radar guns pointing at them from behind the backstop, clocking every pitch. Hoping to impress, some youth pitch to the guns instead of the batters, trying to register high velocities.

The stopwatch is the other basic tool used by scouts, principally to measure running speed. Many older scouts say they do not need a stopwatch to tell if a player can run. Younger scouts often agree that veterans are incredibly accurate. But running speed is also deceptive. One scout described it this way:

> The little guy with a quick stride can look like he is flying down the line, and you sit there thinking this guy can really run. But if you look at the stopwatch you see he ran to first in 4.5 seconds. That's below average.[15] You say, doggone, he looked a lot faster than that. Then there is the smooth runner, the kid with long legs, and who often doesn't look like he is running that good. But if you look at the watch you'll see he ran a 4.1. Without the watch you'd probably rate the first guy as being faster than the second guy.

The stopwatch is also used to time how quickly pitcher and catcher release the ball with a man stealing.[16]

Radar guns and stopwatches have brought some precision to scouting and in some ways made the scout's judgment more objective. Yet another technological innovation—the aluminum bat—has made scouting more difficult. First approved for use in college baseball in 1974, the aluminum bat is now used throughout the amateur ranks. It has different properties than the wood bat used in pro ball. For one, aluminum-hit balls travel farther, so home-run hitters in amateur baseball may not be home-run hitters in pro ball. Scouts must factor in the aluminum effect in assessing a player's potential. How well will a player make the transition to wood? Only a few amateur leagues in the country use wood bats (e.g., the Cape Cod League), and not surprisingly, scouts love to work them. As one scout said, "On the Cape, what you see is much closer to what you are going to get. It gives you a better picture of the kid's potential."

Scouts always think in terms of what the player is likely to become with maturity and good instruction. Unlike professional football and basketball, where most players go straight from college to the NFL or NBA, baseball's major leagues require a long apprenticeship. Only one in twelve minor league players ever make it to the big leagues. And they spend an average of four years in the minors. New York Yankees director of scouting and player development Bill Livesy explains the process of producing a major leaguer and why the emphasis in scouting must be on potential ability:

> It is not unlike how you make a diamond. You find the right piece of carbon and apply a lot of pressure, a lot of pressure, over a lot of years. If the carbon was what you thought it was going to be and you applied the right amount of pressure, then down the road you are going to get a diamond. But if you applied all that pressure to the wrong piece of carbon, all you are going to get are a lot of little pieces of coal. It's the scout's job to find the right piece of carbon.

The measure that scouts use in judging lumps of carbon is called the OFP, or "overall future potential," rating. To arrive at an OFP rating, the scout scores the player on all talents (running, fielding, throwing, etc.) on a scale from 20 to 80, with 20 being poor, 80 being excellent, and 50 being the major league average. The points for each category are then averaged to produce the OFP. Garciaparra's OFP of 58 (see page 12) means he has the potential to be a better-than-average major leaguer. The scout may adjust the OFP by a few points, according to his intuition about the player.

For example, a catcher who does not run well—who scored, say, just a 25 in that category—may have his score boosted a bit, because running speed is much less important at that position.[17]

When a territorial scout turns up an exceptional prospect like Garcia-parra with an OFP rating above 50, the organization will send in a "cross checker," or scouting supervisor, for a second opinion. Top prospects may be evaluated by four or five scouts and supervisors from each organization. The time and expense of so many people, flying in from around the country, to scout a single player is justified. If a player is chosen in the first round of the draft, the organization will invest two million dollars or more just to sign him, and then there is the additional cost of years of development in the minor leagues before he is ready to play in the big leagues.

Besides a player's physical tools, scouts must also think about his psychological makeup, his work ethic, coachability, and self-confidence. Scouts refer to these elements as "the intangibles." Bill Livesy explains it this way:

> Think of the physical side of players, the tools they have, as being like a bunch of cars. It's what we can see. All the cars are at the starting line, all gassed up and ready to make the trip. They've got, physically, what it takes to get to the destination, but you are not sure about the driver. The driver is the player's mental makeup. And you've got to know, does the driver want to make the trip? Can he read the maps? Will he persevere through the storm or will he turn around and come home?
>
> A kid may have the physical ability to play in the big leagues, but without the desire, without the determination to continue that trip when things get rough, without being able to stop and ask directions when he needs to, he's not going to make it. You need to know how important becoming a major league player is to the kid. We want people who want to be major leaguers and who have the work ethic and are prepared to make the sacrifice that it takes to go all the way. We're not in the business of just signing professional players; if I sign too many of them I'll be out looking for a job.

The psychological dimensions cannot be detected from the stands. Rather, it requires that the scout spend time with the player and his family. Hep Cronin described his approach and its importance: "I try to go in and interview every kid that I think I might get [might recommend to be drafted]. I give them a personality profile test and an eye test. These are basically small tools and are more of an excuse for me to get into the house and meet the family. I want to have some coffee and sit down and spend an hour and a half or so with them." Orioles scouting supervisor, John Stokoe, said it is the responsibility of his area scouts to "dig out" the player's "mental makeup":

The area scout has to get out there and talk to the coach, to the people at the games. The coach will always give his guy a good grade, so you don't want to rely on him too much. That means that you have to ask around.

"What kind of guy is so-and-so?"

"Well, he's all right if you can wheel him home after he's been drinking."

"Oh, does he drink?"

"Yeah, he has a few drinks."

So now you know that you have a potential problem, and that's important. Today we also have to worry about drugs. You have to find out all you can—the background of the family and of the kid. That is, if you're seriously thinking of drafting the kid.

Nearly every player remembers when he first discovered that a scout was showing interest in him. A pitcher usually becomes aware of it when he sees radar guns aimed at him from behind the backstop. Other players are taken more by surprise. Matt Allen, a catcher with the Jamestown Expos, who was first scouted as a senior in high school, speaks for many: "The scout left his card and a form to fill out. It was a real big rush. Nobody else on my team had ever gotten anything from a scout before. I became the center of attention. Everybody was focusing on me to see what was going to happen. I think a lot of other people were just as overwhelmed as I was. For me to get attention from a scout like that was a really big deal." John White first caught the attention of a scout as a freshman playing for Wagner College in Staten Island:

In high school I never had the feeling of being scouted. The first time was my freshman year of college. The scouts weren't really there for me, they were there scouting two pitchers. Anyway, I was playing against them, and I was the lead-off hitter, and this guy is like throwing 91, 92, so this is a really big chance for me because I'd never seen any of that in high school. I hit a pretty sharp ground ball to the shortstop, and he made a nice play in the hole, and I ran really well. I got a good jump out of the box, and I guess I got down the line in good time. When I came back to the bench, I heard the scout say something to our coach, like "What was his name, uhh, John White? Yeah, tell him I'm going to keep an eye on him." That inspired me to do well and not to slack off in the off-season. I wanted to take advantage of some of the tools I was given. I have a really good arm, and I have really good speed, and I hit the ball. So when this scout became interested, I finally said, "Yeah, maybe something is there." I wasn't just looking through rose-colored glasses, I had something to pursue.

Usually the player's parents are as excited as he is. James Bishop first became aware of scouts' interest in him during an American Legion game when he was seventeen: "We had a standout pitcher, and there were a bunch of scouts in the stands. After the game, two of them gave my coach cards for me to fill out. My father didn't know the scouts were looking at me until later, when the scouts started talking to him, asking him what kind of kid I was. He was just thrilled about that."

Being scouted often causes the player to press. QV Lowe, a former pitching coach for the Chicago Cubs who coaches baseball at Auburn University in Alabama, explained what happens to many college players when they discover they are being scouted:

> All of a sudden they start pitching for the guns. They want to do well, they want to be drafted, and they start thinking that they have to throw harder. They don't understand that when they do that, they actually throw less hard. A pitcher throws the hardest when he is nice and relaxed. You can see it in a game, the kid will be going along relaxed, no pressure, no worries. He'll go 0 and 2 on a hitter, and he'll want to strike him out with a high fastball. He tries to throw it harder than any pitch he's thrown all night. He will grunt and grind and say to himself, "if I can just do a little more on this. . . . " But it works exactly the opposite, and his velocity drops off a bit.

Lowe's observations were confirmed in a study by physiologists L. Weinstein, G. A. Prather, and A. F. De Man, who measured differences in velocities of fastballs thrown with and without the known presence of a scout. They found that when the scout and radar guns were present, the average fastball among the fourteen college pitchers they observed was clocked at 75.6 mph, whereas when the scout and radar gun were absent their average speed was 79 mph.

The Draft

All but a handful of players enter the professional ranks through the free-agent draft. In the first week of June, officials from each of the thirty major league organizations take turns selecting North America's most talented amateur ballplayers. Going in rounds, the teams make their picks in reverse order of how they finished in the previous season's standings. In the past, teams drafted as many players as they wanted. Today, they are limited to fifty rounds, and there is talk of reducing that number further.

Two weeks before the draft, all the organization's area scouts are called to town to present their individual draft lists. Afterward, the scouting director, cross checkers, and other staff huddle in a hotel to cull their list and rank their prospects, of which there may be five hundred. "It's like being sequestered on a jury," said the Braves' assistant general manager Dean Taylor. "We lock ourselves into a hotel suite for about three weeks and discuss all the players we are considering for the draft. There are absolutely no distractions. We may have as many as two thousand reports [there can be a half dozen reports on each of the top prospects] and we read every one of them." Everyone on the list will have been scrutinized by one or more scouts, undergone an eye test, and taken an athletic motivation test. The high cost of signing bonuses has made the evaluations of players more critical today than ever.

Unlike the NFL and NBA, where the draft is televised live, baseball's draft is done via conference call. The draft lasts three days, which, says Braves scouting director Chuck LaMar, are "the three most important days of the year for any organization."[18] Each team will draft forty-five to fifty players, but not all of them will choose to sign. There are always a fair number of high school players who decide to postpone their professional careers in favor of college, and there are college players who will choose to stay in school for another year or two before signing.[19] Amateurs in the Caribbean, Mexico, Venezuela, and elsewhere are not presently part of the draft, although there has been talk in the commissioner's office of implementing a worldwide draft.

The baseball draft was introduced in 1965 and was modeled after the drafts used in other professional sports. Its original intent was to reduce competition for players and the resulting bidding wars. In the predraft era a player could sign with any team he wanted, and naturally players chose the organization that offered the most money—the largest "signing bonus." In 1964, the year before the first draft, the California Angels had to pay an eighteen-year-old high school outfielder, Rick Reichardt, $175,000 to get his signature on a contract. As a twenty-year-old, I had a special interest in the draft. I was offered a contract with a modest bonus (enough to pay for two years of tuition at Stanford University) by the Detroit Tigers in May 1965, one week before the beginning of the first-ever free-agent draft. Not having any idea what impact the new draft would have on me, and eager to begin my professional baseball career, I accepted Detroit's offer. Later, when I got to my first spring training and learned the size of the signing bonuses some of my teammates had received, I wondered whether I'd made the right decision.

One consequence of the draft has been less competition among scouts.[20] With the draft, the chance of an organization getting a particular player is, at best, one in thirty (there being thirty major league clubs). With such slim odds, there is less incentive for scouts to invest a lot of time in getting to know players and their families well. We can only wonder at the consequences.

The age at which amateur players are drafted and enter professional baseball has changed over the past two decades. In the 1960s few of my teammates had any college baseball experience. At that time there was a universal preference for high school players. As Dusty Baker, of the San Francisco Giants, explained:

> When I signed, they didn't really want college players as a whole. At the time I could understand that. Unless you were Mays, Aaron, Mantle, nobody played beyond thirty-three or thirty-five years old. If you get a college player at twenty-two, by the time he gets ready for the big leagues, he's twenty-five or twenty-six years old, and then as a matter of investment you only have seven to eight years of that player. Whereas if you got a younger player who signed at seventeen or eighteen, like we did, the guy is in the big leagues at twenty-two years old. Theoretically, you might get a lot more years out of that guy.

Yet since 1977 more baseball players have been drafted from college than from high school.[21] Some organizations, however, still prefer to sign high school players in the belief that it is easier to mold a player when you get him at an early age. Also, many organizations believe the minor leagues do a better job of developing talent than do colleges. "Some of my best friends are college coaches," said the Braves' scouting director Chuck LaMar, "but there's no way they're doing as good a job as the Braves are in development. Most colleges' business is to win games, and if that means abusing a kid every now and then to win games, then so be it."[22] Finally, there are some scouting directors who believe that college players, because they have their education to fall back on if they fail in baseball, do not have as strong a drive as high school players. "They are just not as hungry," said one scout. In one recent year, eighteen of the Atlanta Braves' first twenty draft picks were high school players. The Pirates and Blue Jays, among others, are also known to favor high school players.

How do players learn they have been drafted? Does it make any difference which organization picks them or what round they are taken in? John White was picked by the Expos in the twenty-first round:

> I got a call late Monday from [scout] Bob Johnson. I was very happy just to hear his voice, which I recognized immediately. But what he said was, "I have some good news and I have some bad news." Automatically I imagined the worst, something like "we're not interested" or "something came up" or "we got somebody else." The bad news was that things got closed up early and that I'd have to wait till tomorrow to hear what happened. Sure enough, 11:00 the next morning he gave me the call that I had been drafted. The night before, all these images were going through my mind. It was like, what am I going to say to him? How am I going to react? Was I going to yell? Was I going to be calm? Was I going to cry? So now here is the call; before I hung up the phone I go, "Bob Johnson, you are not going to regret this, I promise you are not going to regret it." Then I hung up the phone, I hugged my mom, called my dad at work, and stuff like that. Just made a hundred phone calls.

That evening his parents had a large party, inviting relatives and his friends. White watched the vicarious pleasure his parents got from his being drafted. "I got a sense of what they were feeling, just watching them float around the party. It was great because my dad has really worked hard all his life just to support the family, and this was the first time in a long time that he had something to really get excited about."

Mike Robertson, a first baseman for the Birmingham Barons, was first drafted out of high school but chose to go to college instead of signing. He was drafted again, in the third round, after his junior year at the University of Southern California. He compared his reaction as a high school student to his reaction three years later:

> In high school, when I first got the phone call, I was just ecstatic, jumping all around the room. . . . I thought that I would go out in the world and play ball and just dominate wherever I went. The next time, when the White Sox drafted me, it was great too, but I wasn't as wildly ecstatic as the first time. I mean I was still ecstatic, but I think I had a little more perspective this time. I was still pumped up, and I was still ready to dominate, but it was more like I had a focus now of what I wanted, where I wanted to go, and what I needed to do to get there. I knew there were certain steps that I had to follow to get where I wanted to go [the big leagues].

Heath Haynes waited for the news with a teammate who was also expecting to be drafted. Both were pitchers at Western Kentucky University, and both had had outstanding seasons, although they did not expect to be high-round picks:

> We were figuring we might go in the forties [fortieth to forty-ninth round]. Day one comes, and we don't expect to hear anything. Day two comes, and there was a slight chance that we might have gone in the first thirty rounds, so we sat home all day. We blew off classes, summer school classes. We both had the same agent, and he said that we could be drafted today and not know until noon tomorrow, but that would be the latest that they would contact you. Well, we sat by the phone, and every time it rang we'd say, kidding, "There they are! There they are!" We were just like kids, as the day got later we turned into childish kids.
>
> It was eight o'clock the next morning when the phone rang. I didn't think it was anybody because it rang on my roommate's telephone, not mine. He told me to pick up the phone, and it was the Expos, and they said they wanted me to play for them. The first thing I did was call my parents and tell them. Then I called my girlfriend. She was kind of upset that I was going to be leaving to play ball without being able to come up and see her. The worst was telling my buddy. He was one of those players they missed. He was real good, 10-3, with a 2.20 ERA in college. I know it was a big letdown for him, but he didn't show it. His agent kept telling him that he'd be able to get him signed with somebody, but it never happened. Finally it just blew over. In the end, he just gave up on it and got into a business school.

In talking about the draft, I noticed that many players said they went in a lower round than expected. No one ever said they were taken in a higher round than expected. Do players overestimate their potential? Social psychologists tell us that most people have inflated images of themselves, or in the jargon, a "self-enhancement motive." Sociologist Richard Felson found that college athletes in particular receive overly favorable feedback about their performance from coaches, parents, and fans.[23] The feedback is usually given simply to be polite or kind, but it has the effect of inflating their self-image and, apparently, their expectations about how high in the draft they will be taken. When I asked recently drafted players what round they were selected in, many immediately followed their answer with an excuse. The following college player's account is illustrative:

> When I heard thirty-ninth [round], I thought everything had fallen apart. What I didn't understand was that they had drafted me thinking there was only a slim chance that I would sign. I still had another year of college, and my coach told me that nobody thought that I would sign if I was drafted after the tenth round because it would hurt my pride. But that's not what it was about. I wanted to play, and I thought I could move up in the organization, so I signed.

A common excuse is that college coaches want their players to stay in the college baseball program, and they discourage the scouts. The coaches, it was suggested, tell the scouts the player wants too much money to sign, that he has an injury, or that he has an attitude problem.

Most players do not know which team is going to draft them, and many are quite surprised at who is on the other end of the telephone notifying them. Occasionally the player had no contact with the organization and had not even met the area scout before being selected. University of New Haven pitcher Nick Sproviero was drafted by the Expos. Sproviero said, "They were the team that had shown the least amount of interest in me. I was taking eye tests with Phillies, White Sox, Pirates—they were the teams that were calling me all the time, so it was a surprise when the Expos called." Darren Paxton, a pitcher at the University of San Diego, recalled:

> Being from Kansas, I thought that the KC Royals would be nice, because every kid in my area grows up dreaming of playing for the Royals. So when Montreal drafted me, it just didn't feel right. I had no idea it was going to be Montreal. It just came out of the blue. I had never talked to them or anything. I just about died. Now I think it is fine. Montreal moves people up pretty quick, and they will let you know straight out if you have the talent or not.

Generally, the round the player is drafted in is more important to him than which organization picks him. Few players know enough about the quality or characteristics of the different major league organizations to have strong feelings about who drafts them. Of course, some hope to be drafted by their hometown team or a nearby major league team. Players drafted by losing teams are sometimes pleased, since there may be more opportunities for them to advance. Beyond that, it does not matter; most are simply glad for the opportunity to play pro ball.

Once drafted, the player must decide whether to sign or continue his education. This is often a difficult decision, especially if a large bonus is involved. It can be risky as well. If the player elects to stay in school and fails to develop as expected, or if he is injured, he may be drafted in a lower round the next time or not all. High school stars often fail to make the transition to Division I college baseball. And for pitchers the risk of a career-threatening injury is always present. The human arm was not designed to throw a baseball overhand with all one's force, and each year more than a few promising professional careers end before the individuals ever have a chance to sign a contract. Nonetheless, many players decline the chance to play pro ball in favor of staying in school, hoping to go in a higher round the next time. Derrick White, who grew up in a low-income neighborhood north of San Francisco, is a good example. He was drafted by the Minnesota Twins in the thirty-second round after his freshman year at Santa Rosa Junior College:

> The Twins first offered me $2,500, and, after I turned that down, they eventually got up to $11,000. I thought that if I didn't sign, that I could easily double that in the next draft. The next year the team did really well, we came in third in the state of California, and I did well as MVP. I had some scholarship offers. Me and my cousin were the first ones in our family to have a chance to go to college, and I was thinking I would like to go to the University of Oklahoma, at least for a year. I figured that it wouldn't hurt to be a year closer to my degree, but I was also waiting to see what round I would go in the draft.
>
> I went in the ninth round, to Philadelphia, and then had to decide between them and school. The Phillies were offering $18,000 at the start, and in the end, with a package deal of eighteen cash and thirteen for school, it was a $31,000 deal. It wasn't really that much money for the round I went in. And I figured if I went to Oklahoma and proved myself in Division I, it would increase my value, and it wouldn't hurt any going to school for another year. So I went to school.
>
> But there was a lot of pressure in knowing that I could fail. I actually had to go to the doctor due to all the stress I had. I was working out [weight lifting] one time, and I just blanked out from the stress.

Derrick was drafted in the sixth round by the Expos after his junior year at Oklahoma in 1991, and he signed for three times the previous offer.

Darren Paxton was picked in the thirteenth round out of high school. He decided to go to college. "My parents had always said that education is something that will stay with you for the rest of your life, and you couldn't be sure that baseball would. In baseball a lot of other people are making decisions about your career, while in the business world you can pretty much stake out your own route." Darren got a degree in business and marketing at the University of San Diego, but by the time he was drafted again he had dropped twenty-five rounds in the draft and received no bonus.

Most of the coaches that I interviewed, even those who had not been to college themselves, believe that high school graduates are better off going to college for a while before turning professional. Take the advice of the Padres' Gene Roof:

> It's tough to tell an eighteen-year-old kid who is being offered $600,000 to turn it down and go to college, unless he comes from a very rich family. That's a lot of

money, and if you put it in the bank and can take care of it for the rest of your life, you won't have to hit it too hard. You can live off the interest. When the kid can't get a lot of bonus money, then I think he should go to college. College makes him grow up and mature a little bit and gives him independence, which is what they need in baseball. You shouldn't be getting into pro ball at eighteen and still be dependent on your mom and dad. If you are, then chances are you won't survive in this game. In this game you are out on a limb by yourself. You play together as a team, but it's really up to you.

Negotiating the Contract

Teams like to sign their draft picks as quickly as possible. In one recent draft the Cincinnati Reds signed twenty-four of their first twenty-seven picks within ten days of the draft; the Colorado Rockies signed thirty-seven of their fifty picks within a week.[24] There are strong incentives to sign players quickly. Once a player gets an agent, the amount of money he seeks escalates. Also, college coaches review the draft list. When they see a high school player the scouts liked, they will offer a scholarship, hoping to lure him to their school. As the Orioles' John Stokoe explained:

> A kid drafted in the twentieth round, whom we might be willing to give a few thousand bucks to, is now all of a sudden presented with a college scholarship that might be worth $40,000. When that happens, there is not much you can tell the kid. He'd better take the scholarship and go to school, because we can't match the value of his scholarship. We did all the work, but they end up with the player. The college coach probably never even saw the kid play.

That is partially the reason Major League Baseball does not publish the results of its draft until two weeks after the event.

How does a ballplayer, sometimes still in his teens, negotiate a contract with a corporation? Usually with an agent. In the sports pages we hear about agents like Scott Boras, who advised J. D. Drew to ask for an unheard of $11 million from the Phillies. Boras, in particular, has gotten a lot of attention not just because of the huge bonuses he requests for his clients, but also because he often prevents players' families from talking directly to the organization. Team officials accuse him of isolating players and their parents from the team, forcing negotiations to consist only of team offers and yes-and-no answers from players and parents. Whatever one thinks of Boras's tactics, they have succeeded in wresting unprecedented millions from major league teams.

Players selected after the fifth round often do not have agents to help them negotiate a contract, though many will acquire one during their first year or two of pro ball. Instead, it is usually parents or a family friend who helps. The background and intelligence of the parents can be important in determining how much money a young athlete receives, as one veteran scout explained:

> You walk into a home that has a mother and father, and the father is a lawyer and the mother is a doctor. Well, they know exactly what's going on. You go into a home in the middle of Tennessee someplace, and no father and the mother is working at McDonald's. They have no chance. I mean they don't know. I'm not giving out any secrets by telling you that baseball doesn't like agents. But sometimes when you see a situation like that, no father and mother not educated, there is a place for somebody. It doesn't have to be an agent, but at least the family should get a lawyer to sit in and listen, so at least they have a chance of getting a decent contract. They are at such a disadvantage, the mother and the seventeen- or eighteen-year-old son, sitting there and trying to negotiate a contract, compared to that doctor-lawyer family. It is really an unfair situation, because the kids with the same ability from these two backgrounds are not going to get the same bonus.

While the vast majority of athletes enter pro ball through the draft, there are exceptions. About 5 percent of major league ballplayers in any given year got there without ever having been drafted.[25] Most of them signed as "free agents" after attending a "tryout camp." And among them have been all-stars such as Bobby Bonilla and Kevin Mitchell. How is it possible that players of this caliber could have been missed? How many Bonillas and Mitchells are there around the country who will never be discovered and never have the opportunity to play professional baseball? Given the enormous number of amateur players, estimated at 1.25 million, and the fact that some rural regions are not well scouted, not all of the nation's best talent has an equal chance of being seen. Moreover, baseball performance is highly variable—even the best players have slumps. There is always the chance that a talented player may be observed by scouts when he is not playing well and therefore dismissed. Also, players mature at different rates, so that a player who does not look good, say, in his junior year may as a senior have blossomed into a genuine prospect. Nonetheless, the number of genuine prospects who are overlooked is probably quite small, and certainly less than during the pre–World War II era when fewer sports competed for young boys' devotion—practically every boy played baseball, and practically every town with more than a thousand inhabitants had its own team. Furthermore, few organizations had an effective scouting system at that time. As Hall of Famer Paul Waner once observed, "There were so many teams along there in the middle states, so few scouts, that the chances of a good player being discovered and getting a chance to get into organized ball were one in a million."[26] Not so today.

2. Breaking In

I flew into the Mets' minicamp in St. Lucie, Florida. It was scary at first. I got in at night so I didn't meet any of the guys till the next day. It's my first night, and my roommate was a Latin player who didn't speak much English, a guy from a totally different background than me. The next morning we got up and got our uniforms. At first, nobody explained how things worked there, no fanfare or anything. They told me who I was going to play for and that was that.

It was a real adjustment, a real wake-up call, like "Hey, I am playing professional baseball now, that's why I am here, it's going to be my job." The first couple of days you want to prove to everybody that you deserve to be there. You're happy to be there, but you're really nervous too. It was tough because everybody was so good; great pitching every day and you hitting with wood bats. That was a big adjustment in itself. There were some guys with great baseball backgrounds, like Division 1 all-American and all that. But everyone was pretty down to earth. There was this sense that everybody was in the same boat, everybody was fresh, everybody had a long road ahead of them, and that nothing was going to come easy anymore. (Anthony Valentine, Pittsfield Mets)

Minicamp is the player's introduction to pro ball and to the norms and peculiarities of the specific major league organization they have signed with. In some respects minicamp is like freshman orientation for college students. Coaches tell the new players, like orientation advisors tell the new students, what will be expected of them on and off the field—from dress to drinking and curfew.

Tri-City ValleyCats playing pepper during pregame. (Photo by Morgan Gmelch)

Most players arrive in camp not knowing anyone. They may have played against one or two of the other players while in college or in a summer league, but otherwise all faces are new. Everyone feels pressure to perform well—from the high-round draft picks who want to show the organization that they were worth the big bonuses they received down to the low-round picks who want to show everyone that they are better than the round they were taken in. Andy Dziadkowiec, a catcher drafted out of high school in the third round by the Toronto Blue Jays, remembers his minicamp in St. Catharines, Ontario, a week after his high school graduation:

It was the toughest two weeks of my life. Physically, every day was a grind. You'd get up at 8 o'clock, eat breakfast, and be on the field at 9:00. Then it was all day long. I did more in those two weeks than I did in two years of high school. Every day we'd throw, catch the pitchers, work on situational baseball, and, then after that was finished, you'd work individually on separate things. They spent a lot of time with me on my mechanics, throwing to second. . . . I threw more in those two weeks than I ever did before, and my arm got sore. I didn't want to tell anybody, you want to impress them, so you don't want to tell them that you can't handle it, or that maybe you're injury prone. Physically you're sore, but mentally you try to get through it.

It was weird meeting guys from all different parts of the country. I was so green, I was just eighteen, and I didn't know where to go or what to do or what to say. There were lots of things that were new to me, with laundry and all that. So I asked lots of questions.

At least the climate in St. Catharines is hospitable. Most rookies endure day-time workouts in hot and humid Florida or torrid Arizona where most minicamps are located.

After the first few days of camp, the players are assigned to a team. Rosters change according to how the players perform and how the coaches assess their readiness to play at a certain level. When the training ends, the camp breaks, and the two teams travel by bus or plane to the towns where they will play. Rarely in my interviews did a player remark on the journey itself. I found that odd, perhaps because the journeys at the end of spring training were momentous occasions for me and my teammates.

I still remember well one train journey our team made from the Tigers' spring training base in Lakeland, Florida, to the Carolina League town of Rocky Mount, North Carolina, in 1967. The trip took twenty-four hours, and I spent a good deal of that standing on the platform at the rear of the train getting my first glimpse of the South—tarpaper-roofed shanties clustered near the tracks, black people sitting outside on crates and makeshift benches. Having grown up in a middle-class suburb of San Francisco, I had never seen real poverty before, nor had I seen so many African-Americans in one place. In 1992, while beginning the research for this book, I retook that same train journey. It was not the same. There were still some shanties, but in other ways the South looked much like the rest of the country—the same fast-food restaurants, gas stations, and retail outlets built in the same design one sees everywhere else in America. Perhaps it is because the country has become so homogenized that players today do not find the journeys remarkable.

Arriving in their new towns, players are most excited to see the ballpark. Most are pleased, as minor league ballparks at all levels have been upgraded in recent years. Players from Division I universities with major baseball programs, however, are sometimes deflated. "I was a little disappointed," said Pat Listach about his arrival in Beloit, Wisconsin, to play in the Class A Midwest League. "The ballfield wasn't in the best of shape, and the clubhouse wasn't what I was used to at Arizona State." "When I walked into the clubhouse the first day," recalled Mike Saccocio about his arrival in Jamestown, New York, "the trainer gave me a uniform that didn't fit. The pants were really big, and he didn't have any others. I had always envisioned how I would look in this great, tight, major league uniform; and here I was walking onto the field for my first pro game in this baggy thing." Mark Larosa, who had played for college powerhouse Louisiana State University before signing with the Expos, was even more critical of Jamestown, "I am used to the college atmosphere, big towns and campuses where there are many things to do. In college we traveled by airplane and concert-tour buses, tour buses that had beds in them. This bus here is nothing compared to what we had in college."

Teams in the low minors may have smaller staffs than some major college programs, so players may not get the individual attention that they were accustomed to either. Darren Campbell played for the University of Michigan before signing with the Chicago White Sox, where he was sent to their farm team in South Bend, Indiana:

> When I got to South Bend some of my stuff hadn't come on the plane with me, and I needed a jock and some sliding shorts. When I was at the university I would go to our equipment manager and get whatever I needed. They have a huge budget. No problem. They give you what you need. Well, when I got to South Bend, I needed some gear so I went to the clubbie and asked him if he had a jock for me. He pointed me to a locker where there was a big box of used jocks and used sanitaries [socks]. I looked at that, and I thought, "He must be kidding, I can't wear any of this stuff." That was my first impression of pro ball.

Choosing Roomies

Like all newcomers, the first thing players must do is find living accommodations. Since most first-year players are single, they typically share apartments with other players for companionship and to save money. Consequently, the twenty-four young men who compose a team must divide themselves into six or seven residential groups.[1] On what basis do they select "roomies"? The living arrangements of the 115 players that I recorded from five minor league teams show that players look first to other players of the same race for housemates—blacks with blacks, Latinos with Latinos, whites with whites. The tendency is strongest among Latinos (95 percent roomed with fellow Latinos), mainly, they said, because of language. Anglo players said they would not want to live with Latinos mostly because of language and cultural differences. "I'd never feel like I could communicate well enough with them," said one player. "I love these guys to death, and I have fun trying to talk with them in the locker room, but I couldn't live with them. I mean that wouldn't be much fun for either one of us, because we wouldn't be able to communicate, and we don't always think alike."

Players also tend to live with others who play the same or similar positions, with the primary distinction being between pitchers and position players. This was true of 65 percent of the players I sampled. When asked, most players said they had more in common with teammates who play the same or a similar position. As outfielder Joe DeBerry noted about rooming with fellow outfielder Lyle Mouton, "I can go home and talk to Lyle about our game, about my swing, and things like that. We can talk hitting, whereas if I was living with a pitcher it would be tougher to talk about these things because he is thinking about a different part of the game." The pattern also has its origins in minicamp and spring training, where pitchers, infielders, and outfielders practice and train much of the time in separate groups. Frequent interaction leads to friendships and then to sharing quarters. Sometimes, of course, the selection of roommates is haphazard, as when only one or two players remain who have not yet arranged their accommodations.

With each new season, as players become better acquainted with their teammates, the tendency to choose roommates from within one's own ethnic group and playing position declines somewhat. Players begin to room with teammates who share interests outside of baseball. Those who like to party and pursue women tend to room together, as do the sportsmen who golf, hunt, or fish. Players who are religious likewise tend to room together. Several scholars have argued that bonding between male athletes is based more on sharing activities than on conversation and self-disclosure.[2] So in an environment where few make a real effort to get to know their teammates intimately, it is not surprising that they choose roommates with whom they can do things.

Rookies who join a team late, and therefore have not yet formed friendships, can have difficulty finding roommates and a place to live. Glenn Kinns is a good example of this. After spending his entire first spring training with one team, Kinns was reassigned to a different team when camp broke.[3] His new team was comprised of veteran players, none of whom he knew. Kinns wrote in his journal about the difficulties that followed:

Thursday, April 8: We arrived at West Palm Beach about 1:30 P.M. and are staying at the Sheraton Hotel. The Expos are only putting us up for tonight, so after that we are on our own. I can't find anyone who needs a roommate so I don't know what I'm going to do. There aren't many places that I can afford in the classified ads, so I called Homehunters to help. . . .

Saturday, April 10th: The living situation is really depressing me! I walked around the city today (at least 12 to 15 miles) looking at places within my monetary and walking range (from the stadium). No luck. The neighborhoods were incredibly terrible, and I'll be darned if I'll live in anything that terrible. I tried to get in with Mike Vaughan, Rick Miller, and Randy Budd, because they lost a roommate to someone else, but for some reason Vaughan doesn't want me. . . . I really can't believe anyone would be so selfish and downright cruel, especially to a teammate. I was feeling severely depressed. I called Dad and told him the situation, and he told me not to worry and that he would send me some money so that I could stay at the hotel while I'm looking for a place to live. I'm not going to be concentrating on baseball enough if I have to worry about this much longer.

After two more days of looking without success, the team manager allowed Kinns to stay in the clubhouse until he could find a permanent place to live. He slept on the training table for several days until, finally, two teammates made space for him in their apartment.

Increasingly, young players today are getting assistance from their club's front office who prepare a list of suitable accommodations for the players. Some teams have booster clubs who help get the players settled. Kinns described the reception and ease of finding accommodations in Gastonia, North Carolina, the following season where they were met by the booster club:

Early this morning a dozen or so boosters were at the hotel grabbing players left and right and almost forcing them into their cars. The players had already grouped themselves into twos and threes and fours, so it was pretty straightforward. The boosters knew the apartment complexes that were available, so it didn't take long for most of us to get settled. Except there were a few problems for the black and Puerto Rican players, because prejudice runs pretty high down here.

The Grind

Overwhelmingly, rookies say the most difficult part of being in professional baseball is playing everyday. Many have just come from college programs where NCAA regulations limited their baseball time (practice plus games) to twenty hours per week. Baseball was important, but it was

Top: The Staten Island Yankees arriving at Pittsfield's historic Wahconah Park. (Photo by Philip Kamrass, courtesy *Albany Times Union*) *Bottom:* Pittsfield Mets rookies Maurice Bruce and Brandon Copeland. (Photo by William Mesick)

only part of their college or high school lives. They also had classes to take, exams to prepare for, and they were busy with fraternities and other school organizations. Pro ballplayers' lives revolve solely around baseball; they are at the ballpark seven hours per day, seven days a week. Add the many hours spent traveling on the road, and minor leaguers spend about sixty hours per week at baseball, three times the maximum allowed in college. "My body just wasn't prepared for it," said one rookie catcher. "You're just not used to it, your muscles and your body. In high school we played twice a week, three times if you're lucky. Then all of sudden you're just thrown into it [playing everyday] and sometimes your body just doesn't want to do it. In the beginning its physical, but after a while it becomes mental, too. And it gets worse if you're not playing well." Robert Eenhorn, who was raised in the Netherlands, compared baseball in the minors to European sports:

> There isn't any sport in Europe that's as tough on you as American baseball. You're out there day after day. My friends at home [Rotterdam] don't understand how tough it is. They don't know anything about mental part that goes with playing every day, or the exhaustion at the end of the year. . . . I remember my first season at Oneonta [New York–Penn League] which being a short season league has only seventy-two games. But I thought it was the longest season in the world. Especially in your first year in pro ball, you tend to think about baseball all day long. That's why lots of young players wear themselves out. You have to learn that you can't be thinking about the game all the time, you have to learn to leave the game at the ballpark.

Playing every day is such a strain that by midseason players are pining for a day off. They joke about praying for rain and repeat stories about the extraordinary lengths others have gone to to secure a day off. Ron Shelton, writer and director of the popular film *Bull Durham,* drew on his minor league experience for the scene in which Crash Davis (played by Kevin Costner) leads his teammates into the ballpark late at night to turn on the sprinklers in order to get a day off and a break from losing. There is seldom any real escape, however, since canceled or rained-out games are made up as doubleheaders.

When I was a rookie in the New York–Penn League an incredibly rainy month washed out so many games that five doubleheaders in five consecutive nights had to be scheduled. My teammates were already grumbling about the extra games when the first game went twenty-one innings before being called at 1 A.M. In the nineteenth inning my girlfriend fainted in the

Newcomer to the New York–Penn League, Jamestown Jammers manager Jim Saul, left, and pitching coach Mark Ross, look over maps to find out where they will be traveling this season. (Photo by Jim Riggs, *Jamestown Post-Journal*)

nearly empty stands. We resumed the suspended game the next day—before the scheduled doubleheader—and played seven more innings (a total of twenty-eight innings and eight-plus hours) before the game was ended by an exhausted plate umpire who called a runner, who clearly had been tagged out, safe at home. I got one hit in ten at bats.

The Competition

Even at the lowest levels of pro ball, the competition is tougher than anything the rookies have experienced before. Every night pitchers face teams that are far better than the best team on their collegiate schedule. "In pro ball," Jamestown Expos pitcher Jim Ferguson said, "the number eight and nine hitters [in the batting order] were number three and four hitters in college. There are no easy outs." In the words of Marlins coach Rich Donnelly:

It's a rude awakening. What happens is that in high school you are the star, but now in pro ball you're playing against other teams where everybody was a star. Everybody you play against is like you. Everybody is all-American or all this or all that. . . . Some of the kids have never known failure because all along it's always been easy. Some kids come out of small high schools where they've just dominated, now they're in pro ball, and they go "Hey there's a seventeen-year-old kid here who can do what I can, and I'm twenty-one. Wow, he's from Puerto Rico, how did he do that?"

Similarly, Joe Vavra, manager of the Dodgers' Yakima Bears team, said of his rookies, "They've all had a lot of success where they've come from. They get here, and all of a sudden they are just one of many. When they come down to earth, and its like, wow, am I really that bad? The kid thinks here I was [at home] hitting third, leading my team in every category, and now I'm hitting under .200, and I'm homesick. And then everything kind of closes in on him." One rookie described his reaction to his new team-mates, "I can't believe how many of them had been all-state, all-American, or even all-American in other sports besides baseball. It's been humbling, and it's made me realize I am not so special."

Many players are not as successful in this environment as they were in high school or college. Some sit on the bench for the first time in their lives or are platooned, playing only against right- or left-handed pitching. Many lose confidence. They begin to wonder if they are really good enough to go all the way to the big leagues or if they are even good enough to play pro ball at any level. A common reaction is for them to try to elevate their play. "Trying to play beyond one's ability" is the phrase ballplayers use. Pitchers may try to throw harder; hitters may try to hit with more power. Heath Haynes talked about his first month as a rookie: "My mentality was all wrong. I was trying to throw hard, because I thought that's what they wanted. I got a little bit out of control. Then the pitching coach gave me a speech about speed. He said that, 'You made it here, so we are not worried about your speed anymore. Don't try to do more than you're capable of.' That's what finally settled me down."

The little changes players make, such as pitchers tinkering with their wind-up or hitters changing their stance, can upset their natural rhythm, which in turn can precipitate a slump. Slumps take a heavy toll on rookies who have not been in pro ball long enough to have known real success. Unlike the veteran player who can remember himself being successful, and therefore can ride out the bad times, the rookie does not know that he will regain his "old form." As manager Joe Vavra noted, "Once they start going downhill, they have a hard time stopping it, because they don't know how to stop it. That comes with experience, and rookies don't yet have much."

Wood

Not only is the competition unyielding, but players must adjust to hitting with wood bats. Some said this is the most difficult adjustment of all. Today's players, unlike those of previous generations, grew up hitting with aluminum bats. The difference is considerable. An aluminum bat is hollow and weighs less than a wood bat of the same length, enabling the hitter to swing it faster. "Bat speed" confers two advantages on the hitter. One, it gives him more time to see the pitch before deciding whether or not to swing. By one estimate, a four ounce reduction in bat weight gives the batter an extra five feet to eye the ball before swinging.[4] Secondly, it is the speed of the swing, more than the weight or mass of the bat, that determines how hard the ball will be hit and the distance it will travel. All else equal, a player will hit more balls to the fence and beyond with an aluminum bat than a wood one. Wood bats also have a smaller "sweet spot"— the best part of the bat to hit the ball—about two to three inches long versus four to five inches on an aluminum bat. This means there is less room for error when hitting. The extra weight of a wood bat also means the hitter must shorten his swing and learn to "throw" his hands at the pitch more quickly, and this often requires a batter to change his swing. The difficulty in making this adjustment is easily seen in the number of bats broken by rookies, especially during the first month of the season.

Players who were power hitters in college may find that they have trouble reaching the fences in pro ball. Scott Tedder averaged ten home runs a year during his college career at Wesleyan but only three a year in pro ball, despite playing over twice as many games. "It's been tough. With wood you have to hit it right on the nose to get results," he said. One sportswriter refers to former great high school and college home-run hitters who could not make the adjustment in pro ball as "aluminum heros."

The Cape Cod League, a summer league for talented college players, switched in 1984 from aluminum to wood bats. The league's batting and pitching statistics offer a good measure of the difference between the two. In 1984, the last year that aluminum was used, the league batting average was .273 and the ERA was 4.86. Five years after the wood bat was introduced, the league batting average had declined to .252 and the ERA to 3.68. Runs scored per game had dropped from twelve to under nine and home runs from over two per game to under one.[5]

For the 1997–98 season, Amherst (Mass.) College coach Bill Thurston, a member of the NCAA rules committee and a fierce proponent of removing high-performance aluminum bats, compared the batting statistics for seventy-five college players who also played in the Cape Cod League. Swinging aluminum bats, they collectively hit .339 in college versus just .232 with wood bats on the Cape. Their slugging percentages also declined by over two hundred points, from .552 to .327.[6] In 1999 the top Italian baseball league switched to wood bats after it was announced by the International Baseball Association that only wood would be used in international play, including the Olympics. Sixty-six home runs were hit by the league's nine teams in the three weeks before the switch; in the first three weeks of the "Wooden Age," that figure dropped to two.[7] The switch left team officials with "wooden expressions," worried about selling tickets to low-scoring games.[8]

It seems logical that what is a liability to hitters should be a boon for pitchers. But rookie pitchers also must make changes. In college and high school they usually pitch on the outside part of the plate, where the chances of retiring the hitter are the greatest because of the tendency of most amateur hitters to try to "pull" the ball. Once in pro ball, they must learn to pitch to the inside part of the plate to be effective. (Since hitters cannot get wood bats around as quickly and the handle on a wood bat is thin, batters cannot do much with a pitch on the hands.) Some pitchers make this adjustment better than others. For future players wood bats may be less of a problem because the NCAA has adopted new standards that require aluminum bats perform more like wood, by being heavier, with narrower barrels, and a slightly smaller sweet spot.

Putting Up Good Numbers

It is not long before rookies learn that professional baseball places great stock in statistics. And that their chances of moving up or just keeping their jobs depends on "putting up good numbers." Self-esteem and status on the team are also directly affected by one's numbers. When players are first discovered on high school and college ball fields, as we saw in Chapter 1, scouts translate their present and potential skills into numerical values on a twenty-to-eighty-point scale. Once in pro ball, nearly every aspect of a player's performance is measured—batting average, on-base percentage, batting average with runners in scoring position, runs batted in, stolen bases, hit by pitch, etc. After each game, an official scorer compiles this data on every player who entered the game. The information is then faxed to Howe Sports Data International, who overnight crunch the numbers and fax the updated averages back the next morning. Although nightly every minor league manager also provides some narrative and qualitative assessment in his report to the major league front office, which players never get to see, it is still the player's numbers that speak the loudest. At the end of the season, it is these numbers that are the yardstick for measuring the kind of year the player had. His numbers will be the major factor in determining the kind of contract he is offered for the next season. Although it only takes a dozen infield singles over the course of a season to make the difference between hitting .250 and .300, to the organization and in the mind of most players, those fifty points represent the difference between a mediocre and a great year.

Like the statistics used to quantify performance, everything else in baseball is ranked. The rookie player's first exposure to baseball's hierarchy comes shortly after arriving to minicamp. While all players are friendly, everyone soon learns approximately where in the draft each of their teammates was selected. They also learn how much money many received as a signing bonus. The hierarchy really becomes apparent, however, the following March when the entire organization is assembled for spring training, and players are sorted into six or seven grades (i.e., leagues): Rookie, Short-Season Class A, Low A, High A, Double A, Triple A, and the major leagues. In spring camp a player assigned to a Class-A club would no more assume the liberty of socializing with a Triple-A player, than a midlevel supervisor in a large corporation would invite the vice president home to dinner.

Small Towns

First-year players must also adjust to a new environment—small-town America. Many of the towns in the Rookie and Short-Season Class-A leagues have populations under 50,000, such as Auburn, Batavia, Jamestown, Oneonta, and Utica, in the New York–Penn League. In the Rookie Appalachian League, the Bluefield Orioles, Princeton Blue Rays, and Pulaski Rangers play in towns with only 10,000 inhabitants. Yet, most of today's ballplayers come from the suburbs surrounding large urban areas. California, the state that produces more players than any other (both in total number and per capita of population) is the most urbanized in the nation. Nearly 96 percent of Californians live in a metropolitan area.[9] The other three states that produce the most pro players are also highly urbanized: New York 91 percent, Florida 91 percent, and Texas 82 percent. Fewer than one-third of the players on the five teams I surveyed came from small towns similar in size to the places they were now playing in.

Players from urban and suburban areas often complain that the towns they must live in during their first season are "boring" or "dead." About Jamestown, New York, for instance, a rookie from Los Angeles said: "There's really nothing to do here. Nothing to go walking to, nothing interesting to see. There's just nothing here." "Nothing," of course, is a matter of perspective. To the people of the surrounding rural Chautauqua County, Jamestown is a thriving regional center with several good restaurants, cinemas, a public library, and various services. The players are no less critical of the other towns in the New York–Penn League they stay in during road trips.[10] Andy Dzhadkowiec, raised in Chicago, was assigned to the prairie town of Medicine Hat, Alberta, in the Pioneer League:

> In Chicago I was used to seeing a lot of people on the street. When I came to Medicine Hat I didn't see anybody. There just weren't a lot of people around. There weren't people to associate with. It was just farms. . . . Once the game was over you were very limited. We lived in a hotel on top of a strip bar. There wasn't any other place in the town available. Our life was very limited—go to the game, go to the strip bar, go to bed, go to the game. That was pretty much it. We hung out most of the time, played cards or Scrabble, just tried to stay occupied, because you can only get so much from a strip bar. Once you see that a few times that's pretty much it, unless you're really into that kind of thing. It was not a very good influence for a kid just out of high school.

Not having an automobile contributes to the players' boredom. Most players have a car at home, but because of distance and travel time they are discouraged from bringing them to minicamp and then to the rookie leagues. Rarely do more than a few players on any rookie team have their own transportation.[11] Yet, like most young American males, they grew up being dependent upon their cars to get around and for entertainment. In the small towns in which most now find themselves, there is even more need for a car than there was at home, since public transportation is limited or at best infrequent.[12]

The High School Player

The seventeen- or eighteen-year-old who signs for a team right out of high school often finds the adjustment to pro ball especially difficult. To begin with, he is living away from home for the first time. Unlike the college athlete, he has never been away from family, friends, or his girlfriend before. In some respects, the adjustment required of these youthful rookies is similar to what first-term college freshmen face. The ballplayer, however, has the added pressure of trying to succeed in a highly competitive professional sport. Bo Kennedy was only a week out of high school when he was sent to Sarasota, Florida, in the Gulf Coast League:

> Baseball was a time to grow up in a hurry. When I went to Sarasota I was eighteen years old, living with three guys, all of them were several years older than me. Beer was there any time you wanted it, right in front of me, everyday, no one was there to say no or that it's time to stop. Like a lot of young kids I got carried away. It was getting to the point that I was drinking pretty heavily. We would come home from the games, it was hot and that sort of thing, and we would start drinking. The guys that had experienced the college life knew what to expect and could handle themselves better. To me, to go get a twelve pack of beer almost everyday became my normal thing. That was my big thing. I was borderline becoming an alcoholic.

"The high school kid," said QV Lowe, a veteran pitching coach and manager,

> is like a tiger on the loose, chasing his freedom. He doesn't understand what is out there. He will get into drinking and gambling and this and that, and he doesn't know how to handle it. Away from mom and dad he doesn't have to answer to anybody. . . . I've seen a lot of them become very lonesome, and they start calling home. They haven't used long distance before, and before they know it they run up a six- or seven-hundred-dollar bill calling back to mom, to their girlfriend. They can be extremely jealous of their girlfriends back home. The guys who went away to college have already experienced all that and gotten over it. They're finished with it. But for the high school kid this is the first time he has been away. And it happens at a time when he has other pressures on him. Even though the kid wants that freedom, wants to get away from home, now that he's away, he doesn't know how to handle it, not without someone to talk to.

The high school player must also learn, without much guidance, how to set up a bank account, budget his money, do his laundry, and eat a balanced diet. Some coaches say the transition to pro ball is too harsh for eighteen-year-olds, and that most would be better off going to college first. "It's really tough on them," said Birmingham Barons broadcaster Curt Bloom, who spent five years traveling with Class-A teams as a broadcaster, "You've got the travel, you've got the long hours, you've got the terrible eating habits, and you've got the groupies. That is a lot for an eighteen-year-old."

Unlike the past, however, today's players are offered free counseling whenever they need it. Since the mid-1970s, major league organizations have employed psychologists to help their players with emotional, alcohol, or drug problems. The players are given the phone number of the organization's psychologist and encouraged to call if and when they need help. The players are assured that all conversations are confidential, that nothing will get back to the organization. Few players, however, admitted to ever having used this service, and the few that did had done so for drugs or alcohol.

One ameliorating factor in many players' adjustment is the companionship offered by the young local women who befriend them. Most are roughly the same age as the players and are often just looking for excitement and something to do during the lazy, hot summers. The players initial interest in these girls—who they collectively label as "groupies"—is usually sexual, but friendships often ensue as players and women get to know one another (see Chapter 9). As surrogate girlfriends, they fill voids created by the absence of the players' female friends back home. Occasionally, they become real girlfriends. Either way they offer a pleasant and much-needed diversion from baseball, and they often help with household chores and errands and console players during slumps. In various ways they give players emotional support, and their companionship helps rookies overcome homesickness. It does not replace the support the players enjoyed at home, but it does help.

The Latino Player

One in every four rookies comes from the Spanish-speaking Caribbean or Latin America. In addition to the challenges all young players face, Dominicans, Puerto Ricans, Venezuelans, and other non-Americans must contend with a foreign culture—different foods, customs, and language. Compounding the difficulties, most Latinos are younger than their American teammates. Most have little or no knowledge of English. Carlos Rodriguez was sixteen when he signed out of a Mexican league and was sent to spring training in Florida:

> It was hard for me to even understand the coaches. We used to have a translator, and that was a help, but when the camp broke and the season started my team didn't have a translator. I used to cry because I was homesick. My food is different than what you all eat here. . . . I had to learn how to cook and wash clothes and pay bills. The other thing was that I wasn't old enough to go with the other players to bars or the places where people hang out at night. I remember asking myself what am I doing here. Every time I wrote to my mother, I would say that I was doing fine and she didn't have to worry about anything, but it wasn't true. When I left home, she was crying. I can remember her hiding behind the door, and I knew she was crying. My dad took me to the airport. He did the same thing. He turned around and walked away; he didn't want me to see him crying.

Carlos Arroyo was also sixteen when he signed with the Philadelphia Phillies after his second year of high school in Puerto Rico:

> The first day in spring training they [the coaches] go introduce themselves, and they talk about what they expect from us and all that. But it was all in English, so I wondered what was going on. Everybody was posted into working groups. They said go to your groups. I went out to the fields, we had four fields, and I was wondering where I was supposed to go. I was wandering around until finally I saw a couple of kids in my group. From then on wherever they went, I went with them. It was funny. That was the way I got around spring training my first year.

As Arroyo noted, a common strategy for Latinos with limited knowledge of English is to first observe and then imitate their teammates. They avoid being first in line for an instructional drill, so that they can watch how their teammates do the drill before it is their turn.[13]

The language barrier creates other difficulties. With half a player's life spent on the road, he must eat out often. Latinos may have trouble reading menus and ordering. "For the first month I only ate cheeseburgers and the french fries in the Burger King," recalled Oreste Marrero, who began his career at seventeen in Helena, Montana. "That was all I knew to say." Not speaking English also makes it more difficult for Latinos to explore and get around town. Both on road trips and at home, Latino players spend more time in their hotel rooms and apartments then do their Anglo teammates.

Communication difficulties can also affect their confidence and self-esteem. Coaches in the low minors said that many Latinos struggle on the ball field for the first season or two because of language and culture differences. Some Latinos believe that their advancement in baseball is slowed, because they do not know "the system" as well as Anglo players. As Oreste Marrero said, "I care about learning English, because I know if I speak English I get to the majors faster." Latinos are sometimes treated condescendingly by their American teammates who mistake deficiencies in English for lack of intelligence. I remember some of my own teammates speaking to Latinos in a simplified pidgin even when their English was adequate: "Juan big boy; Juan throw ball hard."[14]

Most Latino players make a serious effort to learn English, usually by watching a lot of television, practicing their English in restaurants, and talking to teammates. Some always carry an English dictionary. They also learn on the field what Latinos call "baseball language." Playing baseball for two seasons in French-speaking Quebec in the 1960s, I experienced some of the same problems as Latinos in the United States in that I had to learn enough French to buy food, eat out, get around, understand the public address announcers, read the sports pages, and communicate with my Francophone girlfriend who spoke little English. I also remember the initial oddness of listening to the line-up announced in French over the public address system, "*lancer* [pitcher], *receveur* [catcher], *premier but* [first base]. . . ." However, because my manager and most of my teammates were English-speaking Americans, I had it far easier than Latino players do in the United States.

Some Latinos may also have to deal with racial prejudice. Much of it stems from North American conceptualizations of race. In Latin America and the Caribbean, people are labeled according to skin shade, such as, "high brown," "brown," "light," "clear," and so on. Because these subtleties are absent in North America—replaced by a crude black and white dichotomy—a Latino player with brown or light-brown skin finds himself simply labeled "black." The treatment he receives varies and depends in part on where in the United States he is playing. In ballparks in the South he may even hear a few fans call him "nigger," in restaurants waitresses may be slow to wait on him, and, if he is out with a white or light-skinned female, he may get hard stares from some locals. Elsewhere, racism is usually more subtle but still hurtful.

Recognizing the difficulties that Latinos may have in coping with such racism, at least one organization has tried not to assign young Latinos to teams in the Deep South. Their concern has been that racism, by making the player's adaptation to the United States difficult, may also hamper performance and perhaps even sour him on playing ball in the United States.[15] Overall Latino players have had an easier time in the Southwest, where there is a large Spanish-speaking population.[16] Baseball is popular among Mexican Americans, who support Latino players both at the ballpark and in the community. Many restaurants and stores have Spanish-speaking employees, and the warmer climate of the Southwest makes it easier for them to play well than in the Midwest and Northeast, especially in the spring when temperatures are often too cool for baseball.

While there is little overt racism on most professional baseball teams, cultural differences between Latinos and their teammates often result in social distance, and sometimes friction. *Machismo,* the Latin cultural expectation that males be manly, virile, tough, unsentimental, and sexist, can be interpreted by American teammates as arrogance, cockiness, and bravado. Anglo players often stereotype Latinos as being temperamental, hot-headed, and less than hard-working. For example, I came across the following passage in the journal of a white player: "Pat [a teammate] and I are the same mentally, hard work is our motto. We both share the same attitudes toward the Puerto Ricans, it's not that we are prejudiced against them from the start, but they are lazy and aren't willing to work harder than they have to."

Language differences often allow such generalizations to go unchallenged. Given such differences in language and culture, it is not surprising that Latino players stick together. As rookies they not only share quarters, but also eat, go to the ballpark, and go out together afterward. In the words of Dusty Baker, who spent his career in two organizations—the San Francisco Giants and Los Angeles Dodgers—both with many Latino players, "Hispanics have always been a separate group because of the language. As long as some players are not speaking Spanish, then there's going to be a separate group. If Hispanics have a choice between struggling in English or speaking in Spanish, then they are going to speak Spanish. And that's unlikely to change."

The intense competition, the strain of having to play every day, the new work tools (i.e., wood bats), the loss of the social support provided by family and friends, and the relative boredom of small-town life, exacerbated by the lack of transportation, are the tough conditions of professional baseball faced by all rookies. The adjustments required are especially difficult for young high school players and for Latinos.

Contrary to what I had expected, few players complain about the travel. Most say they actually enjoy being on the road, aside from all-night journeys at the end of a road trip. Road trips introduce variety into their lives: new scenery, new stores to browse in, new ballparks, and, for some, new women. And the hotels they stay in while on the road are usually better than the apartments they rent; they at least have firm mattresses and cable TV. Although some players recounted the horrors of a particular trip—the time the driver got lost and drove fifty miles in the wrong direction or the times the air-conditioning broke down in sweltering heat—these were exceptions.[17] Yet, torturous, long journeys in unreliable, run-down buses and staying in cheap hotels is one of the most enduring stereotypes of minor league baseball, in both fiction and film. Clearly the popular image of the minors is dated. It has been at least two decades since Rookie league teams routinely traveled in old buses or stayed in declining downtown hotels, three players to a room. Today, the buses are modern—many are equipped with VCRs—and the teams usually stay in modern, inexpensive motels (e.g., the Ramada, La Quinta, and Quality Inn chains) on commercial strips.

Despite the difficult adjustment required, none of the players I interviewed had regretted being in pro ball. Most are proud to be professional baseball players, proud that after years of hard work they are finally on a track that could take them to the major leagues. Many feel privileged. Their image is on a baseball card, fans request their autographs, radio broadcasters seek them out for pregame and postgame interviews, they are pursued by young women simply because they are professional athletes, and their folks back home boast of their being "away" playing pro ball. Though the challenges rookies face are considerable, most cope. No one I spoke with ever talked seriously of quitting, and virtually no one does.

3. Learning the Culture

Some aspects of a baseball player's education are deliberate and formal, such as learning baseball strategy. Coaches run drills and give instructions on positioning, cut-offs, relays, pivots, and so forth. They also lay out the organization's philosophy and what behaviors are expected. A handbook with the organization's rules and regulations is given to each player. The Florida Marlins call theirs *The Marlin Standards Book;* the Baltimore Orioles, *The Oriole Way.*[1] Compared to most occupations, baseball has many rules and exerts a lot of control over its players' lives, both on and off the field.[2] I still remember arriving in Lakeland, Florida, for my first spring training thirty-three years ago and receiving a sheet of regulations telling me when I had to be in bed, when the lights went out, what time I had to get up, and how I was to dress, all in sharp contrast to the freedoms I enjoyed at college and even at home. "Tigertown Rules and Regulations" contained over fifty edicts grouped under the headings "Dormitory," "Cafeteria," "Clubhouse," and "Field."[3] "Learn and live by them," my manager said, "or you will be heading home before you can blink."

Baseball's rules fall into two broad categories: performance and professionalism. The former proscribe behaviors that might negatively affect job performance. Curfews, which aim to ensure that players get adequate rest, are a good example. Curfews are universal in the minor leagues (in the low minors it is usually 1 A.M. or two hours after the game). Curfews are a little looser in Double A or Triple A, where the players are older and more mature; and they may only be "advisory" in the big leagues. Atlanta Braves manager Bobby Cox explained, "We have all kinds of rules in our club, and we expect them [the players] not to break them. But at this level we don't need to check their rooms every night. This is a grueling sport now: 162 league games, 33 spring training games. . . . If somebody is going to break curfew, I don't know who it would be. I really don't."

Another performance-related proscription is never missing stretching. Stretching is done as a group, under the supervision of the team's trainer and is taken so seriously that the penalties for missing it are often as severe as those for being late for a road trip. Both for health and image reasons, all minor league players are banned from using tobacco products—chew, dip, and cigarettes—at the ballpark. Individual managers often add other rules beyond those required by their organization. One manager who thought golf was bad for his hitters banned it; another forbade his pitchers to sit with their pitching arms next to bus windows where the air-conditioning vents blew cold air onto them. I played for a manager in the Florida State League who would not allow any player on the beach after 11 A.M., concerned that the sun and sea would sap our strength.

Rules pertaining to professionalism try to ensure that players behave in a manner appropriate to Major League Baseball. A strict dress code governs their appearance on the field (e.g., undersleeves must be the team color, hats or helmets worn at all times). One team I played for imposed a twenty-five-dollar fine for merely altering the height or look of one's stirrup socks. Team caps or jerseys may not be worn outside the ballpark. Similarly, players are prohibited from, and may be fined or even removed from the game for, throwing a bat or helmet in anger. I watched the Jamestown Expos' manager remove his starting catcher in the fourth inning of an important game when he slammed his helmet on the ground after striking out. Clubs also forbid players from using profanity near fans. Britt Burns, roving pitching coach for the Florida Marlins, said, "We want them to be solid citizens and that means no f-bombs near fans, especially kids. If you must say 'fuck,' go up the tunnel, don't do it near the stands. We want to promote the family entertainment value of professional baseball."

Players may argue an umpire's call but must never bump, touch, or make any physical contact with him. The umpires' locker room and the scorer's booth are off limits to players at all times, not even to seek an explanation of a call or ruling. Players are not allowed to mix with umpires away from the ballpark; umpires and teams often purposely stay at different hotels. Players are also forbidden from fraternizing with the opposing team while on the field, although this rule often is not enforced. This rule usually comes as a surprise to rookies fresh out of high school and college, who are accustomed to talking to opposing players, many of whom they know from summer leagues.

Off the field, ball clubs are particularly strict about drunkenness, drug use, shoplifting, and any other criminal activity. While traveling with the Jamestown Expos, I learned of two players who were swiftly and summarily released the day after they had been picked up for shoplifting. "We don't tolerate theft," said the manager. "There are a lot of things that have a grace period, but when it comes to theft and the evidence is strong, we send the player home." Similarly, a teammate of mine in the Florida State League who had come to the ballpark somewhat intoxicated and missed a fly ball in the first inning was released that very night.

All clubs also have a dress code for when the team is traveling. In the minor leagues it means no collarless shirts, cut-off shorts, or sandals. "I try to remind them that they are representing the Cleveland Indians," said Jim Gabella, manager of the Indians' Double-A team. "I don't like slobs," said the Marlins' John Boles. "If a player looks slovenly, that is the way he plays." Most major league teams require jacket and tie on the road. Rules about appearance vary between organizations. Some clubs prohibit earrings, beards, and long hair, while others are more lenient.

A ban against players' having women in their hotel rooms, however, is universal. It bridges both performance and professionalism. Managers say that players who escort women through the lobby or hotel corridors to their rooms sully the club's image, and, in small towns, players sleeping with local girls may create resentment. It also creates the risk of sexual assault charges and lawsuits. And there is the concern that womanizers and their roommates will not get to sleep at a reasonable hour. A few managers still believe that sex, whether with a groupie, girlfriend, or wife, saps a player's energy. I overheard one manager, a proponent of the old myth about women's ability to rob men of their physical strength by draining them sexually and psychologically, blame his first baseman's slump on his having too much sex with a girlfriend. I wondered how he knew.

Organizations exert far more control over the behavior of their minor leaguers than their big leaguers. Players in the low minors are young, usually single, not always mature, and, as newcomers to pro ball, they are still learning their way. Many of them need structure and guidance, and hence strict rules may be important to keep them out of trouble. Players in Triple A or the big leagues are four or five years older and are usually more responsible and professional; many are also married. The greater media coverage in the upper echelons of pro ball also means they have lost much of the anonymity of the low minors, and therefore have to be more careful about how they behave in public. But, even if they wanted to, clubs are not able to dictate the off-field behavior of players at this level. Major league players belong to the Major League Baseball Players Association (MLBPA), one of the most powerful unions in the world of sports. The MLBPA prevented baseball from extending its minor league ban on smokeless tobacco to big leaguers. Agents, which most players have by the time they reach Double A, may also inhibit clubs from imposing their will in some areas.

Breaking a rule usually means a fine. Typical levies in the minor leagues are $10 for missing a sign, $25 for throwing a bat or helmet, $50 for being late to the ballpark or the bus, and $100 for bringing a woman to your hotel room. Some managers use smaller fines to remind players of their responsibilities. "It says listen, the only way you're going to remember this is if I fine you, so I take two dollars. And by God it helps," said the Yakima Bears' Joe Vavra of his mostly rookie team.

Most players think the rules are reasonable. "They're fair enough," said Yakima Bears pitcher Adrian Burnside. "We're here to play baseball, and I don't know how you're supposed to do that if you're out partying all night. . . ." But managers and coaches do not find all players compliant, and some say that in recent years it has gotten harder to enforce the rules. Speaking about his rookies, Vavra, a sixteen-year veteran, put it this way:

> It's the way society is. The way the lads react today is the way society has gone. They'll test you on it. There is no more of this, "Yes, sir. No, sir," type of thing. Today they're talking out the sides of their mouths a little more than they used to. . . . On the field you [manager] get a little less respect than you used to. With dress code, you'd think you asked them to commit a grave sin by having them wear a collared shirt and not to wear a hat in the restaurant. It seems like they've never heard that type of thing. To me, that's standard. I was told once and that was it. I don't think they understand that once you sign that contract you're a professional. We expect you to uphold what has been passed down.

The formal rules of baseball are the ideal, what players are expected to do. They do not, of course, always reflect real behavior. Although team curfew may be two hours after the game, some players stay out later, taking a chance that the manager will not be doing a bed check that night. A club's enforcement of its own rules may vary, usually depending on how well the team is performing. When teams are winning, managers loosen up—curfews are relaxed, sloppy dress may be overlooked, and there may even be beer on the bus. But when the team is losing, everything tightens up—the rules are strictly enforced and extra practices are called.

Beyond rules and instruction, the player's education is mostly informal and unstructured, just as it is in most professions, whether teaching or practicing law. Each player receives a constant flow of signals and impressions from his teammates, coaches, media, and others, which combine to mold his attitudes and understanding of the culture of pro ball. Players learn that besides playing well, they must conform to their coach's expectations if they are to advance. Baseball is not the pure meritocracy that the heavy reliance on statistics suggests.

Players learn that some level of conformity to the norms of the team is required if they are to fit in and be accepted. As is true of life in general, behaviors that are reinforced and rewarded by coaches and teammates tend to be repeated, while behaviors that provoke comment or criticism tend to be avoided. The patterned regularities that result from this kind of learning usually remain implicit, that is, they rarely rise to the level of conscious awareness. Indeed, apart from baseball strategy, players have difficulty articulating what they have learned or what the norms of pro ball are. Nonetheless, some patterns are evident.

Local knowledge is a term that some researchers use to refer to shared information that is not learned formally, but that is essential to perform one's work and get along with colleagues. Even something as simple as where to sit on the team bus often involves a protocol that players must learn. Manager, coaches, trainer, and broadcasters sit in the front, sometimes in specific seats. Movie watchers sit in the seats behind the coaches and staff for proximity to the TV and VCR, and card players sit in the middle where there are usually fold-out tables. Each player gets two seats. When there are not enough seats to go around, it is the rookies and other newcomers who double up. (Players communicate that they do not want company by stretching out or by putting gear or a bag on the empty seat next to them.) The rookie is never told where to sit, instead he learns by observing or by making the mistake of taking the wrong seat and being chased off or ribbed. By the time players enter pro ball most are sensitized to the idea that there might be right and wrong places to sit. From their first bus trips in high school, for example, they learn that coaches sit up front and that the freshman team doubles up, while the upper classmen get the back of the bus.

Teammates congratulating Barry Bonds with high fives after a home run. (Photo courtesy the San Francisco Giants)

Small violations and grievances are often brought before the players' Kangaroo Court. Held in the clubhouse, it is usually organized and presided over by a few veterans, one of which may even don a wig and cape, with a baseball bat as a gavel. Court convenes every few weeks, when a sufficient number of charges or complaints, which are recorded on paper or in "the book," have been filed. While the charges are usually minor—Joe Smith left his bubblegum on the dugout bench and I sat on it, or Joe Smith forgot his photo ID and delayed our flight for twenty minutes—they do carry a message about behaviors that are inappropriate or at least annoying to others. The "trial" is conducted with much humor, and the small fine that is levied usually goes into a kitty for an end-of-season party or extra tips for the clubhouse manager. As pitcher Orel Hersheiser explained, besides reinforcing norms, Kangaroo Court "is a good way to get something off your chest in a light way. You've got a guy who is pissing you off. He is doing something wrong, maybe he is always late to dinner, or doing something to the postgame meal, like leaving the milk out, and you'd like him to stop. So you charge him." The court is usually conducted in a good-natured fashion that promotes communication and camaraderie among teammates.

Showing Respect

An often repeated idiom of pro ball is "showing respect for the game." Players are expected to show respect by acting in a professional manner— by hustling, by wearing the uniform properly, by not throwing a helmet in anger, by never showing up a teammate on the field, and by, as one manager said simply, "playing baseball the way it is supposed to be played." In a much publicized altercation, catcher Carlton Fisk chased after and berated the opposing hitter, Deion Sanders, for not running out a pop fly. Sanders was not showing respect for the game. Some say showing respect also applies to how players relate to the fans. "It's what guys like [Derek] Jeter, [Bernie] Williams, and [Tino] Martinez do—they sign, they talk, they wave, and when they're interviewed they're humble," said ex-Giant and now Yankees batting-practice pitcher, Nick Testa.

The importance of showing respect was made clear to me in my second season when my own regard for baseball was called into question by a teammate. At the time I was writing occasional articles about life in the minor leagues for a San Francisco Bay–area newspaper. Some of my articles were mildly critical of baseball, and some of my teammates read what I wrote. One day in the clubhouse, a teammate from South Carolina who had just been released was clearing out his locker and saying his good-byes. I offered my hand. He shook it but, in parting, warned me in a slow, deliberate drawl, "Watch what you write. If I ever read anything of yours that tears down baseball I will come looking for you."

For some coaches, "respect" also means knowing something about baseball's past. After the release of Ken Burns's documentary film *Baseball,* there was talk in the media and criticism among some veteran baseball people that some stars did not know the major milestones in the history of the game, such as the contributions of players like Curt Flood, whose refusal to accept his club trading him to the Philadelphia Phillies paved the way for free agency. Ken Griffey Jr. was reproached when he candidly admitted to not fully understanding Jackie Robinson's accomplishment. In a private moment one Double-A manager expressed to me his deep disappointment over how little his players seemed to care about baseball's history. He recalled how different it had been in his day, that in the low minors he and his teammates were always interested in knowing what major leaguers had played for the team in the past. "Today most of my guys don't know and don't care. They're fixed on the here and now." Ex-Giants manager Roger Craig said of his players, "They don't want to hear anything about the old days. They don't really care what Mickey Mantle, Roger Maris, or Babe Ruth did; their scope is right now." I was surprised that players who knew that I had played pro ball thirty years before with the same teams they were on seldom asked what it had been like.

Some fans, too, are disappointed that many of today's players seem to care little about baseball's storied past. But then, fans do not realize how different their perspective as a spectator is from that of the players, whose major concern must be their own performance. Kevin Kalal, director of media relations for the Tacoma Rainers, said:

> If I went down to the clubhouse right now and said, "Do you remember what a great hitter Jim Rice was in '75," they'd say, "Who cares" or "Who is he?" It has no bearing on them. The fans compare today's game and today's players to the past. That's okay. But the players must live for the moment. The nostalgia, the tradition, and all the stuff about the national pastime is for the fans. The other evening we had a turn-back-the-clock night to 1960 when we had Juan Marichal and Gaylord Perry on our team. It was nice for the fans to see the old uniforms and all that, but it didn't mean much to the players. Some thought it was a big distraction.

While players may not have as much interest in the legends, folklore, and history of the game as many fans would like, their interest in the contemporary game is deep. Indeed, a part of almost every player's daily routine is watching ESPN's *Baseball Tonight* and reading the sports pages and the national baseball weeklies.

Team before Self

In postgame interviews and in conversations with teammates and fans, players are expected to be modest and always put the team first. Players quickly learn that around teammates, and especially coaches, they must not talk or show too much interest in their personal statistics. Although most hitters keep tabs on their batting averages and pitchers watch their

Author George Gmelch interviewing in the Pittsfield Mets' clubhouse. (Photo by Philip Kamrass, courtesy *Albany Times Union*)

ERAs, they must not do it openly. Individual statistics are computed daily by Howe Sports Data International and faxed to each team, whose media relations office prints them for the press, broadcasters, and coaches. Copies are usually available to the players. But players must not be seen or overheard talking about their "numbers." I witnessed a player being scolded by his manager for talking about his batting average in the dugout. Another was reprimanded for computing his ERA in the dugout before a game. Brett Mandel described his Pioneer League coach ripping the stats away from a player and tearing them up.[4] A pitcher for the Double-A Albany-Colonie Yankees was released the day after he went to the scorer to persuade him to change a hit to an error. The change would have marginally lowered his ERA, while giving an error to a teammate. The manager was incensed; the player had violated team policy in approaching the scorer, and the pitcher had tried to improve his own numbers at the expense of a teammate.

Certainly, we can think of major leaguers who display little humility and whose behavior seems designed to attract attention. But even superstars may be scorned if they overdo it, as Barry Bonds was in 1997 for doing a pirouette while starting to circle the bases after hitting a home run in a playoff game. In baseball, there is still little of the showboating that has become commonplace in professional football and basketball. It is almost unthinkable for a ballplayer to celebrate hitting a home run or making a spectacular catch in the fashion that NFL running backs and wide receivers celebrate touchdowns with dancing, gestures, and posturing in the end zone. Baseball players sometimes jump around, hug one another, and shout, but it is mostly confined to celebrating a team victory or a teammate's achievement and not one's own. And such displays usually occur at or near the end of the game, not in the midst of the game or after each home run. Admittedly, in baseball the opportunity for the pitcher to retaliate for such flaunting may also contribute to the absence of showboating. "If I show up the pitcher," explained Birmingham Barons Scott Jaster, "the next time up he may drill me. In other sports, there is nothing like that 90 mph fastball being thrown at your head to keep you in line."

In public forums, the player is expected to give credit first to his teammates. In some spring-training camps, major league prospects are lectured on how to talk to the media—focus first on the team's achievement and give praise to teammates. Consider the behavior of players at an end-of-season awards luncheon for the Pittsfield Mets, put on by the team's booster club, which I observed and recorded in my field notes:

> Tables and chairs had been set up under a large tent in front of the stadium. At one end was a barbecue and a table full of food, all prepared by the boosters. Toward the end of the meal, the president of the boosters club got up and made the awards—MVP, Best Pitcher, and Most Improved Player. Each winner came to the front to receive a plaque and a Pittsfield T-shirt. All were humble, exceedingly so. The MVP seemed uncomfortable with the attention focused on him. What little the winners said was to credit the team and to thank the boosters for their support, and that they had enjoyed their season in Pittsfield. Hardly a word about their own individual achievement. When they returned to their seats only one player openly put his plaque on the table where others could see it. The other two tucked them away, out of view, almost as if they were embarrassed to have been singled out.

Admittedly, the players' reserve may have stemmed partially from their being rookies, but it also reflects an ethos common at all levels of pro ball.

Hard Work

Baseball leadership puts great stock in the value of hard work. Most players entering pro ball already have a strong work ethic; without good work

Rochester Redwings taking batting practice at Frontier Field, Rochester, New York.
(Photo by George Gmelch)

habits few could have developed their skills to the point where they were good enough to be drafted. Pro ball expects even more. "A lot of players bleed baseball," said the Tacoma Rainers' Steve Gajkowski. "They're here taking early batting practice by themselves or working off the tee, and doing whatever they have to do to get better—extra ground balls, extra swings, extra sprints, you know, whatever it takes." Rookie Wynter Phoenix was surprised at the work habits of his teammates on the Yakima Bears, "In college I was always recognized as someone with a great work ethic. When I came here [Yakima] I found other guys who were just like me. Not everybody, but there're a good few."

Rookies learn that they must continue to work hard if they are going to survive in pro ball. In locker-room talks and individually, beginning the first day of spring training, managers and coaches communicate the importance of playing your hardest, that your days in pro ball are limited, that careers are short, and that you never want to look back and regret not having played the game harder. In conversation there are references to players who made it all the way to the top not because of great natural talent, but because of their work habits. Similarly, coaches never tell a talented player that he is going to make it to the big leagues, rather they tell him that he has the *potential* to make it if he works hard. Managers also talk about work in terms of giving baseball "the effort it deserves." If you do not play your hardest, if you do not give 100 percent, they say, you are not only cheating yourself but also the game. Some add that you are also cheating the fans who have paid to watch you play.

Some coaches talk about the need to be totally devoted to the game, that the player must "live, eat, and sleep baseball." One player, a college English major who read the works of Marcel Proust on the team bus, said of his manager, "He always gave me the impression that he would rather see me reading *Baseball America*." I played for a manager who got annoyed when on road trips some players wanted to listen to music rather than a late-night baseball broadcast from the West Coast.

While most players understand the values of pro ball, they do not always live by them. Research by cognitive anthropologists has shown that values and social messages are not necessarily prescriptions for action, because they are not internalized by every individual the same way. Different social class and cultural backgrounds invariably mean that players will interpret and act upon the values of pro ball differently. The Latino player from a Dominican barrio, for example, is unlikely to interpret his coaches' pronouncements in the same fashion as his middle-class, suburban-raised and college-educated American teammates. The considerable cultural diversity of pro ball, where one-third of the players come from outside the United States, also means that the common values of the sport are not always as powerful a cohesive force encouraging conformity as, say, the values of a corporation, university, or law firm, where employees have more homogeneous backgrounds.

Learning the "Talk"

The education of the ballplayer also involves learning "baseball talk." Like most professions, baseball has its own specialized language. Each work setting within baseball—front office, press box, concession stands, grounds crew, and the dugout—has its own jargon. Newcomers must learn the linguistic shorthand used by coaches and veterans if they are to communicate effectively and function as members of the group.[5] Although no one has actually counted the number of terms, the size of baseball's vocabulary is probably larger than that of any other professional sport. This is not surprising given the enormous amount of time players spend at the ballpark, much of it allowing for conversation. Several books, including Paul Dickson's *The New Dickson Baseball Dictionary,* Mike Whiteford's *How to Talk Baseball,* and Patrick Ercoleno's *Fungoes, Floaters, and Fork Balls: A Colorful Baseball Dictionary,* are devoted entirely to baseball jargon. There are few such books for football, basketball, or other professional sports.

Most baseball terms and phrases describe performance. A home run is also known as "a dinger," "big fly," "tater," "bomb," or "scud," among others. To hit a home run is "to go downtown" (presumably because home runs once left the urban parks in the direction of downtown), "to park one," or "to go yard." A pitcher with a good fastball may be throwing "smoke," "heat," "gas," or "mustard" (all are hot); or "seeds," "aspirins," "BBs," "pills" (all are small and hard to see); or "cheese," "cheddar," or "queso." While the fastball pitcher has "a heater," an outfielder with a strong arm has "a gun." A sharply hit line drive can be a "clothes line," "linea" (Spanish for "line"), "frozen rope," or "rocket." To go hitless in a game is to "take the collar." An infielder who is adept at handling ground balls has "soft hands," while one who does not field well may have an "iron glove." The latter is a player who will have to "make his money with his bat." A player who is a bit timid in the batter's box, perhaps after being hit and injured by a pitch, is "gun shy." "Damaged goods" refers to a player who has been injured and whose career is in jeopardy. There are also terms for personnel, such as "bussie" for the driver of the team bus, or "skipper" for a well-liked manager, and "clubbie" for the clubhouse manager. Some baseball terms are abbreviated, such as "uni" for uniform. Some observers suggest they are like pet names and that they relate to the childlike aspects and love of playing baseball.[6] The inclusion of Spanish terms (e.g., "linea" and "queso") in baseball talk is a sign of the increasing internationalization of the sport. One in every four major league players today is a native Spanish speaker. Martinez is now the most common surname in baseball, followed by Rodriguez.

Generalized behaviors also have their own vocabulary, such as "bush," an adjective that means lacking class or having the characteristics of an amateur player, as in "that play was bush" or "he is a bush leaguer." Managers, ballparks, and towns may also be described as "bush" or "bush league." "Big leaguer" or "hot dog" refers to a flashy player. The phrase "putting on your game face" refers to getting focused or mentally prepared for the game; to "stay within yourself" is to play within your ability and not try to do more than you are capable of.

David Wright, Mike Piazza, and José Reyes stretching during pregame at Shea Stadium. (Photo by George Gmelch)

While jargon is, above all, a form of shorthand, allowing expression of ideas and sometimes complex behaviors in a single word or short phrase, it also establishes the boundaries of the occupation.[7] Knowing the jargon sets members apart from nonmembers. The person who does not understand the slang must not be a ballplayer. When I began the fieldwork for this book, after having been away from pro ball for so long, I was concerned about not being accepted. That I was able to gain the players' and coaches' cooperation had a lot to do, I believe, with my being still fluent in baseball talk. Although some terms had changed, I could still communicate like an insider.

Jargon aside, a liberal use of profanity is also a characteristic of baseball talk. Among many players, it seems that no statement is complete without an obscenity, with "fuck" and "motherfuckers" being favorite modifiers. Brett Mandel quotes his manager: "I have never seen anything fucking like this in my whole fucking life . . . you have got to have fucking pride in what you do. And I know it is pressure. I understand that. But that is fucking baseball."[8] The profanity, however, is mostly confined to the all-male context of the ball field, locker room, bus, and hotel rooms. Its use is unacceptable, especially its cruder forms, in the presence of women and near baseball fans. The use of profanity among ballplayers is similar to the pattern found among the Portland longshoremen studied by anthropologist William Pilcher.[9] On the waterfront, like the ball field, profanity reinforces the worker's masculine and tough image; it also releases frustration and tension produced by a difficult work environment. As among longshoremen, when a ballplayer calls a teammate an obscenity it is usually in the context of a "joking relationship." In short, profanity, much like derogatory nicknames, is another way of expressing personal regard and group membership.

What's in a Name?

Acquiring a nickname is also part of becoming a member of a team. Nicknames, or "baseball names," are as much a part of pro ball as is jargon, and it is an aspect that fans know well since sportswriters and broadcasters often make them known. Nicknames imply a degree of intimacy and closeness, which are often lacking with given names. Players who are not well liked generally do not have nicknames or they are little used. "Having a nickname is part of arriving," said infielder Mark Grudzielanek. "If you are worth giving a name to, it means your teammates think you're okay and that you're going to be around for awhile." For example, Rick Reed had been snubbed and ignored by his teammates for having been a replacement player—a scab—during the 1995 Major League Baseball strike. Two seasons later, with a different ball club and pitching well, he knew that he had redeemed himself when his Mets teammates began to use his nickname, "Reeder."[10] When rookie infielder Adam Kennedy came to the Anaheim Angels in a trade, his new teammates called him "AFK," as in JFK. It is a starter nickname, said bench coach Joe Madden, good enough until they get to know him better.[11]

The most common nicknames come from a player's surname.[12] Some are abbreviations—Ash for Ashford, Chad for Chadwick, Doobie for Duboise, Furg for Furguson. Other nicknames are based on a prominent personal trait, often relating to appearance. A player with red hair was called "Rojo" (Spanish for "red"); a teammate with a long penis was called "Snake," another, with a bent penis, was known as "Hook." Some nicknames stem from a player's weakness. When I first broke in and made a bunch of errors, my teammates nicknamed me "I-beam," likening my glove to a steel girder. The nickname lasted only a season, as the next year my fielding woes disappeared; "I-beam" became "Moonbeam" to some, based on my having come from California (it was the 1960s), and my habit of spending several hours a day in a library at home and on the road. The infamous Phillies pitcher Mitch Williams, who walked the bases loaded and contributed to his team's loss of the World Series, was called "Wild Thing" because of his poor control. Truly derogatory nicknames, however, would not be used if their recipients objected.

Catcher Darren Campbell's explanation of the origin of his name "Soup," shows how nicknames come about:

> I got it my first year. It was Tony Franklin, my manager, who gave it to me. We were taking infield one day, and I was throwing the ball real well and hitting the ball great in batting practice. I was just playing great. He said, "Soup's on today," like the commercial, "Soup's on." It just stuck after that. Ever since then the guys call me Soup and Soupy. That night we had a three-hour rain delay and when we came back on the field, we played horribly. After the game Tony was balling everybody out, and he was calling out names. "Scott you did this dammit; White you didn't cover the base damnit." And when he came to me, he said, "Now, Soup blah blah blah." It just stuck after that. My parents and friends at home still call me D or DC, but in baseball its Soup or Soupy.

Original sobriquets, like "Soup," that are not derivatives of surnames, are less common today, according to sociologist James Skipper.[13] Measuring the frequency of nicknames in the major leagues by using data from the *Baseball Encyclopedia,*[14] Skipper found that the percentage of players with nicknames rose steadily until the 1920s and then dropped sharply after that.[15] (The *Encyclopedia,* however, does not list ordinary baseball names like Chad for Chadwick.) The decline in real nicknames may reflect changes that have occurred both in baseball and in society generally, such as increased individualism and impersonalization. The high mobility of today's players, who change teams more often than in the past, may be another factor. Also, the public may have become less inclined to use players' nicknames as their image of ballplayers has changed from larger-than-life folk heroes to hard-headed entrepreneurs, a change that implies impersonality and may also reflect a degree of resentment.[16] The enormous salaries of today's players and the recent baseball strikes have alienated not only fans, but also some sportswriters and broadcasters, who help popularize player nicknames.[17] Though original nicknames may be less common today, ordinary baseball names are as widespread as ever; and they remain a colorful example of the special linguistic environment of ballplayers.

Pranks

Pranks are an integral part of pro ball and may serve a useful purpose. Although some are ingenious, most involve fairly typical horseplay, such as stuffing things in the fingers of a teammate's glove, applying eye black on a catcher's mask so that when he puts it on it blackens his face, leaning a waste basket of water against a teammate's hotel room door late at night and knocking, and applying shaving cream to the telephone receiver. "Hot foot" is the surreptitious igniting of another player's shoelaces. An accomplice engages the victim in conversation, while the prankster sneaks up from behind or under the bench and lights his laces, which smolder like a damp candle wick until the victim feels the heat. In the "cake slam" or "spoiled cake trick," a cake is brought into the locker room and shown around with the perpetrators saying something like "it smells funny," in order to get the intended victim to take a close look or sniff, whereupon it is thrust into his face. The high cost of cake and the small salaries of minor leaguers make this prank more common in the big leagues. Some big league pranks, like the cake slam, also play to the TV cameras.

Some pranks can only be played on naive newcomers unfamiliar with the trick. Hence, rookies are a common target. Glenn Kinns described an incident during his first spring training:

> When you're a rookie, you do whatever they tell you to do. So, when Dick Williams, the pitching coach, said to me, "I forgot to bring out the stuff from the training room, go back in there and bring out the box of sliders," it never dawned on me what he was asking for until I got there. I was thinking about sliding pads or something like that. But anyway I had run all the way from the far field, it's a long haul, back into the training room, and here I was looking all over the place for what could be sliders. I didn't want to go back out there with nothing. I was in there for about ten minutes, then I began to think that I better get back out there because they're going to miss me. So I ran all the way back out there, and now everyone is in on it, and they are all laughing it up. And Williams says, "Where's my box of sliders?" I felt like a complete idiot.

Mike Saccocio described a prank called the "mo-fledge" that his Jamestown Expos teammates played on newcomers:

You, the rookie, would be sitting in the dugout during the game, and naturally you wanted to make a good impression on everybody. The team had one player, a black guy nicknamed Mo, who was a master at starting a sentence that you could understand but then mumbling through the rest, the "mo-fledge" we called it. This guy would say to you, "Mike, did you ever notice when that pitcher comes over the top he . . . mumble, jumble, gobbledygook . . . the ball is hard to see." The sentence wouldn't make any sense at all, but the last thing you wanted to say is "Hey, black guy from Cincinnati, I can't understand your accent." You'd say, "Yeah, yeah, sometimes it bothers me too." And then maybe you would start adding things, and he would come right back and mumble something else. The rookie, of course, is just pleased that this guy is talking to him, taking an interest in him. When it happened to me, I looked back and saw the guys had their hats over their faces laughing so hard, shoulders shaking. I guess it was funny because when a new guy joined the team I remember setting him up for the "mo-fledge."

Pranks help break the tedium of road trips and long days at the ballpark. When not hanging out in hotel rooms, the players are at the ballpark about seven hours a day. During the pregame period, there is a lot of idle time. The games themselves are often long and slow-moving (during a typical game the ball is actually in flight for only ten minutes). Having only nine players in the game at any one time means that fifteen others are sitting on the bench or in the bullpen watching. Rain delays mean more down time. It is easy to see how pranks serve a useful function; players readily recognize that the mischief, by introducing humor and laughter, provides an escape and relieves some of the pressures of pro ball. "Sometimes things get serious, and you need a little giggle to take the edge off," said pitcher Steve Gajkowski.

Pranks, in the words of Tacoma Rainer Paul Torres, "help kill time. You're sitting in your room bored out of your mind, and that's when you come up with these ideas. You say to your roommate, 'Hey, let's do this, let's do that.' That's usually how it starts, and then you got the payback time. A guy pulls a prank on you, and then you plan something to get him back, and on it goes." Because pranks often require cooperation, they can contribute to camaraderie among teammates.

Like a Kangaroo Court session, pranks can also carry a message. On occasion a stunt is aimed at a player who has behaved inappropriately. Take the case of Glenn Kinns, who was playing for the West Palm Beach Expos. In the second week of the season, after a game in which the relief pitchers had performed poorly, the manager called a clubhouse meeting. Kinns described in his journal what happened:

> Junior [manager] really lit into the relievers, especially Waymire and Maria because of their lack of aggressiveness, which was really apparent. Neither of them do any more than they have to do to get by. Rick Williams [pitching coach] spoke awhile about those guys that really want to pitch, Randy Budd, Barry Branum, Greg Pope, then he looked at me and said "Shit, Kinnsy would chew through the fence to get the game ball." At the time it made me feel good, because I knew he knew that I was working my tail off.

Kinns had a reputation for working harder than any other pitcher on the club. He ran more than the others and nearly always finished first in the sprints and distance runs. Some players viewed him as a rate buster, and resented him for making them look like "slackers." When Kinns arrived in the clubhouse the day after the pitchers were "chewed-out," he found a section of cyclone fence nailed to the front of his locker. On the other side of the fence was a ball hanging from a string, and attached to it a note— "I'm the game ball, chew through and get me." The prank, a leveling mechanism of a sort, encouraged conformity.

Professional football and basketball players, who have fewer games per season, have faster-paced games, much less down time, and shorter road trips, do not engage in practical joking nearly as often as baseball players. Their games are also high-intensity, high-adrenaline affairs in which teammates playing pranks on one another would be distracting. In baseball, on the other hand, practical joking is so pervasive that it has become part of the game's culture and image. News and magazine features on individual players sometimes describe pranks in which they have been involved. Pages upon pages of player biographies recount ingenious practical jokes. Some biographies, such as Jay Johnstone's *Temporary Insanity,* are full of such zaniness. TV cameras are quick to zoom in on the horseplay. (As I write, it is only April, and I have already seen one cake slam on TV before a spring exhibition game and a shot of a player sitting on the bench sporting a large bubblegum bubble on top of his cap.)

Hazing

Hazing—the taunting, ridiculing, making a fool of, hectoring, twitting, or teasing someone—is often part of initiation into a new group, whether an occupation, a secret society, or a tribal age-set. In college fraternity houses, for example, new initiates or "pledges" may be forced, despite antihazing laws, to endure physical ordeals, sent on fools' errands, or required to dress and behave clownishly in public. Even the Boy Scout troop I belonged to in the mid-1950s hazed its new recruits. (On our first camping trip, we were taken blindfolded deep into the woods at night to be branded with a hot poker, or so we feared. The hot poker was actually plunged into a pail of water near the initiate's face while dry ice was applied to his bare skin.) Sociologist Michael Messner noted that ritualized testing and hazing of rookies is common where new players on a team pose a threat to the veterans, such as taking over a starting position.

When beginning the research for this book, I assumed that rookie ballplayers would be hazed as part of their initiation into pro ball. This assumption was based largely on my own experience as a rookie. It was a single incident that happened shortly after a teammate, Bob Felber, and I had been promoted from a Rookie League to a Class-A League. It is one of the most common pranks in pro ball, though as rookies we had never heard of it.

The hazing began with a group of players arguing about whether a teammate, Carl Solarek, could really lift three men off the ground. Others, all confederates in the prank, stolidly professed disbelief, offering to wager. A hat was passed and forty dollars was collected. I was selected to be in the middle; as a rookie I was happy to be included. I described what happened next in my journal:

> I was on the floor, in the middle of George Korince and Ken MaGowan. My arms and legs were locked, and somehow they got me to strip down to my jock to lighten the load. . . . There was a big crowd around us cheering Carl on when the next thing I knew he jumped back and everyone else began dumping some condiment, ointment, soda pop, etc. on me. With my arms and legs locked, I couldn't escape. My chest was painted black with shoe polish, topped with catsup and mustard, my legs were painted pink with merthiolate, my genitals and pubic hair were coated with analgesic balm, zinc oxide, ice cream, tuft skin, pine tar, and merthiolate. Lucky the game was rained out, because I couldn't have played. Every hair was stuck to my body.

When they finished with me, they called Felber into the clubhouse and, telling me to keep quiet, did the same to him. Jim Leyland, then a twenty-year-old catcher and, until recently, a highly accalimed major league manager, was the ringleader (a portent of his future leadership skills?).

I've always thought of this experience as hazing. So I was surprised when none of the players I interviewed said that they had been hazed as rookies. Even after much probing, they still denied it. The most logical explanation is that rookies are on teams composed mainly of other rookies, not veterans. Would college fraternity pledges be hazed if there were no upperclassmen? Not likely. Bob Felber and I had been "lifted" only after we were promoted to a team of veteran players. As newcomers, we were unwitting. Other researchers have noted that in blue-collar, skilled occupations, where new recruits work alongside old hands, hazing is a common rite. And it often takes the form of "body-centered games," similar to baseball's three-man lift. Miners, for example, may grab a novice, remove his trousers, and coat his genitals with grease;[18] New York City firemen lure the "probationary" onto a stretcher, tie him down, remove his pants, douse him, and then leave him upright, strapped to the stretcher, standing outside against the firehouse wall.[19]

Autographs and Baseball Cards

As rookies become acculturated into the world of pro ball, they develop an identity and a sense of themselves as professional baseball players. The passage begins when the player is drafted and signs his first professional baseball contract, with all the news coverage and celebration with family and friends these entail. That he is now a "professional," however, does not really begin to sink in until he arrives at minicamp or spring training and is surrounded by the organization's other players. As he learns the organization's style and strategy, his sense of being a professional grows. Particular events and interactions with teammates and coaches incrementally add to this growing awareness. Most players I asked about this were able to recall such significant events. Some talked about receiving their first paycheck and suddenly realizing that they were *actually* being paid to play ball. Others spoke of watching people filing into the stands during the opening days of their first season, and knowing that they had bought tickets—paid money—to watch them play. Their performance was now a commodity with value.

Two of the most frequently mentioned catalysts in the crystallization of the player's identity as a ballplayer are requests for autographs and the publication of his own baseball card. "The autographs cemented in your mind that you were playing pro ball," said outfielder Matt Luke. In the words of another athlete:

Yankees farmhand signing autographs in Albany, New York. (Photo by Darren Mrak)

During my first year at Jamestown, I signed so many autographs that eventually it became a nuisance. I would sometimes even stay away from the fans to avoid their requests. Then the next year when I played for Gastonia [North Carolina] in the Sally League, there was much less local interest in the team and fewer fans, especially fewer kids around looking for autographs. And it made me feel less like a pro ballplayer.

Players learn that they are expected to sign autographs, at least up to a point. Most requests come before the game, when fans are able to stand at the low fence along the sides of the field and are near enough to attract a player's attention. Club rules forbid fans from asking for and players from giving autographs during a game. (In fact most players will not sign autographs once they begin their final preparations to play.) After the game, autograph seekers wait outside the clubhouse or near the gate leading to the parking lot. The Rookie and Class-A players I spoke to estimate that they sign about fifteen autographs per game.

Although most players enjoy having fans request their signature, the satisfaction fades when they realize that many autograph seekers do not have a particular interest in them and sometimes do not even know them by name. Kids often ask just because it is something to do; adults sometimes

Brian Bowles

P I T C H E R

Brian Bowles's rookie card.

ask just in the hope that the player will make it to the big leagues, and his autograph will then be worth something.

For many players, the singular event is receiving their own baseball card. Cards are a concrete symbol of their professional status and put the player in the same stratum as big leaguers.[20] One player talked about his first card: "When you are in grade school and middle school you are always flipping and trading cards. Then one day, all of sudden you see your own picture on a card, and you say, 'Hey, I am a professional baseball player.' I don't think I really realized what I was doing, what I had achieved, until the day I saw my own baseball card." Having a card begins when a rookie signs a contract with a card company.[21] Topps and Stadium produce minor league player cards that are nearly identical to the major league variety. That is, they have a color picture of the player on the front along with his name, position, and team. On the reverse side are biographical details: height, weight, right or left handed, birth date, residence, year drafted and in what round, college attended, and a short blurb, such as "Brian attended Boston College for three years, leading the Big East in innings pitched, complete games, and strikeouts as a junior. Looney also earned the All Big East honors as a junior."

Upon receiving their packs of complimentary cards from the manufacturer, the players usually first sign and exchange them with their teammates and then mail the rest home to be distributed by proud mothers and fathers to neighbors, friends, and distant kin. The cards are also sold in the concession shops of every ballpark in the league. Former Angels first baseman Dan Ardell said one of his "great regrets" is that he never had a baseball card. When Topps offered him the standard card contract and a check for five dollars in the early 1960s, he turned them down. He held out for ten dollars, but Topps would not budge.

Requests to be interviewed on pregame radio broadcasts also contribute to the player's sense of being a professional, as does reading the coverage of the team and seeing his own batting or pitching statistics published in the local newspaper each morning and in *Baseball America* and *Baseball Weekly,* the national baseball publications. Being recognized on Main Street and being pursued by young women just because he is ballplayer were also mentioned by some players.

Although players develop a professional identity by the end of their first season, most do not yet feel an allegiance to their parent organization, whether it is the perennial World Champion New York Yankees or a last place club. Many still root for the favorite teams of their youth, rather than the big league organizations they work for. And away from the ballpark, some even wear the baseball caps of their favorite teams. For them, the big leagues is still a long way off, and they know there is a chance that even if they do make it to the majors, it might not be with the organization to which they now belong. When they read the sports pages or watch ESPN's *Baseball Tonight,* minor league players are more interested in the performances of friends or former teammates than they are in the teams themselves. A rookie on the Pittsfield Mets spoke for many young players: "Our manager calls us New York Mets, that's pretty much his motto. But we know we are the Pittsfield Mets. You don't think of yourself as a real New

York Met until you get to New York, or maybe if you get to Double or Triple A that changes, but not down here."

Some contact with the major league players in spring training would probably encourage minor leaguers to identify more with the parent organization, but they do not have that opportunity. Minor league players are housed separately and workout on different fields. Moreover, the parent organization does little to foster corporate spirit or loyalty down the ranks. The discrepancy in salaries, meal money, and travel and working conditions between the minors and the big leagues is enormous. Minor league players watch the parent club pay out multimillion-dollar salaries to so-so big leaguers and then skimp on them and the minor league franchises. It is only when they reach Double A and the odds of making it to the big club dramatically improve, that players begin to truly identify with the parent club.

4. Moving Up the Ranks

The ambition of all rookies is to play in the major leagues. From the time they were kids and first dreamed about being a ballplayer, the goal was always the majors. Even the greenest rookie understands that a major league career will bring financial security, while most minor leaguers barely make enough to scrape by. The recognition and financial rewards of pro ball go disproportionately to those who reach the top and are grossly out of proportion to the small difference in skills between major leaguers and players in the high minors.

In baseball, the ladder to the top has more rungs and is more difficult to climb than any other major professional sport. Every major league organization has five or six minor league teams, collectively known as the organization's farm system. What this means is that in addition to the twenty-five players on each major league roster, every organization has another one hundred or so players under contract. Standing between the rookie leagues and the major leagues are five levels of pro ball—Short-Season Class A, Low A, High A, Double A, and Triple A—each level more difficult than the one below. In contrast, National Basketball Association and National Hockey League teams, with few exceptions, have only one minor league affiliate. The National Football League has none, although its teams carry additional players on a "practice squad."

Nearly every professional baseball player, including first-round draft picks who sign for upward of one million dollars, starts out in the minor leagues. Since 1965, the first year of the modern-day baseball draft, fewer than twenty players have gone directly from the amateur ranks to the majors. And less than 10 percent of the forty to fifty players drafted and signed annually by each club ever make it all the way to the top. Those who do make it will have spent, on average, four years in the minors before being called up, some much longer.[1] Billy Taylor became the closer for the Oakland Athletics after fourteen years in the minors; Trenidad Hubbard finally joined the L. A. Dodgers after thirteen years and 1,305 hits in the minor leagues, to name just two recent examples.

The Rookie Leagues

Rookie ball is the bottom rung of the baseball ladder. Rookie leagues are designed for high school and college players who have just been selected in the annual June draft—hence the names "Rookie League" and "rookie ball."[2] Because they do not start until after the draft, Rookie League teams play only about seventy games, half as many as the other minor leagues.

There are four Rookie Leagues.[3] In the far west is the Pioneer League, with eight teams stretched north from Utah to Canada. In the East is the Appalachian League, with ten teams scattered across North Carolina, Tennessee, Virginia, and West Virginia. The other two leagues—the Arizona League and the Gulf Coast League—are less advanced and have all their teams based in spring-training complexes. Using these facilities lessens the organizations' expense, offers multiple fields for drills and training, and permits closer supervision of young athletes.[4]

The emphasis in rookie ball is on instruction, especially in the Arizona and Gulf Coast Leagues. In Arizona, for example, teams have 7 A.M. workouts followed by a game at 10 A.M., all to minimize the impact of the summer heat. The Gulf Coast routine differs only slightly, with games starting at noon, after instruction and drills. In both leagues the pressures of winning, of playing before fans—crowds are negligible despite free admission—and of dealing with the media are all lessened. In Arizona, where all six teams are based in the greater Phoenix area, no road trip takes more than thirty minutes. While all this creates favorable conditions for instruction and lessens the pressure of playing pro ball, it also means that the game itself seems less professional to the players. Outfielder Anthony Valentine talked about the Gulf Coast League shortly after he was promoted to Pittsfield in the Short-Season Class A New York–Penn League, "Up here you feel like you're really in pro ball. There are real crowds. People know who you are; they want your autograph. There are real road trips. Down there nobody even comes out to watch us play. It just wasn't what I expected pro ball to be."

In interviews I routinely asked rookies if they believed they would make it all the way to the big leagues. Nearly all said yes. "I wouldn't be here if I didn't think I could play in the big leagues," was a common refrain. Nevertheless, I often got the sense that they were not entirely convinced they had the required talent. Wynter Phoenix, a leading hitter on his Yakima Bears team, typifies the uncertainty many players feel:

> In my time alone at night, when I'm thinking about baseball, I think about my ability and my potential and how far I've come and of where I want to go. The big leagues is my dream, and at times I have a lot of confidence. But the game of baseball is so humbling, each day it checks your confidence. Sometimes I lose faith and take a step behind, and it's frustrating and disappointing. In your heart, if you love the game and believe in yourself, you never lose confidence. But in your mind, you ask, am I going to make it, what are my chances really?

Managers are even less sanguine about their players' chances. Of the six rookie league managers I spoke with, most figured no more than a quarter of their players believed "deep down" that they would one day play in the major leagues. "Trying to get my players to believe in themselves is one of my biggest challenges as a manager," said Pittsfield Mets manager Doug Davis.

> [In baseball] we deal so much in failure. It's in everything we do. A player gets four at bats, and most of the time he is going to fail in three of them. The game of baseball is hugely how you deal with failure. I find that even at this level, with kids who have been successful all the way up [amateur ranks], they still have a difficult time believing in their abilities, difficulty believing that they can go out there and be consistent every day.

Many rookies have a timetable in mind for their advancement. Some talk about the big leagues being four or five years away; with five levels between rookie ball and the majors, they figure they should advance one level each year. Players with college experience usually have shorter timetables because of the extra experience they gained in college ball. Others talk mostly about getting to a certain level, usually Double A, within a specific period of time. Rookie pitcher Darren Paxton's comment is typical, "I am assuming that if I haven't made it to Double A in three years, then I probably won't pursue baseball any more. If I am still in A ball, then I wouldn't think my chances would be very good, and the Expos wouldn't be very serious about moving me up." Like Paxton, most rookies, especially those with college degrees, say that if they do not progress up the ladder they'll get out of baseball. In truth, very few, including college graduates, ever leave the game voluntarily.

For many players, optimism is further dampened when they attend their first spring training the following March. There, among all one-hundred-odd players in their organization, they see the depth of talent ahead of them at their position and question their previous ideas of how quickly they will advance. But for now—playing rookie ball—they are focused on trying to fit in, on making a good showing ("putting up decent numbers"), and on just surviving.

Short-Season A

A small step above the Rookie Leagues are the two Short-Season Class A Leagues, which are also heavily stocked with rookies. In the East is the fourteen-team New York–Penn League, which, despite its name, also has teams in Vermont, New Jersey, Massachusetts, and Ontario. In the West is the eight-team Northwest League. Both leagues play an abbreviated seventy-game schedule from mid-June to early September.

From the local team owners' perspective, a major benefit of short-season ball is that it concentrates the season into the profitable summer months when the weather is good, school is not in session, and attendance is best. Full-season teams often draw twice the gate between July and August than they do between April and May. Nonetheless, minor league fans are always fickle; it is not uncommon for teams at this level to enjoy good attendance for a period of years and then lose local support, sometimes forcing the sale and relocation of the franchise to another town. Overall, good weather and clever promotions are as important to filling the stands as having a winning team.

Class A

Baseball looks more professional at the Class-A level, since most players are now veterans of at least one or two seasons, and the less talented have been released. Nonetheless, each player must still prove himself—the position player must show that he can hit better pitching, and the pitcher must show that he can get out the more-experienced hitters.

There are five Class-A leagues, subdivided into High A and Low A.[5] The high or advanced leagues are the California, the Carolina, and the Florida

State Leagues. The most fortunate players are those assigned to the Florida State League, where the teams play in plush, big-league spring-training stadiums. When I was promoted midseason (1966) from the Florida State League to the Carolina League, at that time a step up, the decline in the quality of the ballparks made it feel more like a demotion. Compared to the Florida State League, the Carolina League stands were smaller, the lights dimmer, the clubhouses cramped, and the infields less manicured. Only the size of the crowds and the support and knowledge of the fans were better, and that, unfortunately, was not enough to prevent me from growing nostalgic for the luxuries of the Florida State League. The current required upgrade in ballpark standards, however, is fast reducing the unevenness. The two lower level Class-A leagues are the Midwest (with teams in Indiana, Michigan, and Wisconsin) and the South Atlantic Leagues (stretching from New Jersey to Georgia), which each have fourteen teams and play 142-game schedules.

Most organizations have three Class-A teams and one Rookie team. Seven organizations, however, have only two Class-A teams but two Rookie teams. The wealthy Altanta Braves have three and two. For fans, Class-A ballparks offer intimacy as the small stands are close to the action. At this level of pro ball fans have access to players, and players willingly sign autographs and participate in idle pregame chat along the sidelines and near the bullpen. And fans get to see and know the players over the entire season, unlike the high minors where there are frequent roster changes as players are shuttled to and from the big leagues.

Most Class-A teams have names and logos of their own, rather than that of their parent organization as in the lower leagues. Carolina League teams, for example, are named the Bulls, Keys, Hillcats, Cannons, 97s, Avalanche, Blue Rocks, and Warthogs. Only the Kinston Indians use the name of its parent organization. Some team names are poetic and have endeared fans to them such as the Thunder Bay Whiskey Jacks, Carolina Mudcats, Hickory Crawdads, Erie Seawolves, and the Rancho Cucamonga Quakes. At the higher levels the Toledo Mud Hens, Durham Bulls, Carolina Lookouts, and the Portland Seadogs, among others, have engendered similar affection. Likewise, Class-A teams and above have their own distinctive uniforms and caps, rather than wearing major league look-a-likes. Today, the market for these unique minor league caps is booming, as is evident from a glance at the ads for team paraphernalia in every issue of *Baseball America* and *Baseball Weekly*.

With the big leagues still three or four jumps away, the players in A ball do not yet think of the major league players as their competition. There are plenty of minor leaguers immediately ahead of them to worry about. But even they do not receive that much attention since the overriding concern is playing well enough to stay in the starting lineup and to be promoted to the next level. Players who are not having much success become increasingly pessimistic about their chances and begin to lose their enthusiasm for baseball. The itinerant lifestyle of the minor leagues becomes more difficult to bear when you are not playing well or are sitting on the bench. Photographer Andrea Modica got to know the rookies on the Oneonta Yankees as she photographed them over a season for her fine-art book, *Minor League.* Two years later she revisited her former subjects, then playing for Greensboro in the South Atlantic League, and found that those who were not having good years had lost some of the excitement they had during the first year. She said, "They seem a little tired of riding the bus, tired of eating pizza, tired of working so hard and not getting very far. . . . It seems like the honeymoon is over, and they are worn down by the grind."

Even so, hardly anyone quits. Some resign themselves to their situation, adopting the attitude, "Well, at least I'm in pro ball." They console themselves about their fading dreams; at least they will always be able to say they were once professionals, that they got paid to play ball, and that they wore a major league uniform, even if it was just in A ball. They remind themselves of their many teammates from rookie ball who have been released; at least they have played well enough or shown enough promise to have survived this long. Some lower their sights and redirect their goals. Instead of the major leagues, they will try to reach the highest level of pro ball they can. "When I leave, I'd love to be able to say that I made it to Double A," one Northwest League pitcher with a high ERA and more losses than wins, said to me. For now, they will enjoy what perks and status pro ball has to offer. For those who have had several good years—who have put up good numbers—optimism grows about their chances of making it. They enjoy playing more than ever and are beginning to watch more closely how the guys above them on the ladder are doing.

Double A

Players say the biggest jump on the ladder is from A ball to Double A. In Double A the players have been around for an average of four years and have mastered most aspects of the game. They have seen the same plays so many times that playing their position becomes second nature—they do not think, they react. Most can make the same plays as the big leaguers, just not as consistently. I asked Double-A players and managers to compare the quality of play in their league with the levels below. Here is a sampling of typical responses:

On fielding: There were always holes where you were getting hits in A ball. Here there aren't. Guys here make the plays, and they often make them look routine. (Scott Tedder, Birmingham Barons)

On pitching: Down there [A ball] you can get away with working behind the hitters. Here you have to get ahead of the hitters, and if you make a mistake, there's a much greater chance that you're going to get hurt. Here you got to know how to work the hitters. (Jason Bere, Birmingham Barons)

When you are sitting on a 1-0, 2-0, or 3-1 count in A ball, you are going to see a fastball usually. In Double A you are just as likely to get a curve ball, slider, or change-up. At this level you just don't keep throwing fastballs. (Gene Roof, manager)

On hitting: If you make a mistake in Double A, the hitters are going to capitalize on it. If it's 2-0 and you throw one down the middle, they are going to hit it hard somewhere. Down in A ball you might get away with it, but not here. Not often. (Bo Kennedy, Birmingham Barons)

At each level the game increases in power and speed. The hitters are stronger, so you have to make less mistakes as a pitcher. The runners are faster, so the infielders have to come and charge the ball. If you are going to survive here you have to be faster and sharper at everything you do. (Brian Keyser, Birmingham Barons)

Players also receive less instruction in Double A. "In Rookie and Low A you sit there, and the coaches tell you everything you did wrong, as if you were in high school," said one player. "Up here we have very few team meetings where the coaches scream and holler and press us. We know what we have to do. At this level all that hollering is uncalled for." For their part, coaches say there is less to teach, though some also complain that too many players think they know more than they actually do. "The guys think they have all the answers and don't need you anymore," said one disgruntled Expos coach, who uncharacteristically chose to return to the low minors, where he could do more teaching.

The facilities also improve as one goes up the baseball ladder. The sta-

Hoover Met Stadium, home of the Double-A Birmingham Barons. (Photo courtesy the Birmingham Barons, Marty Morrow)

diums are larger, the lights brighter, clubhouses and lockers more spacious and better equipped, and the pregame and postgame food is better. Attendance and media coverage are also greater. Dividing one month of research between Class A and Double A teams, I sometimes jotted down differences in my field notes. The following entry was written while traveling with the Double-A Birmingham Barons after having spent a week with the Short-Season A Jamestown Expos:

> The lights are certainly brighter here in Birmingham. It not only makes the game easier to view, but the grass looks greener and the colors are more vivid. Many clubs have the players' names on the back of their jersey, unlike in A ball, and their shoes are always black, always having been polished the night before. (They're supposed to be polished in Jamestown too, but they don't always get it done.) Here they have three umpires instead of two. The GMs are older and the front-office staffs are three or four times as large. While Jamestown was drawing one thousand a night, Birmingham is averaging about three or four times that. Even the tickets are better produced here: glossy and sometimes with a picture on them. The teams are more geographically dispersed down here, making for some

very long bus rides. For this trip (Birmingham to Orlando, 534 miles) we'll be on the bus all night.

Each major league organization has one Double-A team, which adds up to thirty clubs spread over three Double-A leagues: the Eastern, Southern, and Texas Leagues. All play a 144-game schedule and, like most minor leagues, have a split season and end-of-year playoffs in which the winner of the first half plays the winner of the second half for the championship. Rob Evans, probably the first broadcaster to have worked in all three leagues, compared them:

> The Eastern League is more of a pitcher's league, the Texas League is tilted more toward the hitters because of the smaller ballparks and hot, dry air, and altitude. They played the highest scoring game in baseball history there, 35 to 21, El Paso over Beaumont. The Southern League is the most balanced and, because of that, it's where you get the best judge of talent. In terms of ballparks and facilities, the Eastern League is by far the poorest of the three. After spending a few years up here in Binghamton I can understand where a lot of eastern people get the idea that minor league baseball is bush league. The Southern League has better and bigger ballparks and cities to visit—Jacksonville, Birmingham, Memphis.

Many Double-A players are in their midtwenties and are more mature than players in the lower leagues. In rookie ball an average of one player per team is married, in A ball two or three, but in Double A half of the team may be married. As husbands and sometimes fathers, players have responsibilities to more than just themselves; they are now breadwinners with dependents to support. All this contributes to a more serious approach to their profession. In the words of Birmingham Barons pitcher Brian Keyser, "Every level up, there is a little more of a professional attitude. In Double A you see less of the mindless stuff that goes on in A ball. You go out there and play the game, get on the bus, and you are quiet for the most part, win or lose. You're more steady, as they say." The players' salaries (a minimum of about $1,600 per month compared to $900 per month for rookies) have finally reached the point where they do not have to eat fast food all the time or rely on a parent's credit card to get by. One pitcher partially credited his fine performance in Double A and his promotion to the big leagues to finally having enough money to eat properly and to avoid the stress of living on a very tight budget. Similarly, the Jamestown Expos' Heath Haynes said, "It's important to get into a routine. You have to be able to come out each day and do the same thing, feel the same every day. The key to baseball is being able to feel good every day. If you're doing different things and having to worry about if you have enough money, it takes away from your game."

Double A is the crossroads, the point at which a minor league player first gets the sense that he is close to the big leagues. A player knows that he has put together several good years and that he is well regarded by his organization. If not, he would not have made it this far. A generation ago players advanced slowly, one level at a time. Today, a player having a great year in Double A may go straight to the majors, skipping Triple A. So many top players jumped straight to the major leagues in one recent year that *Sports Illustrated* columnist Tim Kurkjian wrote a piece entitled "Who Needs Triple A?"

For the first time players now have teammates who are called up to the major leagues, or who have already spent time with the "big club" during spring training or as September call-ups the previous year. This makes them realize that the difference between their skills and those of the players at the top are not great, and that with a few breaks they too can make it. Players often describe themselves as "turning it up a notch," and working even harder at perfecting their game. "When you get here [Double A] you realize you are this close to the big leagues," said Mark Grudzielanek, spreading his thumb and forefinger an inch apart. "Your confidence jumps. You know that if you work a little bit harder, it's possible, you might make it." In retirement, ballplayers never want to look back and wonder what might have been had they just worked a little harder. "I always want to know that I gave them one hundred percent. I don't want any regrets. I don't want to be wondering some day if I could have done more and didn't do it," said Heath Haynes, whose words speak for most players. About half of all players who reach Double A eventually play in the major leagues, though many for little longer than the proverbial "cup of coffee."

Triple A

Triple A is the final step before the big leagues. Here, team rosters are more diverse than at any other level. Playing alongside one another may be a thirty-five-year-old veteran trying to make it back to the big leagues and a twenty-one-year-old phenom who has raced up the minor league ladder. Over one-third of the players on most Triple-A rosters have already spent some time in the majors. Some are veterans that are trying to hang

Hammons Field, home of the Double A Springfield Cardinals. (Photo courtesy the Springfield Cardinals)

on for one more shot; some are working on a particular weakness or developing a new pitch; some are on rehab assignment and expect to go back once they are healthy. Many players get stuck in Triple A. Many could play in the major leagues if given the chance.

Compared to Double A, where most players are upwardly mobile, in Triple A there is more uncertainty and sometimes less enthusiasm. Players who have been sent down from the big leagues are not sure if their careers are on a downward trajectory or if they will, with extra work or a break, be called back to the big club. Some are "holding on," trying to establish themselves as future coaches, managers, or scouts. Because some players have been demoted, there is more disgruntlement and disillusionment in Triple A. Stepping down the ladder, even if it is to the penultimate rung of the minors is never easy. "When you come back down from the big leagues," said Derrick White, who has been up and down with the Expos, Tigers, and Cubs, "It's like you failed. You've already proven to everyone that you can play in Triple A. It's like being in college and someone telling you to go back and do your freshman year over again. And, if I hit ten home runs down here they'll say, 'Yes, he was supposed to do that,' and if I don't hit ten home runs they'll say, 'Hey, I told you he wasn't ready.' It's tough to reprove yourself."

The high turnover of players can make the social milieu in Triple A less agreeable than in the lower leagues. Many players' friends have now been traded, signed with other organizations, or released. As Derrick White explained, "In A ball and Double-A ball you are with all your buddies, and you are thinking we're going to go to the big leagues together. By the time you get to Triple A a lot of those guys are gone, and a lot of new guys are around. You don't know them as well. We don't stick together as much up here."

At this level, being involved in a trade becomes a real possibility. For players, trades are usually unexpected and sometimes devastating because they can dash a player's hopes of taking over a spot on the big club. On the other hand, if the player's new organization is weak at his position, a trade can be an opportunity to get to the majors faster. I asked players about some of the other differences between Triple A and Double A. Here are some representative responses:

On hitting: The hitters up here [Triple A] are more selective. In Double A the guys are younger, pretty much all prospects, and they like to swing the bat a lot. Up here you got some veterans who spent quality time in the major leagues and they're more selective. A pitcher like me—I'm not a power pitcher—has to try to throw a lot of strikes and get ahead of the hitters because they are so selective. (Steve Gajkowski, Tacoma Rainers)

Up here it tends to be more of a mental game, and they know when to do things. They're a whole lot smarter. (Paul Smith, Tacoma Rainers)

On pitching: The pitchers are around the plate more, and you can pick up on their tendencies easier than at lower levels. Up here, if a guy is painting the black on you consistently, you know that's what he is trying to do. That is his plan. At lower levels the pitchers have less control, and it's more difficult for them to carry out their plan, and more difficult for you to counter. Also there are a lot more older guys here, and it's a lot more relaxed. . . . You can focus a lot more on your game, and I think that helps out. (Scott Jaster, Birmingham Barons)

The pitchers are better. They exploit your weaknesses right away, and they'll keep doing it until you make adjustments, if you can. (Paul Torres, Tacoma Rainers)

On teammates: In Triple A you are with a bunch of guys that have already been there [major leagues] and that's not always fun. They're all thinking that they should be back up there. Whereas in Double A few guys have been there, and they're hungry because they want to make it, and they are all pulling for each other. (Doug Henry, San Francisco Giants)

There are two Triple-A Leagues. The fourteen-team International League (IL) is centered in the Midwest and East, with teams spread from

Ohio east to Rhode Island, and from Ontario south to North Carolina. The Pacific Coast League (PCL) was based until recently in the western half of the United States and Canada. Today, after absorbing teams from the now defunct American Association, it also has teams in the Midwest and Southeast. Unique to Triple A is a World Series in which the winner of the PCL plays the winner of the IL.

Unlike bus travel in leagues below them, Triple A clubs fly. They do not, however, have the luxury of flying in their own chartered planes with schedules arranged for their convenience, as do major league clubs. To economize, they fly on early morning commercial flights, a less than ideal arrangement. Having played the night before, players have seldom gotten to bed before 1 A.M. This gives them only a few hours of sleep before a 4:30 A.M. wake-up call. Some players say the long bus rides in Double A are actually less taxing. "At least the bus takes you from door to door, from the ballpark to the hotel, without all the changes, layovers in airports, and having to get up in the wee hours," complained one veteran.

Triple-A teams average about 380,000 fans per season, or roughly 5,000 fans per game.[6] That is about 20 percent higher than Double A, and 100 to 200 percent more than most Class-A teams draw. The Triple A International League's Buffalo Bisons drew more than one million fans per season for six consecutive years (1988–93), more fans than the 1988–90 Atlanta Braves and the 1991 Montreal Expos drew.[7] The players, of course, prefer the larger crowds. As Steve Gajkowski said, "You can hear the fans a lot more, especially when you do something like strike out the side. It always helps to have good crowd support, so I'd much rather pitch in front of a crowd up here than down in A ball."

As I traveled from league to league, I wondered how well players understood what they personally had to improve on to advance. Nearly all did, and most described particular skills or parts of their game that needed work. Players in Double and Triple A, however, were usually more specific and also were likely to mention only one or two aspects of their games, while players in the low minors were more general and tended to talk about an all-round elevation of their skills. Here is a sampling from each level.

Triple A: I have been a little anxious [too eager] at the plate. I need to start taking a couple more pitches . . . getting pitches that I want to hit instead of ones that they are making me hit. (Mark Grudzielanek, Jamestown Expos)

One of the new generation of luxurious minor league stadiums, the Syracuse SkyChiefs PNC Stadium (named after a local grocery chain) seats 11,604 people. It has an open-air concourse, and a restaurant in the right-field corner. The field is astroturf requested by the parent Toronto Blue Jays, who play on the same artificial turf. (Photo courtesy the Syracuse SkyChiefs)

Double A: I need to work on my slider and change up. I am refining those and trying to stay mechanically solid. I just turned twenty-one, and I am in Double A, so I am ahead of the game. I would say in a year or two I'll be ready [for the major leagues]. That's the time frame they are giving me. (Jason Bere, Birmingham Barons)

Single A: I just need to keep throwing strikes and being successful. I've gotten this far in a relatively quick manner, so I don't think that I have to change anything to really get to the next level. I just have to keep with the same plan that I always have and see where it takes me. Unless somebody tells me different, I'll just keep on doing what I've always done. (Brodie Purcell, Watertown Indians)

Consistency. I gotta be consistent. I can't go out and have a good game here and then have a bad game. And I've got to watch my walks. And I have to throw strikes. I am in a closer role now, so I can't afford to walk a guy when I come in with men on first or second and one out. I got to keep throwing strikes and keep the ball down. (Mark Larosa, Jamestown Expos)

Short-Season A and Rookie: Pretty much everything. Every part of my game is strong, but in every part there's two or three things that I would love to really, really improve. I try to work on those things every day. I look forward to getting better at everything. It's like a big part of how I go about my business, wanting to learn, and get better every time I'm at bat. I want to learn something from the next at bat. So, every day I try to learn something. (Adam Kennedy, New Jersey Cardinals)

I need to work on my control a little bit so I don't walk as many people, and I need to develop my curve ball, I think that's what I have to do to get to the next level. Just work on getting my breaking ball over, getting ahead of the count, and just a stronger fastball. (Adrian Burnside, Yakima Bears)

Three of the players quoted above (Grudzielanek, Bere, and Kennedy) were promoted to the big leagues within a year or two.

The common idiom that came up in these discussions was "consistency," as in "I've got to get my game to where I am more consistent." The third baseman, for example, charging the slow roller, has got to make the barehand grab and underhand throw to first most of the time, not just some of the time. Players like to say they can make the same plays as the guys above them, just not as consistently.

A mistake players make when they are promoted is to try to elevate their play or, in baseball talk, "to play beyond your ability." Often players forget that it was their good performance that earned them the promotion, and then they fall into the trap of thinking they have to do more to succeed at the new level. I know the syndrome well. Midway through my second season I was promoted from the Florida State League, where I was my team's leading hitter, to the Carolina League. I had not hit many home runs in the large parks and heavy air of Florida, and, being a first baseman, I thought I would now be expected to. I changed my swing to pull the ball more and went into a bad slump. After getting only a few hits in my first thirteen games, I was sent back to Florida with the feeling that I was a failure. There, going back to my regular swing, the base hits returned, but not my confidence to play well at the next level. Likewise, pitchers, upon being promoted often give too much credit to hitters, thinking they have to throw a little harder to get them out. The importance of having confidence is the primary reason major league organizations are careful today not to advance players too quickly. Young players are often easily discouraged and intimidated by the tougher competition, and they do not always bounce back. When facing talented veteran players, they often do not understand that with experience and maturity they too will someday succeed at that level.

Mobility: Money and Chance

The amount of money or signing bonus a player receives can influence his chances for advancement, especially early in his career. Like any business, every baseball organization wants to make good on its investments. The reputations of the area scout and scouting supervisors are also on the line. So, high draft picks who receive large bonuses get preferential treatment. At the start of their careers, they are guaranteed to be in the starting lineup. Their managers are instructed by the front office to play them, whether or not they are performing well. They get extra instruction and more opportunities to move up. As Atlanta scout Hep Cronin put it:

> Nowadays money is dictating a lot as far as who gets to advance and who doesn't. Let's face it, in any business, if you sign somebody for a half million dollars, I don't care if they hit .200, you are not going to release him. You have a half million invested in the kid that your scouts have picked in the third round, or whatever, and he is going to get every chance in the world. . . . Years ago, that same kid would have got released if he hit .200 a couple of years in a row. I can cite instances of kids who are first-round draft picks who haven't produced, and, after four or five years, they are still there.

Similarly, a New York Yankees player and high draft pick, who wished to remain anonymous, said, "Money means everything. I know that I am going to get more chances than everybody else. Clubs like the Yankees act like they have to prove why they drafted a guy and gave him so much money. They don't want to admit that maybe they made a mistake. So, they stick with the guy and give him all the chances in the world, even though he has already shown that he doesn't have what it takes."

Even in rookie ball, players are aware of the influence of money. Listen to a rookie pitcher, drafted in the thirty-ninth round, talk about his chances of promotion at the end of a winning season in the New York–Penn

League, "I've done better than most of the higher draft picks this year. Now it's just a matter of whether Montreal will move me up next year, or will they move up some other guys who got more money than me." One of his teammates, drafted in the forty-first round, added: "It's tough being a low-round draft pick, because if you have a bad year they can look at it as if we don't have that much money invested in this guy so it won't be a big deal if we release him and try somebody else." Favoring bonus babies because of a club's investment goes against the fans' notions of baseball as a meritocracy, in which players who put up good numbers always advance and those who do not are demoted or released. Having to keep underperforming high draft picks in the lineup can also frustrate managers who always want to win.

There may be some small justice, however, in that preferential treatment means bonus babies are sometimes not as hungry as teammates whose survival is more precarious. Knowing that he has more time to prove himself can weaken a player's work ethic and his urgency to perform well. The attitude of one top draft pick I knew well was that he had the organization over a barrel, that even if he never made it to the major leagues he would still have their money and a lot of it. In his mind, make it or not, he could not lose. In five seasons he never got beyond Double A. The influence of money becomes less important in the higher levels of the minor leagues and after a player has had repeated failures. There finally comes a time when every organization loses patience and cuts its losses.

Chance, or getting a break, also plays a role in mobility. The most common break is an injury to a competitor. When playing behind a star player with big money, an injury may be the only chance a younger player will have of being called up or of breaking into the lineup. One major leaguer who had been to eight consecutive spring-training camps as a utility player, confided, "It wasn't that I wanted my buddies to get hurt, because I didn't. I wanted them to get hurt just a little bit, enough to give me a chance to get into the lineup." Every season does bring new injuries that create openings on rosters and in lineups, especially in the majors. Once given the chance to play in the big leagues, many players become fixtures. Pat Listach had averaged just .250 over four seasons in the minor leagues when he was called up to the Milwaukee Brewers in 1991 after all three shortstops ahead of him went down with injuries. He hit .290 and was named American League Rookie of the Year.

Which minor leaguers have the best chance of going all the way to the big leagues? Players, coaches, and scouts all agree that it is difficult to predict who will make it, and equally difficult to predict who will succeed in the major leagues and stick around for more than a few years. Certainly, there are a handful of new draft picks each year who are so blessed with talent and attitude that they are talked about as "can't miss." And though many of them will make it, even in this select group there is no certainty. The single best statistic to support this point comes from the annual free-agent draft. Since the draft was instituted in 1965, nearly two-thirds (63 percent) of all the players selected in the first round never made it to the major leagues. And among the 37 percent who did make it, many were only there a short while. Double-A manager Gene Roof said, "If I knew who was going to make it I wouldn't be a manager down here. I'd be up in the front office, and I'd be making as much money as anybody in the world."

Fortunately for Major League Baseball, there are just as many happy surprises as there are disappointments. Jason Bere was a thirty-sixth-round draft choice out of a Massachusetts community college. Most scouts thought the odds were long of him ever wearing a major league uniform. He could not break into the starting rotation on his rookie level Gulf Coast League team, and in his first season he lost all four of his decisions. But the following year, as he got bigger, stronger, and threw harder, he became a prized prospect. Two years later he was in the Chicago White Sox starting rotation and won twelve games.[8] A bigger surprise was Mike Piazza, today baseball's premier power-hitting catcher with a $91 million, six-year contract. Piazza was a "courtesy pick" in the last round of the 1988 draft. Had he not been the "god-nephew" of then–Dodgers manager Tom Lasorda he may not have been drafted at all.

Obviously it takes a great deal of talent to get to the big leagues. But baseball people are quick to point out that talent alone often is not enough. They talk about the intangibles—the elements apart from players' physical tools that influence performance, notably a player's drive and his confidence. Pittsburgh Pirates coach Rich Donnelly put it this way:

> He has to have drive to make it. He has to be a competitor. There are competitors, and then there are guys who play. It's the competitors who are going to advance. The guys who go out there every day, whether they are sore or tired or what, and compete. If you play a pick-up basketball game with them, they are still competitors, they are still going to try to beat the pants off you. I've talked to all kinds of coaches about this, and there is a common thread, and that common thread is being a competitor. That's the kid I want. A lot of guys are happy playing four

days a week, they don't want to play the extra three days because they're tired. Well, a competitor is not tired, a competitor plays every day. It's not the money that makes him play hard, it comes from inside him.

Players and coaches also talk about the importance of confidence—the player believing in himself and in his ability. "Those who don't have confidence reveal it, and they don't last long," said one Double-A manager. "You got to believe that you can make it. Success in this game is 50 percent mental, and if you don't have it you simply aren't going to make it." Some players said it is important to show the organization that they really want to make it and that any equivocating, anything that shows that baseball is not their top priority, will hurt their chances. Former Expos farmhand Glenn Kinns thought the turning point in his failed career had been turning down his organization's invitation to play in the fall instructional league, because he had hepatitis. "Even with hepatitis, I still wanted to go, but my father, being a doctor, told me it wouldn't be safe. Not going to instructional league when you are invited is a big thing. I think they thought that I just didn't want to go. They just got down on me after that."

Getting to the big club not only requires putting up good numbers, but also being at the right position at the right time and having the particular combination of skills that are needed. As Oakland A's pitcher Mike Oquist said, "There are a lot of guys that can play in the big leagues. But there are only so many teams and so many spots, so you have to wait your chance. Timing has a lot to do with it. There has to be an opening at the right time, and you have to be in the right spot." "There are lots of guys that have good years and get passed over," said the Braves' Jeff Treadway. "It's tough, you just have to mentally keep going, keep trying. If you get too discouraged, you're finished."

How well a major league team is doing, can also affect a player's chances. When the big club is consistently losing, management makes more changes in personnel. One Triple-A coach recounted to me a clubhouse conversation he had just overheard in which some of his players were expressing their disappointment over the parent club's twelve-game winning streak. They knew that when the big club played well, there was less likelihood for one of them to be called up.

There are also other reasons it is easier to advance in some organizations. Organizations who routinely lose players to free agency—usually because of an attempt to keep payrolls in line—advance younger players more quickly to fill the openings. The Pittsburgh Pirates are a small-market club without the resources to retain stars or sign expensive major league free agents. Hence they emphasize the rapid development of the talent in their farm system. Consequently, a young player in the Pirate organization is likely to advance more quickly than a player of equal talent in a large-market organization, like the Yankees or Braves. Having just arrived in Double A, Mark Grudzielanek told me he had a good shot at being called up to the Expos, another small-market team that regularly loses their best talent to free agency. Indeed, a year later he was in the big leagues, and in 1999 he became a free agent himself and signed a multiyear, multimillion-dollar contract with the Los Angeles Dodgers.

For a number of reasons, today's players get to the major leagues quicker than in the past. Expansion (four new teams since 1993) has created more openings, and many great athletes who once would have played baseball are now siphoned off into other sports, shrinking baseball's talent pool. Also much-improved college baseball programs now offer an excellent apprenticeship before young players enter pro ball, reducing the time they need to spend in the minors. Finally, with the enormous salaries today's players command, some clubs cannot afford many high-priced veterans, and that creates more opportunities for minor leaguers to move up. Of course, the old-timers often complain there are too many players in the major leagues who need more seasoning.

5. Making It

This chapter could be called "The Show" since it is about life in the major leagues. But "The Show," a popular expression among baseball writers, has never seemed right to me. Players do not view themselves as entertainers, nor is professional baseball show business, although there are some parallels. If anything, the phrase is better applied to the minor leagues, where management organizes nightly stunts, contests, and promotions to attract and entertain fans. In any case, this chapter is about the major leagues, what it means to finally arrive and what everyday life is like there.

Whether a player survives the final cut on the last day of spring training or is called up from the minors in midseason, making it to the big leagues is the greatest milestone in a baseball career. "It's about the most exciting thing that can happen to anyone," said Kevin Kalal, director of media relations for the Triple-A Tacoma Rainers. "I still remember when Brent Gates got called up. He was standing in the locker room, and I was asking him to autograph a baseball. He had the ball in his hand, and he was just shaking. Here is this all-American college player, a great athlete, and his hand is just shaking." Teammates, many of whom started out together in pro ball share in the excitement. Exuberantly, they offer congratulations and wish him luck. There are always a few, of course, who are jealous and some who feel it was they who should have been promoted. Coaches are also pleased since their mission in the minor leagues is to produce major league caliber ballplayers. "So when one of theirs gets called up," said Kalal, "it's a feather in their cap, too."

Shortstop Paul Noce was playing for the Triple-A Iowa Cubs when he got the call. Like most players, he remembered the details as though it happened yesterday:

I knew they [the Cubs] were going to make a move, but I didn't know it was going to be me. But you hear things, that someone is going to be sent up. I'd been playing very well, and I had just come off a good spring training too, and I knew they liked me. I was in the training room getting my shoulder rubbed down when I heard the phone ring in the manager's office. His door must have been open. I told the trainer, "That's for me." I don't know if I was just being cocky or saying it for the fun of it, but then Dick Pool came around the corner and said, "Hey! Larry wants to see you in the office." I went in there, and he told me, "You're going to Chicago tomorrow." You can imagine how excited I was. I had made it. Even if I was just going to be there for a day, I was going to be in the big leagues. All the hard work had paid off. And for once, there was the chance to make some good money.

Noce was not scheduled to travel to Chicago until the next day and, since he was still an Iowa Cubs, would be in the lineup that night. Aware that any injury could cancel the decision to bring him to Chicago, he asked his manager if he could skip the game. "He goes, 'Yeah, get out of here.'" Noce said, "So we packed and left Des Moines that night and drove half way to Chicago and stopped at some motel. I remember telling my wife, 'You know, they can never take this away from us. We made it, even if it's just for a day. This is something we'll always have.'" The next morning Noce and his wife drove straight to Wrigley Field, arriving five hours early. He was in the lineup, and after striking out his first at bat, he got his first major league hit.

How do the players react to their first days in the big leagues? "Goose bumps," said one player. "The awesomeness of it all was overwhelming." "I thought I'd died and gone to heaven, baseball heaven," said another. Paul Noce said, "I felt like I'd won the lottery or like a peasant walking into the castle. Spoiled rotten." Former Giants outfielder Cory Snyder described being in a daze for the entire first week: "You are so excited because this is something you've strived for your whole life. And then it's here. It takes time before it all sinks in—I've made it. It was just so exciting. When I went to the plate, it didn't matter what I did. It didn't matter if I struck out, because I was just so happy to be there, to finally have arrived."

Derrick White's first game with the Montreal Expos was not what he expected:

I was expecting to be nervous, not knowing how to handle it all. All those dreams I'd had of how it was going to be when I walked out there, being numb, hearing the crowd, looking up into the big stadium. But it was totally the opposite. I was completely into it and not really fazed at all. I guess because I was so numb. I ended up going 0 for 5. It wasn't until the next day when I came to the park that I was nervous and began to realize where I was—in the big leagues. Before I got up to bat the second night I was really nervous, unlike the first night, but I got two hits.

San Francisco Giants pitcher Shawn Estes said:

> I was very, very intimidated. I started the season in Low-A ball, as low as you can go, and in September I was in the big leagues. I'd been in the Low-A ball for four years before being traded to the Giants. Then in one season I went from Low A to High A, to Double A, and then to the big leagues, and when I got up there, they inserted me into the rotation. It was like "Whoooa, that was fast!" My head was spinning. I hadn't really had time to reflect on what was happening. Then I got intimidated, thinking, "Do I really belong here?" I was kind of in awe, because I'd grown up as a San Francisco Giants fan, and now I was playing with these guys—Matt Williams, Barry Bonds, Robbie Thompson—who I'd watched on TV. It was a time I'll never forget.

What players notice most about the big leagues is that everything is larger and better—the stadiums, the crowds, the lights, the playing surfaces, the clubhouses. Even the lockers are twice the size of those in Triple A. On top of that, interns and clubhouse attendants are at their beck and call; messengers and gofers perform almost any service they desire. In one Yankees rookie's words, "Better, better, better! Better food, better money, better traveling, better hitting backgrounds, better bats, better fields, bigger crowds."

Most players are also unprepared for the attention they receive from fans and the media. "I was kind of overwhelmed by the attention," said Bernie Williams. "I was used to playing before ten thousand fans at most. And now all of a sudden, overnight, there are thirty thousand people watching me. It was a lot to deal with, especially the first couple days when I was trying to get used to the playing conditions, trying to get settled in. It was really exciting, but it made me nervous, too." Television coverage and the number of sportswriters in the big leagues is a quantum leap beyond the media attention given to the minor leagues. "Everything is so magnified in the big leagues. The smallest things you do are recognized, because the games are on TV and covered by national newspapers and that type of thing," explained the Braves' Kevin Millwood.

Derrick White felt like he was under a microscope.

The Cincinnati Reds coming off the field after a win (Photo courtesy the Cincinnati Reds)

> You know that if you make a good play you could be on ESPN that night. Or, if you make a bad play you could be on ESPN that night. The media are always looking for something. They want to know how you feel about the manager. How you feel about being called up? Are you ready? They're always looking for background angles, like are you related to anyone? Were you this guy's paperboy?

One of the "angles" a sportswriter found newsworthy about White was that he had once been a paperboy for John Bocabello, a former teammate of the Expos' vice president. White thought this connection was silly at best.

The media hype accompanying the arrival of highly talented rookies to the big leagues adds to the pressure they feel to perform well. "A rookie today comes in with a lot more fanfare," observed Giants manager Dusty Baker.

> Even before some of these guys get here, they've been on the cover of *Baseball America*. It's big business to build up a rookie, so that people will want to come out and see the new kid. Years ago rookies didn't really get hyped until they got up here and did something. Maybe it's good for baseball that everybody is hollering for this kid or that kid before he gets here, but on the other hand it sometimes haunts the kid, too.

Before the Mets' Paul Wilson, twenty-four, had thrown his first major league pitch, the Mets' television crew displayed a split screen picture likening him to Tom Seaver.[1] Eager to live up to the billing, he overthrew his fastball and slider and strained his shoulder. By the end of the season he had a 5-12 record, a 5.38 ERA, and a lame shoulder, and doubted that he would ever regain his 90-plus mph hard fastball.[2]

Some players cannot forget the huge crowds in the stands who they imagine are scrutinizing every move they make. One player who was unnerved during his first few weeks in the big leagues told me that every time he came to the plate, he would look up at the giant scoreboard and see his lowly batting average in numbers six feet tall, staring him in the face.

Most rookies arrive unsure of whether they can succeed in the major leagues. Most feel they have to prove themselves all over again. "When you were down there in the minor leagues, you were a prospect, and it was all about development," said Kevin Bass. "When you get up here, it's all about fulfilling your potential as a player. That puts a lot of pressure on you. If you can handle the pressure, then you've won a big part of the battle." Not all players can, however, as coach Rich Donnelly explained:

> Some kids can't handle it. A lot depends on their background and makeup. It's like being thrown in the water to learn to swim. If you can dog paddle, you stay on top and pretty soon you learn how to swim. Some do it; others just quit and grab the wall of the pool. That's what happens here, too. Some just go slump and give up. They can't take the pressure. They just don't have the mental toughness. I've seen a lot of guys who've had great years in the minors and then get up here and freeze. They see six decks of stands full, and, oh boy, they just get rattled. They need to block all that out, forget about what the paper says about them—the media can bury a player—and go out there and play ball. Forget the other stuff. Just play the game like they've always played it.

"Some guys let the pressure ruin their careers," said Pirates coach Bill Virdon. "They have major league talent, but they don't cut it. I've seen it happen a lot of times." It's not until most players have some success that they gain enough confidence not to feel the pressure. Former Giants manager Roger Craig believed too many of today's rookies arrive in the big leagues scared:

> Nowadays very few of them come up with the attitude, "I worked my butt off to get to the big leagues, and I'm here to stay. I'm going to show them my abilities and not worry about or think about going back to the minor leagues." That's how guys talked when I went up [in the 1950s]. Nowadays, a big percentage of them come up, and their thought is, "Man, if I don't pitch good, I'm going to be sent down. If I don't play good, if I go oh-fer [hitless], I'm going to be sent down."

You can't think that way and survive. A player's got to walk in here with the attitude, "I busted my butt. I'm ready. I'm not afraid. I'm not in awe. I'm gonna do things and see what happens."

Playing the Game

It does not take long for most rookies' nervousness to recede. "I'm going to go out and play the game the same way I always do," Greg Colbrunn told himself over and over during his first week with the Montreal Expos. "It's important to stay within yourself, to do what you did down there [minor leagues] that was good enough to get you promoted up here. And if that's not good enough, then I will have to do something else." Likewise, Kevin Seitzer said, "Once I got over the awesomeness of the major leagues, it was just like any other game. You keep the same approach and go about your business just like you did in the minors. It's actually a lot more fun up here."

The consistent high quality of the pitching is one of the big differences between major and minor league play. "In Triple A, in five days you might face two top-quality pitchers. In the big leagues, you're gonna face a top-notch pitcher every night," said Andy Fox. "Mentally you've got to be sharp every night to be able to compete." Rookie hitters find some compensation, however, in being able to see the ball better because of larger backdrops and brighter lights at major league stadiums, and because major league pitchers have better control—their consistency enables hitters to dig in with less worry about being beaned.

Another difference is that big league games are all about winning. Managers are no longer concerned about "development," about giving players game time to reach their potential. Instead, managers usually play their best nine, those who give the team the best chance of winning. If a rookie is in the starting lineup, he must start producing fairly quickly if he is going to stay. But survival is not solely about putting up impressive numbers. The rookie who does things to help his team win—consistently moving over the runner, hitting the cut-off man, etc.—is going to stick around.

No matter how talented the rookie, it takes time to excel. It is significant that no major baseball record has ever been broken by a rookie. In fact, rookie marks are usually considerably below single-season marks, as Luke Salisbury noted in *The Answer Is Baseball*. The disparity is testament to how long it takes for even the most talented and highly touted rookies to play the game on the same level as veterans.[3] By contrast, in pro football and basketball—sports where sheer physical skill may count for more than finesse and training—rookies do break records.[4] Salisbury cites Wilt Chamberlain, who broke a single-season scoring record during his first season in the NBA, and running back Gale Sayers, who as a Chicago Bear broke the single-season record for touchdowns during his first year in the NFL.

Fitting In

Naturally, all rookies want to be accepted by their new teammates. Veterans advise watching and listening. "You don't want to pop off and say a lot, because there are a lot of guys that have been around for ten or fifteen years, and you're just coming up," explained the Braves' Randy St. Claire. "I came to the ballpark, put my uniform on, played hard, and kept my mouth shut," said outfielder Cory Snyder. Infielder Kevin Seitzer said he approached his arrival in the major leagues the same way he approached the transition from junior high to high school:

> As a freshman in high school, you were seen but not heard. You kept your mouth shut. You didn't talk back. You didn't want to do anything that could cause somebody to say you were out of line. When I got to the big leagues, I just sat in my locker and kept my mouth shut. I talked to people when they talked to me. I didn't want to push myself on anybody. I just went about my business during batting practice and everything, and things worked out for me.

"If you come in here all cocky and strutting your stuff before you actually achieve anything on the field," said the Giants' Doug Henry, "then you're gonna hear about it. The veterans aren't afraid to jump on someone when they need to." While rookies are expected to be respectful and defer to their elders, most veterans are, in fact, supportive and generous with advice. Many help rookies with everything from baseball matters to suggesting where to eat and shop. "Get to the clubhouse early, never backstab a teammate, and keep what's said in the clubhouse in the clubhouse," was what Scott Cooper said his Red Sox teammates advised him when he first came up.

Rookies are the predictable target of practical jokes, however, which they are expected to accept without complaint. Stealing a rookie's street clothes from his locker and replacing them with grubby clothes or garish apparel is a common prank. Scott Cooper was forced to wear a soiled gas-station shirt and ragged pants on the plane at the start of a road trip after his teammates switched them for his good travel clothes. Another rookie found clean new clothes in his locker, but the pants were red and the shoes white. After hitting his first major league home run, the Expos' Derrick White returned to the dugout expecting high fives and a hearty congratulations. Instead, he got the silent treatment. "They didn't even get up off the bench. For the longest time, they just sat there as if I'd made an out. It was just a joke." But apart from such good-natured practical jokes and gags, there is not much hazing in the major leagues today. In fact, former Giants Bud Black, who thinks that rookies today are "treated with kid gloves," said, "With all the exposure young players get in the media, in the magazines, and everything, if veteran players start hammering them, their reaction is, 'Why are you hammering me? I'm the man.'"

Frequently, rookies already know many of their new teammates from the minors. If they were on the big club's forty-man roster, they also would have spent spring training with them. Fitting in is easier on "young teams," which do not have a lot of older established veterans. When Derrick White was brought up to the Montreal Expos at age twenty-six, many of his team-mates were the same age. "It was kind of like, 'Hey, congratulations. You're finally here.'" When he later played on teams with a lot of older players, he found that they were more inclined to "give rookies the treat-ment and shy away from the younger guys." Not surprisingly, rookies gravitate toward players they knew in the minor leagues. Most players said the best friendships in baseball exist between athletes who played together in the minors. In the big leagues, players room alone on road trips and gen-erally keep more to themselves. The inequality in big league salaries and status—from high-paid superstar to journeyman to rookie—usually trans-lates into more social distance between teammates than is true of the minor leagues.

Life in the Majors

What is life outside the ballpark like for major leaguers? Fans usually think ballplayers have it easy. "They have all day off and a five-month vaca-tion once the season ends. What a cushy way to make a living," one fan told me. The reality is quite different. Although ballgames do not start until 7 P.M. and last about three hours, players are at the ballpark from early in

Double-A New York Yankees farmhands in a bar after a game. (Photo by Nancie Battaglia)

the afternoon until well after the game ends. Most players typically do not get out of the clubhouse until after eleven. Then they must eat and unwind before they go to bed. "You are usually so keyed up from the game that you have to do something to come down. No matter how late it is, you can't just go back to your hotel room or home, without some unwinding," said Andy Fox. On the road, players often go out in small groups to eat and drink. When they return to their rooms, they listen to music, play video games, make phone calls to family and friends, or watch television. Most players spend an hour or so watching ESPN's *Sports Center* or *Baseball Tonight*. Waleska Williams complained that the first thing her husband, Yankees center fielder Bernie Williams, does when he returns home is "turn on the TV to see if there is another game he might watch. Sometimes I stay up and watch baseball on TV in order to be with him, but often I fall asleep on the couch."[5]

When I was a minor leaguer, I thought one of the benefits of making it to the big leagues would be the cultural and other attractions of big league cities. So, early in my research when I asked players what they had seen in the cities they were visiting, I was surprised to learn that few had been to Central Park, the Statue of Liberty, Wall Street, or any of the museums in New York City, or that they had not visited Alcatraz, Lombard Street, Chinatown, or Coit Tower in San Francisco. Some had not even ridden the cable car to Fisherman's Wharf. In the minor leagues such unadventurousness is more understandable—the cities and towns have fewer attractions, the hotels are often located away from downtown, and players do not make enough money to take cabs everywhere. Some big leaguers, however, said they saved sightseeing for when their wives were along (most teams now invite the wives on one road trip each season). Others said they expected to see some of the historic places and attractions before their careers were over, but not just now.

Contrary to what fans think, the main reason players do not get out more is lack of time. Too keyed up to go to bed before 1 or 2 A.M., it is nearly noon by the time most ballplayers have gotten up and had breakfast, which leaves only a few hours before they return to the ballpark.[6] In addition, the starters do not want to wear themselves out by traipsing around the city, especially in summer heat. Being out in public carries risks, too. Recognizable veteran players attract attention and requests for autographs. I once observed several fans recognizing Alex Rodriguez and a teammate on the street in downtown Seattle. The fans followed them for blocks and in and out of a store until the ballplayers eluded them. One player who did want to get out and see things complained that he could not find anyone to go with him.

So, except when playing golf, most players stay close to the hotel until it is time to return to the ballpark. They do go out to eat and afterward walk or window-shop in the vicinity of the hotel, but most then return to their hotel rooms to watch more TV, play cards, read (*Baseball America, ESPN Magazine,* and *Sports Illustrated* are favorites), or rest. Their lives, especially on the road, revolve entirely around baseball. Players often talk about nonbaseball activities, such as playing cards, watching TV, and doing crosswords, as ways to "kill time" before going back to the ballpark. Although ballplayers are not required to be on the field until 3:30 or 4:00 for night games, most arrive hours earlier to get prepared at a leisurely pace and to hang out.

The clubhouse is the ballplayer's home away from home. Major league clubhouses, unlike their cramped minor league counterparts, are spacious and comfortable. A large carpeted area with a sofa, television set, and large table on which food is set out is usually found in the center. Around the perimeter of the room are the players' lockers. These are roomy and brim-

Visiting team clubhouse, Fenway Park, Boston. (Photo by Robert Rogers, courtesy the Tampa Bay Devil Rays)

ming with baseball gear—multiple pairs of spikes, uniforms, hats, gloves, bats, and other paraphernalia. Each locker has its own safety deposit box.

Off from the locker room are showers, the manager's office, and several rooms where the team's trainers ply their trade, loosening muscles, overseeing players' conditioning, treating injuries, and supervising rehabilitation. Athletic training today is a science, one requiring lots of technology—rubbing tables, whirlpool baths, and diathermy machines, which use electric heat or ultrasound for deep-heat treatment of sore or injured muscles.[7] A refrigerator or ice machine is also standard, producing a steady stream of ice for pitchers' arms. Nearby, are inside batting cages, the video room where players can watch personalized tapes of their hitting or pitching, and a family room for their visiting wives and children. The clubhouse is a sanctuary, a place where players are out of reach and out of view of fans. Although credentialed sportswriters can come and go up to forty-five minutes before game time, the clubhouse is off limits to everyone else.

By 4 P.M. everybody is on the field preparing for the game. Players loosen up by running and then, as a team and under the supervision of the trainer, they stretch. Next, they play catch—slow toss from close range at first and then gradually lengthening the distance and the velocity of their

Head San Francisco Giants trainer Stan Conte stretching Stan Javier during spring training, Scottsdale, Arizona. (Photo courtesy the San Francisco Giants)

throws. In foul territory, some play "pepper" in which a batter softly hits the ball to a line of two to four players who take turns fielding it and throwing it back at the batter. "Flip" is another popular game in which players form a circle and then try to keep the ball moving from person to person by swatting it with their glove hand without catching it, hoping to do it with enough force to make someone miss it. Players sprawl and fall over one another trying to keep the ball in play. If a player allows the ball to fall to the ground or swats it wildly, he is dropped from the group. Gradually, the circle is tightened until only two players are left. Fearing injury, some teams discourage "flip."

Batting practice, better known as BP, is the centerpiece of pregame activities. Home teams are typically allotted ninety minutes; visiting teams get forty minutes.[8] Players hit in groups of three or four and take several rounds. Each hitter starts with two bunts and then gets a prescribed number of swings. Some fudge. "Baseball players all have selective arithmetical amnesia," says sportswriter Alison Gordon, "when they're in the cage, they can't figure out how many swings makes five."[9] The BP pitcher stands in front of the pitching mound, about ten feet closer than normal to the plate, pitching from an artificial-turf mat in order to protect the mound. With a basket of balls at his side and protected from line-drives by an "L screen," he pitches three-quarter speed. The objectives are to help hitters find their batting stroke—to get their timing and swing down before the game starts—and to let them practice hitting particular pitches, such as driving a low and away pitch to the opposite field. Waiting their turn, other players tease, banter, and enjoy the scene—the pitch, the swing, the crack of the wood bat, and the flight of the ball to the outfield or into the seats. Players not at the cage may work on their hitting mechanics in foul territory with soft-toss or by hitting off a batting tee.[10] When not hitting, infielders take ground balls in the infield, outfielders and pitchers shag fly balls in the outfield or run. Baseball players probably spend more time preparing to play than athletes in any other sport. Except for the starting pitchers, they expend more energy in conditioning and pregame practice than they do in playing the game itself.

The 1998 Great Home Run Race and the phenomenal power of Mark McGwire has turned BP into a fan attraction. Where BP used to be just for players, now thousands of fans arrive at the ballpark hours before the first official pitch to watch sluggers hit "rockets" and "bombs" into the seats and occasionally slam one off the scoreboard. Even players from opposing teams often stop what they are doing when McGwire takes his swings.

When BP is finished, the players return to the clubhouse to change their uniform tops. When they return to the field—while the visiting team is taking its BP—they mill around the dugout, talk to reporters, or chat to former teammates on the opposing team. Some players carry around bats and take casual shadow swings to get the right feeling and to reinforce muscle memory. Half an hour before game time the field and dugout are cleared of all writers, broadcasters, and nonuniformed team personnel. The four umpires arrive on the field shortly before game time. They meet with the managers near home plate to collect lineup cards and go over the ground rules. Finally, after the national anthem is sung, the plate umpire formally begins play, and the first pitch of the night is thrown.

Reading a media guide about an upcoming opponent is Tampa Bay Devil Rays manager Larry Rothschild en route on a team charter flight from Baltimore to Toronto. (Photo by Robert Rogers, courtesy Tampa Bay Devil Rays)

On the road, teams move to a new city every three or four days to begin a new series. One of the perks of playing in the major leagues, said the players I interviewed, is flying on a chartered airplane. By using charters, the team can travel after a late-night ball game and reach their next destination in time to get a decent night's sleep. As Paul Noce described it, "The bus takes you straight from the ballpark right onto the runway. You get off the bus and straight onto the plane and don't have to worry about sitting in a terminal for hours or making connections like in Triple A. And then you have the whole plane to yourself to stretch out. If you want food, you just ask the flight attendant, and you get it. Pretty nice." Many players find that the improved travel conditions make playing in the major leagues less physically draining than the minor leagues. "Even though you play twenty more games per year," said Jeff Treadway, "the better travel means you're not as exhausted as in the minors."

Major league teams stay in first-class, downtown hotels, where every player has a room to himself. Accommodations have not always been this good. During the pre–World War II era, teams were often shunned by the better hotels. Connie Mack recalled his Philadelphia Athletics being barred from some hotel dining rooms or else seated in the very back.[11] Once, the proprietor of a third-rate hotel agreed to accommodate Mack's players only if he prevented them from mingling with the other, presumably more respectable, guests. I was curious about whether today's ballplayers caused trouble in hotels and were unwelcome guests, after reading about the rowdiness described in Jim Bouton's *Ball Four.* I spoke to clerks and managers at three hotels; none had any complaints about players, but they did report problems with overzealous fans and groupies who hang out in the lobby and cruise the hallways hoping to meet players and get autographs.

Autographs and Appearances

Part of the job of being a big leaguer is dealing with an admiring public, particularly fans who want a close look and an autograph to take away— a memento or proof of their brief encounter with "fame." Fans line the barricades near the players' entrance to the stadiums, come down to the railing along the box seats, and mass wherever else they can get close enough to players to make eye contact and ask for an autograph: "Hey, Mo, over here, over here." Even in the sanctuary of the clubhouse, boxes of baseballs are set out for players to sign.[12] Baseball management often remind players of their "obligation" to fans. Signing autographs is an important way to establish a connection with the fans and foster support for the team.

For most big leaguers, signing autographs does not have the same meaning or appeal it did when they were in the low minors, where it reminded them that they were now professional ballplayers. Most big league players do not mind signing a reasonable number of autographs, and a few still enjoy it. Oakland A's pitcher Mike Oquist signs autographs every day because, "I can remember when I was a kid trying to get an autograph, and what a great thrill it was when somebody took the time to give me one. So, I always sign for kids." But many autograph requests are a nuisance. Orel Hersheiser, known to be generous with fans, described a common scene:

> You're down there warming up in the bullpen trying to get your game face on twenty minutes before the game and you have twenty kids hanging over the fence saying, "Gimme the ball" or "Stop and sign the autograph, please" or the father saying, "Do it for the kid." There are some naive and immature fans who don't seem to care that you have a job to do. There are some fans who act like they would rather have you sign autographs for three hours than play a ballgame.

David Wright signing autographs during pregame at Shea Stadium. (Photo by George Gmelch)

Players most resent the fans who request multiple autographs and those who they suspect are not soliciting a signature for themselves or their kids but to sell at a card shop or show.[13] "It's all out of whack; it's become a money thing. Collecting autographs used to be a hobby, but now it's become a business," lamented Cory Snyder. "Even the kids sometimes can't be trusted," said Milwaukee Brewers Franklin Stubbs, "some of them are collecting autographs just so they, too, can sell them. My wife says, 'You can't really judge the people who want the autographs, so you just have to sign and let them do what they want with them.' Well, it ain't right." *Washington Post* sportswriter Tom Boswell once described "the eddy of humanity, half-adult and half-child" that swirls around any player when he steps out into the public as one of the ugliest scenes in baseball.

At the Seattle King Dome I watched a middle-aged fan at the front of a throng of autograph seekers ask Cal Ripken to sign a half dozen baseball cards and then mutter when Cal only signed one. Usually there are so many people requesting autographs that players cannot possibly satisfy them all. Some fans are bound to go home disappointed. "Sometimes it's best," said one pitcher, "to just say hi, wave, smile, and walk on by, because if you only sign a few, you're going to disappoint a lot of people. So sometimes it's better not to sign any. But if there are only five people there, I'll stop and sign, because I know I can get through them all."

Players are often pursued by their adoring public away from the ballpark. In hotel lobbies, restaurants, shopping malls, and just about anywhere players go, at least the well-known ones, people gawk and some will ask for an autograph. One hotel manager described how autograph seekers work in concert in his hotel, posting individuals on different floors and cruising the lobby and elevators in search of players. When a player is spotted, they alert their confederates by walkie-talkies. One fan positioned himself beside the ice machine near Cal Ripkin's hotel room, hoping Ripkin might come for ice sometime during the night and give him an autograph. So many fans have pursued Ripkin over the years that in some cities he stays in a different hotel from his teammates.

Players are also vulnerable when they go out to eat, especially if they go in a group. "You don't know how many times I have been out having dinner with my family, when some stranger comes up asking for an autograph," said Cory Snyder. "'I hate to bother you,' they say. Well, if they hate to bother me, don't do it. People can be awfully selfish or maybe they just don't think." Waleska Williams described what it is like to go out with her husband, Yankees outfielder Bernie Williams:

> Sometimes Bernie wears a hat and his prescription glasses so that he will be less likely to be recognized. It's funny because sometimes people will say, "Hey, you look like Bernie Williams." Some people come up and make small talk. Often, I don't mind, and I just keep on my way, but there are times when we are in the middle of something, like a conversation, and we really don't want to be interrupted. Again, it's the timing.

Orel Hersheiser talked about the costs of being a celebrity during his glory years with the Los Angeles Dodgers, "In '88 I couldn't even run to the grocery store to get a gallon of milk without it turning into a half-hour appearance. People would hear that you were there and would find you. It got so my kids didn't want to go anywhere with me." On the other hand, lesser-known players are rarely recognized in public. Doug Davis, a backup catcher for the Angels and later the Rangers, was able to go almost anywhere his entire career without being bothered. About protecting their privacy, Davis's wife, Mary Ann, said, "Doug just wasn't ever famous enough to where people recognized him out of his uniform. We'd go out to dinner and people would never know who he was. And kids have no clue. Sometimes if they discovered he was a ballplayer, they still wouldn't be sure who he was. They'd come up and hand him the wrong card to sign."

At home, most players try to secure their privacy by having unlisted telephone numbers. Even that is not always enough. When I interviewed Pat Listach while he was a fixture for the Milwaukee Brewers, he complained that his phone was still "ringing off the hook," despite having an unlisted number. The amount of privacy a player has depends not only on his status, but also on what team he plays for. Players on teams receiving heavy TV and media coverage, like the Atlanta Braves and New York Yankees, are usually far more recognizable than players on less well-covered teams.

Major league players are also expected to make appearances at charity fund-raisers, openings, and community events. Every day a team is playing at home, the ball club's community relations department schedules one or more events that require guest appearances by players. During one recent trip to the San Francisco Giants, where I interviewed some of the team's community relations staff, the following events were held: two players made a presentation at home plate for the American Cancer Society; two players visited children in a local hospital; one player taped a Public Service Announcement about AIDS prevention; four players were involved in a photo shoot to promote San Jose Day at 3Com Park; and a week earlier the entire team had participated in an AIDS benefit in which they all wore the AIDS ribbon on their uniforms. During the 1998 season, a typical year for the Giants in terms of their participation in community activities, players made an average of seven appearances each; and a few players did as many as fifteen.[14] Every team member contributed something at some point during the season. In recognition of how little free time players have, most ball clubs' community relations coordinators try to schedule events at the ballpark whenever possible, or at a time when players can make their appearances on the way there.

Players receive no payment for charitable events, but they are paid for appearing at business openings, card shows, and corporate functions. While most players are generous with their time, some are not. And critics, like sportswriter Rod Beaton who covers the National League for *USA Today,* are quick to take them to task for it. "There are too many guys who think their obligations begin and end with the foul lines. Everything has been handed to them all their lives, and they come to expect that they are special. So, why should they go out of their way to give up a morning to make crippled kids happy." "The first thing some guys want to know," said

Barry Bonds and a young fan at the San Franciso Giants annual AIDS benifit. (Photo courtesy the San Francisco Giants)

one club official, "is whether it is going to be worth their time, and that means, 'How much are they going to pay me?'" The Milwaukee Brewers' trainer John Adams described how some players get spoiled:

Here's a classic example. We had a shortstop who'd just made the team. The first week of the season our community relations guy asks him if he'd like to do an Elks Club thing. The kid says, "What do you mean?" The PR guy tells him, it's a luncheon—they will ask how you like playing in Milwaukee, how you like the city, and that kind of stuff. The luncheon is right here in Milwaukee, and the team will have someone pick you up at the stadium, and the Elks will pay you

Cincinnati Reds clubhouse at the Great American Ball Park (Photo courtesy the Cincinnati Reds)

$300 for it. "They're going to pay me for it? Yeah, hell yeah, I'll do it," he says. Four weeks later the PR guy asks the kid if he wants to do a similar appearance at the Kiwanis. It's in Thensville. First thing the kid says is, "Well, how much are they paying me? Uh, oh, Thensville is kind of far out, can you get me one a little closer?" That's how quick a kid can change, and it's not like this kid was hitting .400.

On the whole, baseball players are said to do more community appearances than athletes in any other major sport. That is partly due to baseball being a summer game, the season when most community activities and charity fund-raisers take place.

Money

Anyone who reads a newspaper knows how well professional baseball players are paid. For the 2000 season the average major leaguer earned over $1.5 million, while five superstars made over $12 million each, or roughly $74,000 per game.[15] Pitchers Kevin Brown and Pedro Martinez each earn about $300,000 for each of the forty games they start per season. Ballplayers earn other income as well, notably a share of Major League Baseball's licensing fees. Part of every dollar a fan pays for a cap or a souvenir with a team or MLB logo on it goes to the players. Players also earn money from their individual contracts with sports-equipment and sports-memorabilia companies for allowing their names to be used on gloves, bats, baseball cards, and so on. And they also receive $73 per day in meal money for every day they are on the road. I never could figure out why major leaguers required five times more meal money than minor leaguers, who presumably have similar appetites. Also, enough food is set out in major league clubhouses for the players to eat dinner and more without having to spend much of their meal money.

It is the players' salaries more than anything else that gets the attention and raises the ire of nonplayers, including some sportswriters. "Everything is money, money, money," said sportswriter Rod Beaton. "When I was growing up and reading everything there was about baseball, you almost never saw a dollar sign in a story. Now you never see a feature without it— or two or three. It's the paramount issue in the game today." Shortly after interviewing Beaton, I was reading through the journal and notes I had written when I was playing in the 1960s and found no mention of money other than a tally of one month's living expenses.

The attention the media gives to salaries not only turns off many fans, it also affects players. Salary figures appear regularly in the sports pages, in features, in articles about contract negotiations, and in a complete listing of all major league salaries, reminding players of how much their teammates and opponents earn. In the past, said Yankees coach Don Zimmer, "Nobody knew what anybody else made. I didn't know what Pete Reiser made, and he didn't know what I made and nobody cared. Today everybody knows, and it hurts some players. If a guy is hitting .240 and making $3 million, and you're hitting better and making a lot less, naturally you're going to want more." Moreover, when fans know a player's exorbitant salary, they are more likely to ride him when his performance does not meet their expectations. The publication of salary figures means players are under more public scrutiny than ever before.

Columnist Mike Royko began one essay on baseball salaries with, "In a mood for a jolt of envy, some grinding of teeth? Then let us talk of baseball contracts, which can always get the old resentment juices flowing."[16]

Most sportswriters and fans share Royko's sentiments. "The money in baseball," said philosopher Michael Novak, "casts a special pall. . . . There is too much of it. It drowns the sensibility. It makes the spirit wither, it suffocates the life of sport." Former players who retired before salaries escalated in the seventies and eighties, are also sometimes miffed and understandably jealous. The average major league salary in 1967 was just $19,000—that is, one-eightieth of the average salary in 2000.[17] Former Dodger great Duke Snider was quoted as saying, "If I were to get paid a million, I would feel that I should sweep the stadium after I finished playing the game."

Most players object to baseball-is-headed-to-hell-in-a-handbasket-stories about the size of their paychecks. "Why do they make such a big deal out of our salaries when it's no different in hockey or basketball?" asked outfielder Cory Snyder. "Nobody rags on a guy who goes out and makes a movie in six weeks and gets $40 million dollars for it. And what about CEOs who earn more than we do, even when their companies are floundering. They [the public] forget that we only play a span of five or six years, and then we're done." Snyder has a point. The pots of gold earned by pop musicians and movie stars cause little public concern (evident in their salaries being reported in the entertainment section and not the news pages) and their performance life spans are much longer.

Bud Black voiced another of the players' arguments, "There are only seven hundred of us. We are the best at what we do. The top of the pyramid. You take the top seven hundred executives in the world and see what they make. It's a free-market system. I am not defending it, that's just the way it is." Most economists would agree with Black. The public demand to see sports and entertainment stars, the limited number of individuals with star quality, and the bargaining power of the stars relative to team owners or promoters are all accepted explanations for the lavish remunerations that ballplayers and entertainers enjoy. It is unfair to disparage athletes who market their skills for top dollar, and then ignore corporate America's penchant for paying its CEOs enormously inflated salaries and bonuses.

Moreover, some ball players make the point that they paid their dues before they got to the major leagues. When they were drafted and began their baseball careers they did not have any choice about who they would work for or where they would be sent. "An attorney or a doctor finishes college, and he is not told which law firm or hospital he has to work for," said Orel

Hersheiser. "And does anybody remember that players mortgaged parts of their young lives in the minor leagues making one thousand dollars a month to get here? People forget that."

Major league players especially resent suggestions that the "big money" distracts them from doing their job on the field. Most players have financial planners, agents, wives, or partners who look after their investments. I have never seen a player reading the *Wall Street Journal* in the clubhouse. And only once have I heard a player talk about his business interests while at the ballpark. The concern over player salaries should focus on inequity within baseball, in which fewer than 15 percent of major leaguers make more than 50 percent of the money. Worse yet, there is the fate of the grossly underpaid minor leaguers. While major league salaries have shot up eighty-fold over the past thirty years, minor league salaries, when adjusting for inflation, have actually declined. In no American workplace have the rich gotten richer and the poor poorer; in no workplace has the salary gap between the top and bottom become more distorted.

6. The Mental Game

Ask fans what it takes to play professional baseball, and they usually talk about running speed, arm strength, hitting, and power. Seldom do they mention the mental traits, such as focus, concentration, and confidence, that are also required to play baseball at a high level. In keeping with baseball's mania for quantifying everything, players and coaches often put a number on the mental dimension as a way of stressing its importance. "Succeeding in pro ball is 90 percent mental, it's big," said infielder Andy Fox. "Baseball is 80 percent mental," said one manager, "you've got to make players believe in themselves to perform well." Or, in the words of former Kansas City outfielder Jim Wohlford, "Baseball is 90 percent mental half the time."[1] Actually, Wohlford's Yogi-ism probably best illustrates the reality, because some aspects of baseball are more mentally demanding than others.

A lot of evidence suggests these figures of speech are right. For example, how else can we account for the large number of minor league players who have all the physical tools to play in the major leagues but never make it, while less-talented players do. More telling still, over half of all first-round draft picks—the most talented and heavily scouted players in the annual draft—never make it to the major leagues. "The difference between a good year and a bad year is mostly in the head," said Birmingham Barons manager Tony Franklin, who attributed the difference in his .280 batting average one year and .230 average the next solely to a decline in his ability to concentrate. Recognizing the importance of a player's mental makeup, most baseball organizations now ask prospects to take a psychological test, such as the Athletic Motivation Inventory (AMI) or Caliper. So far, these tests have not been very good predictors of success, but they can point out character weaknesses or psychological vulnerabilities that coaches can take into account.

Pregame

The physical preparations a ballplayer engages in before the game—running, throwing, stretching, batting practice, and fielding ground and fly balls—are well known to those fans who arrive at the ballpark early. What is not visible are preparations of the mind. Starting pitchers often begin preparing for their next start the day after their last outing. "The next morning in the shower you start thinking about your next opponent, who their key hitters are and how you're going to pitch to them," said the Giants' Russ Ortiz. Many pitchers will follow their next opponent in the box scores and on ESPN's nightly highlights, and if the games are broadcast, they will try to watch. "I go over their stats mainly to look at home runs so I know who the major power hitters are, and I look at stolen bases so I know who can run," said the Birmingham Barons' Brian Keyser. "It's a gradual progression of concentration up to the day I pitch."

Preparations are particularly involved on the day they pitch. Orel Hersheiser described his routine:

> I get up around nine or ten, after I've had eight hours sleep. I have a light breakfast, then I always eat pasta and chicken around two or two-thirty for a seven o'clock game. . . . At three o'clock or so I will do some light stretching before I take BP. After BP I go back in the locker room and lounge around and watch some scouting tapes or read the scouting report [on the opposing hitters]. An hour and a half before the game I get my massage, and then I go though my stretching with the therapist. That takes me to about forty minutes before the game. For the next twenty minutes I stretch on my own. I go over the scouting report one more time and then talk with the catcher on a one-on-one basis. I kind of reboot the computer in my brain to try to clear everything out, and let things come naturally. Then twenty minutes before the game I am down in the bullpen, starting to throw and going through my warm-up process. I listen for the national anthem, because once it starts I really gear it up to game speed and thinking about hitters. The national anthem is the trigger that tells me that I only have about fifteen or twenty more pitches before I need to go take the mound, or go to the dugout.

The preparations of position players, who are in the lineup everyday, are less elaborate. But most do think about the opposing pitcher and how he has pitched to them in the past, many also look at scouting reports on how to position themselves against the opposing hitters. In the major leagues, some hitters also prepare by reviewing videotapes of themselves and the opposing pitchers.

All major league teams now have a full-time video coordinator who uses four field cameras (first and third base, center field, and home plate) to tape every at bat and every pitch thrown in every ball game. Oddly, in the minor leagues, despite the emphasis on player development and the millions of dollars invested in top draft picks, there is still little use of video. No minor league team that I am aware of has a video coordinator or editing equipment; at best they have a single camera, operated by a player.

In the big leagues all the video footage is computerized and then edited (e.g., all the empty time between pitches is removed) and downloaded into individual personalized tapes. An entire season of a hitter's at bats are compressed into two tapes, and a pitcher's performances into five to seven tapes. There are also tapes of defensive or fielding plays. All tapes are labeled and shelved in the team video room for viewing. In the San Francisco Giants' video room, for example, there are four rows of library shelving filled with videos, each is marked with a players name, "Bonds," "Estes," "Benard," "Snow," etc. There are also game tapes, such as "Giants vs LA, 7-14-98," and a library of opposing pitchers. There is always a videographer on duty to cue up tapes as requested.

In many video facilities, like at Turner Field in Atlanta, players are able to watch and compare good and bad swings or pitches simultaneously on a split screen. Players can also borrow their tape or have copies made to take home for viewing. A few teams are now transferring video to CD-ROMs so that players can view their footage on laptop computers anywhere, anytime. "On the airplane to the next city, they can just throw that little CD-ROM into their laptop and study all their stuff right there in their seat," explained the Giants' video assistant Roger Macias enthusiastically. New video technology also enables players to request highly specific images, such as all their at bats against left-handers, all their at bats with a 3-1 count, all their hits to left field, all their doubles, or all their home runs.

Besides watching themselves, players can view the opposing starting pitcher. "You pick up his tendencies, how he might pitch to you, and the characteristics of his pitches, such as what kind of break he has on his curveball," explained the Dodgers' Matt Luke. Some teams now show video of that day's opposing pitcher on the clubhouse TV for the players to look at as they dress and lounge around.

On some clubs that I spent time with, like the Giants, the hitters were the most frequent video viewers, while on other clubs, like the Braves, it was the pitchers. Everywhere, however, starting pitchers use video more than relievers, and younger players use it more than veterans. The busiest time in the video room is after batting practice, an hour or two before game time. Some pitchers come in after they leave the game to watch how they did, while their arms are being iced. Some players come to the video room during the game to take a quick look at their previous at bat. "They're looking mainly at their mechanics, like if they're pulling out too soon," said Braves videographer Rob Smith. "Or, they'll want to see the location of the pitches, to see how they are being pitched to."

In general, whether pitchers or hitters, players look at video most when they are slumping. Take the San Francisco Giants' Shawn Estes, for example:

> I use it primarily when I am going bad, and not much when I am going good. When I am going good I have a pretty good feel for what I am doing, and I don't want too much information. When I am going bad I can go to video and compare it with my good video. . . . Video doesn't lie. This year we saw where my mechanics and the action of my fastball were not like what they were last year when I was at my best. Last year my fastball was sinking, and this year [1998] it is cutting. You could see that I was getting around the ball rather than on top of the ball and driving down through the pitch.

The Braves' Tom Glavine also does not watch much video except after a bad outing, "then I'll go back and watch to see if it was me having a bad night or if it was that I had a good game and they were just better than me. If it was me, video can tell me if I need to make some adjustments." The Padres' Tony Gwynn became a devotee of video after his wife, Alicia, taped a game during a slump sixteen years ago. He found the tapes so useful that he put up $85,000 to furnish the Padres with a video room, and on road trips he takes along two video machines, a 10-inch monitor, and a bunch of tapes.[2] While most players believe in the value of video, some make little use of it beyond watching themselves hit home runs. Cory Snyder explained, "Some guys don't like to be clouded with too much information. Other guys want as much information as they can get. They like to reinforce seeing themselves getting a hit or hitting a homer. I guess its gets them pumped up or something. It's whatever works for you. . . . Baseball is an individual game, and everybody reacts differently." Pittsburgh Pirates video coordinator Brad Hines found that players who were never exposed to video in school ball, such as Latinos from other countries, are less likely to use it now.

All the coaches I interviewed believe video is an excellent teaching tool, able to show a player precisely what he is doing right and wrong. As Atlanta coach Pat Corrales put it, "Like they say, a picture is worth a thousand words. It is easier to communicate with a player when you can show him what he is doing. He can grasp it right away. Before video you used to sit there and you could talk to him all day long, and he still might not get it."

"I use it to prove a point more than anything else," said Pirates bench coach Bill Virdon. "If you can sit down with your player and show him on video what he is doing, you have a lot bigger chance of him believing you and of him seeing what you're trying to say." And being able to compare present and past performances also makes it easier to diagnose problems. The use of video has been, in the words of manager Jim Leyland, "one of the major breakthroughs in baseball." However, because video is a relatively recent innovation in pro ball, there is still much variation in how players use it and benefit from it.

The newest electronic technology in pregame preparation is Sports-Track, a computer exercise that measures a player's concentration and coordination. Developed for fighter pilots several decades ago and recently adopted by three West Coast teams—the Dodgers, Giants, and Padres—it requires the player to manipulate a rollerball on a keyboard in order to keep a moving symbol in the center of a computer-screen grid. Before starting the game, the player answers a series of questions about his recent travel, sleep, eating patterns, and sources of stress. The player then gets five tries on the computer, after which the results—showing his current level of concentration and coordination compared to his baseline information—are printed out. Hence, the athlete learns before going onto the field how sharp he is likely to be that day and what adjustments he might have to make. Only a handful of the San Francisco Giants, where I was introduced to SportsTrack, were using it regularly, however.

Locking In

"What do you do mentally to prepare?" was the grand-tour question I asked players to start my queries about the mental game. Their answers varied, but the one constant was that baseball players do not try to get "psyched up" like athletes in contact sports. In football, for example, which is played once a week and in which players bash heads, it is the norm to get pumped up. In baseball, which is played every day and is a noncontact sport, it is counterproductive to get so worked up. If baseball players were to expend the same emotional energy for every game as football players, they would never last the entire season. As one player aptly put it, "You can't play baseball with clenched teeth."

In place of the back slapping, shouting, yelling, motivational speeches, and high intensity rah-rah that is so common in contact sports, baseball players turn inward. "Putting on the game face" is the phrase some players use to describe getting mentally ready to play, getting focused on the specific athletic tasks at hand. Baseball is a difficult game to play under any conditions, but even more so if the player is not mentally prepared. Considerable concentration and focus are required to pitch a baseball with velocity and movement to a precise location. The same applies to hitting. A fastball travels from the pitcher's mound to the batter's box in about four-tenths of a second. The batter must make his decision whether or not to swing in the first eight feet of the pitch's trajectory; and for only three feet of the journey, an absurdly short two-hundreds of a second, is the ball in a position to be hit. And to be hit well, the ball must be hit square and on the sweet spot of the bat, which is less than three inches in length. Moreover, the ballplayer must maintain his concentration for the almost three hours it takes to play a game. In contrast, the gymnast, swimmer, or ski racer must maintain focus for the five or ten minutes his or her performance lasts.

With all the stops and starts in baseball and the batter coming to the plate about four different times during a game, it is easy for a player to lose concentration. No wonder that from Little League on up players are implored by their coaches to keep their heads in the game. While most baseball people use the terms *focus* and *concentration* interchangeably, they actually have different meanings. To focus is to bring something to into sharp relief: for a pitcher it might be the catcher's glove; for the hitter it is usually the pitcher's hand and the release of the baseball. To concentrate is simply to pay close attention to something for a period of time. To put on one's game face involves both focus and concentration.

Some players spend time alone or plan "quiet time" to gather their thoughts and concentrate. The starting pitcher particularly can often be seen by himself in a far corner of the dugout, clubhouse, or trainer's room

Getting mentally prepared to play before a Double-A Eastern League game. (Photo by Darren Mrak)

thinking about and visualizing the opposing hitters. On game days he does not sign autographs or do interviews so as not to be distracted. Likewise, relief pitchers banter and joke in the bullpen until the sixth or seventh inning, or until the starter is in difficulty, and then they settle down, turn inward, and mentally prepare to come into the game. As a late-arriving rookie, the Jamestown Expos' Mike Saccocio quickly learned not to fool around with his teammates when they were mentally preparing to play. "They would be carefree and joking, but if you tried to cut a joke with them five minutes before the game, they would just look at you like, 'Who are you?' That taught me what a game face was. They were different people then." Soon Saccocio developed his own routine for putting on his game face:

I knew the trainer well, and he would let me use the toilet in his room where it was quiet. It was a great time to think, and if I could go it made me feel faster. I could hear the announcers announcing the lineup, and you'd hear the music. I'd just sit there with my uniform on for about fifteen minutes, and I'd say to myself, "I am playing professional baseball. People are paying to watch me play. I am playing professional baseball. . . ." Then I'd walk out onto the field, and I'd say,

"Those are the Yankees or Reds or whoever over there." Then I'd be ready to play.

In the 1980s the Philadelphia Phillies even set aside a special room called "the mood room" for pitcher Steve Carlton and others who wanted a quiet place to mentally prepare. Just how focused players become was made clear to me when I asked pitcher Brian Keyser why there is less infield chatter in pro ball than in college ball. He could not tell me, because he was so focused on the catcher that he rarely heard anything. With experience most players become adept at focusing, or what many call "locking in." Listen to Birmingham Barons first baseman Mike Robertson:

> When I step onto the field I turn off what was going on off the field. I put everything behind me and I lock in. What happened during the day, the week, the month is gone, out of my mind. Now it is just focus on the game. From then to the end it is just the game. Just the game. Once I am locked in no one can break me mentally. No one can break my concentration. At the end of the game, when I step off the field I turn it off.

As we will see later, many players, unlike Robertson, have difficulty turning it off once the game is over. But for now, I will turn to one of the primary techniques some players use to prepare.

Visualization

About one-third of the players I interviewed said they visualize before games. Visualization, or what many sports psychologists alternatively refer to as *imagery* or *mental rehearsal,* is used to create and concentrate on the mental images of a physical act before doing it.[3] Cognitively, visualizing is similar to video, except that the player runs the images through his mind instead of looking at them on a screen. For example, a hitter may call to mind images of himself hitting a particular pitch, or a pitcher might conjure up images of himself going through his motion and delivering a pitch to a particular location. One of the advantages of visualization is that it can be done anywhere, even away from the ballpark. "The mind becomes the practice field," said Harvey Dorfman and Karl Kuehl, and "that field is always accessible. In the mind someone is always available to throw BP or, for pitchers, to hit against you."[4]

Visualization is certainly not unique to baseball. In fact, it is more widely and systematically used by elite athletes in gymnastics, diving, running, figure skating, tennis, and many other individual sports. Downhill ski racers with eyes closed going through their moves as they visualize the course before the start of a race are sometimes captured on television. It is used by performers outside of sport as well. A jazz musician once described to me how he prepares for performances by visualizing himself at the piano playing the difficult parts of the pieces he will soon perform.

As with the use of video, how ballplayers visualize varies.[5] Below, six players describe what they do. First those who routinely visualize:

> I started it my sophomore year at school [Cal State Fullerton]. Our assistant coach was really big on visualization, so I got that instilled in my pregame preparation. I do it just a minute or two before we start up. I visualize what I want to do off who is pitching. . . . I see three different at bats, line drives to center, to left, and to right. And I see myself fielding a couple of ground balls. (Adam Kennedy, New Jersey Cardinals)

> When I wake up in the morning the days that I am pitching, I'll visualize the hitters. Before I go into the game, when I am warming up in the bullpen, I'll visualize the first batter being up there and me throwing strikes, hitting spots. It's a mind game. In between innings I'll think about who I am facing the next inning hitters-wise, and I'll visualize how I'm going to pitch them. . . . I think it really helps me pitch a lot better, but sometime I lose track of doing it. (Shawn Estes, San Francisco Giants)

Pitcher Mark Larosa learned to visualize from his girlfriend's father, who is a psychiatrist and who uses hypnosis and imagery in his practice:

> While they are announcing the lineups, I sit in the corner of the dugout by myself and breathe deeply and try to relax, and I see myself on the mound going through the motions, delivering the pitch. I don't see the batter's face or anything, just my arm action and my ball action. Once I think I have it down, that's it. It doesn't take long, just three to five minutes.

> I always do it when I go to sleep the night before I pitch. I picture the arm angle, and I picture the ball going down, and there's a tunnel around it. I see the hitter. . . . If I throw a change-up down and away, I picture him swinging out in front of it, totally missing the ball. (Darren Paxton, Jamestown Expos)

Now, two players who do it casually:

> It's not like I make a point to sit down and visualize. Over the course of the day you will see yourself take the perfect swing or hit a nice line drive up the middle.

When I have a good at bat in a game, I want to duplicate it later in my mind. (Walt Weiss, Altanta Braves)

The biggest thing I do is try to see where the pitch is. I watch the pitcher in my mind and see how he pitches to me. I try to visualize myself hitting that pitch through the middle of the field, trying to take out his eyeballs. I see myself put a nice easy swing on it and try to relax. But I don't do it on any consistent basis. Sometimes you face a guy so many times that you already have the pitch in your head, and it's like you don't have to do it. (Franklin Stubbs, Milwaukee Brewers)

The Giants' reliever Doug Henry returned to visualizing after an entire season in which he could not focus:

I was visualizing pretty well back in '91, and I am back to that point now. When I first started getting back into it at spring training, I was probably doing it five minutes at a time, about three times a day. Now, sometimes I am doing it, and I am not even aware of it. And that's where I need to be. It helps me a lot.

As the comments suggest, players visualize in different ways. Doug Henry visualizes three times a day, while Adam Kennedy does it only once and briefly. Darren Paxton sees vivid images with lots of detail, while Mark Larosa barely even sees the hitter. Sports psychologists have suggested that mental rehearsal is most effective when the images are vivid and detailed, like Paxton's, and when the player can control the image, as when seeing a line drive come off his bat.[6]

Researchers have also found that people differ in their ability to produce mental images. Some of the differences in the players' accounts of their imagery seemed to be related to whether or not they had been instructed in how to use visualization. Those who had been taught, like Adam Kennedy, produced more detailed images. Despite the variation, there were some commonalities. For one, all players visualize alone, not in groups as is done in some sports. One of my former students who plays professional hockey in Europe described his Swiss hockey team visualizing as a group before each game, being led by the coach. Second, the images they conjured up were almost always positive ones—throwing strikes in good locations, hitting the outside pitch to the opposite field, hitting line drives, etc. Research shows that negative imagery—where an athlete fails to execute the desired task—degrades and inhibits performance.[7] Third, most of the imagery used by the players was internal, that is, the player imagined his performance and surroundings from his own vantage point, as seen through his own eyes. In external visualization an athlete imagines the action from the perspective of someone else, as though watching a movie. Internal imagery, according to researchers, is more likely to enhance performance.[8]

I found a wide variation in how strongly players and coaches believed in the value of visualization, and curiously the latter were often the least convinced about its efficacy. Atlanta Braves coach Pat Corrales was one exception. Corrales came across a book that discussed visualization in the 1960s, late in his career, when he was catching for Cincinnati. When relaxing and before afternoon naps, he began visualizing himself at the plate and also catching a tough pitch and throwing out the runner at second base. But he added, "I'd never tell anybody because in those days they'd think I was crazy."

Even Keelism

"Staying on an even keel" is one of the maxims of pro ball. It means to maintain balance—to not get emotionally too high or too low. Along with concentration and focus, say baseball people, it is an essential requirement of surviving in pro ball. As a guiding principle, it is applied to both how the game is played—calm and controlled—and to how players comport themselves after the game. Too much tension produces nervousness that can interfere with a player's ability to make the right decisions in the field or at bat. Even managers try not to rant and rave too much. But even keelism has even more to do with how players handle success and failure. The following quotations capture how players and coaches think and talk about its importance:

> If you live and die with every pitch, it will wear you out after a while. The mental approach is everything. (Brian Keyser, Birmingham Barons)

> If you can stay on an even keel, it makes you accept failure a little better and rebound from it better. . . . When I am struggling, I try not to let it be outwardly obvious to everyone. If the other teams know you're struggling, it makes their job easier. (Jeff Treadway, Atlanta Braves)

> When I am going good, I enjoy it but I try to fight off the euphoria as much as possible. I remind myself that it's not going to last very long. I don't want to go too far up. To play this game you have to learn not to get too down or too up. (Scott Tedder, Birmingham Barons)

Buffalo Bisons manager Terry Collins, in talking about his star twenty-three-year-old shortstop Carlos Garcia, explained why you cannot get down: "The only thing that I am concerned about is that he gets so down on himself. If he strikes out or if he is having a bad night, I am worrying about him the next day. That's where he has to start maturing a little bit, handling the bad times. The good times are easy. When those bad times come you can't let yourself get so down that it makes coming back from them a problem."[9] Manager Tony LaRussa's comments about one of his players reveal the ideal attitude, "Nothing bothers him. He can strike out three times and not really be concerned or lose his confidence. He can get two home runs, and you don't really see a big difference."

The ability to maintain balance is something that most players acquire with experience. Few rookies approach their successes and failures with the evenhandedness of veterans. The Jamestown Expos' Jim Austin was an exception, having learned the importance of balance from his baseball-coach father. When he arrived in Jamestown to start his pro career, he was surprised at how poorly many of his teammates approached the ups and downs of the game:[10]

> I watch a lot of the players, and I think a lot of them won't make it. They have a bad night, and they think their life is done with. We had a player already who broke his hand by punching his locker. He got sent home. I've seen a lot of guys go oh-fer [hitless] and just can't handle it at all. They bring it home. You can't even talk to them at all. They are cussing, screaming this and that. Man, you can't do that. You'll tear yourself up. . . . I was in a slump a couple of weeks ago, like one for twenty-one. . . . I couldn't hit the ball to save my life, but I still just put the helmet down nicely.

The strategy that many players use to maintain balance is to try to forget the game once they leave the ballpark. "When I walk out of that clubhouse at the end of the night," said Mike Robertson, "I leave the game behind me, I don't want to think about it. In college if I had a bad game it might be in my head all week long." Similarly, Yankees pitcher Paul Gibson said, "When I go home I really don't like to talk about the game. It is a done deal. I was there eight hours, and now I don't want to think about it until the next day."

Forgetting the game, however, is particularly difficult for young players. For one, they have fewer outlets for life outside of baseball. They room, eat, and spend all their free time with teammates. And, unlike many

A pensive Pittsfield catcher Travis Stockam during a hitless night in the New York–Penn League. (Photo by Philip Kamrass, *Albany Times Union*)

veterans, they are away from family and friends who might offer diversion and help them keep things in perspective. For young players, there is no escape from the game. "Because there is not much to do," said one Jamestown rookie, "you sit around all day thinking about the game." The traditional postgame going out to drink in bars, I believe, is aimed largely at trying to forget, trying to get the game out of your head. I asked some coaches how they saw it. QV Lowe, who coached in the minor and major leagues for the Cubs, Expos, and Yankees for two decades, said:

> You go four-for-four and you think you're the best, then the next day you go oh-for-four and you hit a real low. These are young kids. They can't handle the ups and downs. So they find that drinking can wash the game right out of the mind. Numbs the senses. But pretty soon it becomes a habit. . . . I've never known a player who could just go back to his hotel room, lie down, and go to bed. You are so worked up after the game that it takes two or three hours to calm down enough to sleep. So you have a few drinks.

By the time most players have reached Double A, however, they are better at leaving the game behind, better at staying on an even keel, and most can do it without the crutch of alcohol. Yankees farmhand Joe DeBerry's approach is fairly typical of veteran players: "If you do it properly you can go home and get away from it [the game]. I go home, I read a lot, watch TV, just relax and really try to stay away from the game. Every once in a while I might take out a bat and shadow swing a little, but really I just try to forget it. I try to do all my work and thinking at the ballpark." Veteran players say that having a home, spouse, and children to return to after the game helps them escape. But even after years in pro ball, some still have difficulty. For all his success, Mickey Mantle admitted that when he had a bad day it really stayed on his mind, and "it got pretty quiet in the room."[11]

Not staying on an even keel can mean that the life of the player becomes an emotional roller coaster: nights of jubilation followed by nights of despair, peaks and valleys. It is the valleys that are of most concern. Remember manager Terry Collins's worry about his star shortstop not being able to bounce back from a bad night. Thinking too much about a bad night can cause a player "to press" (to be overanxious) the next day. Pressing impedes concentration, and reduced concentration lessens performance.[12] If the emotion is anger, said baseball analyst and former general manager Syd Thrift, it is damaging to the "visual systems" critical to hitting. The phrase "I was so mad that I couldn't see straight," argued Thrift, is literally true since the eyes are an extension of the brain.[13]

Slumps

Psychologically, the most difficult thing ballplayers must deal with is the slump. Most of the hitters I asked said that they begin to think they are in a slump after going three or four games without a hit or going more than four games with just a few hits. In the words of former Cub Paul Noce, "After three oh-fers you start pressing a bit, then pretty soon you've got it in your head that you're in a slump." Pitchers said they could be in a slump after a single outing, but usually it takes back-to-back bad outings.

Most players believe that slumps begin with some slight physical or mechanical change in their technique. It might start with overstriding, opening the front shoulder too quickly, or any one of a dozen other little alterations in hitting or pitching mechanics. Sometimes it begins with bad luck—the hitter is making good contact, hitting the ball hard but right at the fielders or the pitcher is making good pitches but the hits are falling. Cleveland Indians prospect Brodie Purcell noted, "You can go out there and pitch just fine, but the other team is really hitting well, and you're getting hurt. You start to doubt yourself, when actually you're doing just fine. It's just not one of your days. But you don't know that so you start to change something about your delivery, and now it becomes a physical thing."

Slight injury, soreness, or fatigue may cause a player to alter his mechanics so that, say, instead of hitting line drives, he is popping the ball up. Whatever the cause, after a few hitless or winless games the slumping player begins to think he must be doing something wrong, and he begins to press. His problem now becomes mental. He turns to teammates and his coaches for advice. And there is plenty of it—everybody has an idea about what needs to be done. So, he decides to change some aspect of his technique, and it may help or it may make matters worse. As baseball impresario Bill Veeck once said, "The best cure for a slump is two balls of cotton. One for each ear." In most instances what the player really needs to do is not panic, not doubt himself, and just continue doing what he has always done. Eventually the hits will start falling again. As one coach said, "Too often guys start to doubt themselves when they are actually doing fine. If they will just stay balanced, stay upbeat, they will ride it out."

Just as the cause of a slump is often mental, so is the cure, namely to make the player feel confident again so that he can perform. As QV Lowe explained, "I might make up something. 'Jim, you're striding a bit too far.' If Jim can think about something he can correct, it will give him confidence that he can hit again, and that gets his mind off the negative. He needs to focus on something he can understand."

We get a sense of the nature of slumps and the players' despair from the following interview excerpts. Here, QV Lowe described one of his rookie's slumps:

> He hit .400 for Wichita State, played on a couple of College World Series teams, and now he hasn't had a hit in the month of July. He can get the ball out of the infield, but it just won't fall. I see him with his head down, and he is thinking "my baseball career is over." I am trying to stay positive with him, but it's awful hard to stay positive when his head is in a hole. He never hears you. He is so mired in self-pity that he is not hearing anything.

Heath Haynes, a Jamestown Expos pitcher, described the behavior of his battery mate and fellow rookie during a slump:

> He had another bad game last night, and he just freaked out. Freaked out when he was in the dugout, when he was in the bus. I am sure that he wasn't the most pleasant guy to be a roommate with last night either. Before he got on the bus, he ripped off his shirt, and all of the buttons came flying. Throwing stuff around and just not caring. About a month ago, he hit two home runs in one game and looked like a hero and thought that everything was going to be easy, that he would make it to the majors in no time. Last night he was probably thinking, "Gee, when are they going to release me?" He has to be thinking that. You can just see that he is so frustrated, that he doesn't want to play anymore.

The following quotations come from veteran players and illustrate the more-measured approach that comes with experience. First, a Boston Red Sox outfielder who has gotten one hit in his last twenty-eight at bats:

> I try not to think about it, but that isn't always easy. Slumps are mostly mental. It's all in your approach to the game and how you deal with the things that happen. If you line out a few times, and you are not getting any breaks, and you start thinking that you are doing something wrong at the plate, then you think yourself into a slump. Then you start hitting dribblers, and getting jammed, and doing things you are not supposed to do. All of a sudden you are in a real slump. And it is caused by thinking too much. So, I try not to dwell on it.

Joe DeBerry, a Double-A first baseman, in the midst of a long, early-season slump after being traded to the Yankees and being eager to impress, said:

> I had such a great spring training. I hit over .350, I did everything I was supposed to, and I got here and thought that it was going to carry over for me. But it didn't. And it's tough because I really want to get off to a good start. You set goals for yourself . . . you want to move up and then bam, the hits stop dropping. At first I got a little pissed off. I felt sorry for myself . . . but now I am getting to the point where, "Hey, this is baseball. This is what it's all about." It's just something you have to battle through. I am not happy about it, but I know, my hits are gonna come.

No player is immune to slumps. Even the best hitters have several per season.

While the importance of the mental element in performance is widely recognized, management has been slow to develop it in players. "It's like it doesn't matter," said one progressive coach. "They treat the mental side like we are all idiots. They are big on the brawn part of it. You have lots of attention going to strength and the physical tools, but the other part they don't worry about." It may be that the mental is too subjective, too illusive.

Despite all of the research that shows performance can be enhanced by visualization, for example, little formal attention is given to it in most baseball organizations. In fact, coaches spend relatively little time teaching mental skills of any kind. One expert, ostensibly drawing on studies by sports psychologists, estimated that only 10 percent of all instruction time in pro ball is devoted to the mental game.[14] When asked about visualization, most of the coaches I interviewed shrugged it off as an "individual thing," not something they felt comfortable teaching. One Double-A manager put it this way, "I don't do a whole lot with that. It's up to the individual. We have a sports psychologist who does that stuff in spring training. I'll leave it to him." One veteran, gray-haired coach said he did not know anything about visualization. When I explained it to him, he said, "Well, I can visualize what I'd like to do with a sexy woman in an X-rated movie, but I can't see how seeing myself hit a baseball would ever be of any help." Jim Leyland, once regarded as one of the best managers in the baseball, curiously saw little value in it as well: "I personally don't believe in it because a lot of times you get the same people working with both teams. So if your [sports psychologist] guy is over in the other clubhouse getting you to visualize striking out my guy, and my guy is in here visualizing hitting a home run off him, who is going to win? But if my players believe in it, hey, that's fine, I am not going to discourage it."

However, as major league organizations become more interested in tapping the advances made in sports science, often applied first in the college ranks, and as they come to rely more on sports psychologists, sound mental techniques are likely to become an integral part of the pregame preparation of players in the future. But for now, too little attention is given to helping players develop the mental side of their game.[15]

7. Rituals of Uncertainty

Baseball contains a great deal of chance and uncertainty. Take the three essential activities of the game—pitching, hitting, and fielding. In the first two, chance can play a surprisingly important role. The pitcher is the player least able to control the outcome of his own efforts. He may feel great and have good stuff warming up in the bullpen, but get into the game and not have it. He may hang a curveball only to have the batter drill it, but into the hands of a fielder for an out; meanwhile, his best pitch may be blooped for a base hit. He may limit the opposing team to just a few hits yet lose the game, or he may give up a dozen hits but still win. Good and bad luck do not always average out, even over the course of a full season. Some pitchers end a season with poor won-lost records but have good earned run averages, and vice versa. In 1990 the New York Mets' Dwight Gooden gave up more runs per game than his teammate Sid Fernandez, yet Gooden won nineteen games and lost only seven, while Fernandez won only nine games and lost fourteen. Both pitched for the same team, which meant they had the same fielders behind them. Regardless of how well a pitcher performs, on every outing he depends not only on his own skill, but also on the proficiency of his teammates, the ineptitude of the opposition, and luck.

Hitting, which Hall of Famer Ted Williams and other observers have called the single most difficult task in the world of sports, is also full of risk and uncertainty. Unless it is a home run, no matter how well the batter hits the ball, fate determines whether it will go into a waiting glove, whistle past a fielder's diving stab, or find a gap in the outfield. The uncertainty is compounded by the low success rate of hitting: the average ballplayer gets only one hit in every four trips to the plate, while the best hitters average only one hit every three trips.

How does the risk and uncertainty of pitching and hitting affect players? How do they try to exercise control over the outcomes of their performance? These are questions I first became interested in many years ago as a college student during the off season, while taking an anthropology course called "Magic, Religion, and Witchcraft." As I listened to my professor describe the magical rituals of the Trobriand Islanders, it occurred to me that what these so-called primitive people did was not that different from what my teammates and I did to bring us luck.[1]

Routines and Rituals

The most common way ballplayers attempt to control chance is to develop a daily routine—a course of action that is regularly followed. Talking about the routines of players, Pirates coach Rich Donnelly said:

> They're like trained animals. They come out here [the ballpark], and everything has to be the same. They don't like anything that knocks them off their routine. Just look at the dugout, and you'll see every guy sitting in the same spot every night. It's amazing, everybody in the same spot. And don't you dare take someone's seat. If a guy comes up from the minors and sits here, they'll say, "Hey, Jim sits here, find another seat." You watch the pitcher warm up, and he'll do the same thing every time. And when you go on the road, it's the same way. You got a routine, and you adhere to it, and you don't want anybody knocking you off it.

Routines are comforting, they bring order into a world in which players have limited control. Sometimes practical elements in routines produce tangible benefits, such as helping a player concentrate. But what many players do goes well beyond mere routine. Many actions are purely *rituals*—prescribed behaviors in which there is no real connection between the means (e.g., tapping home plate three times) and the desired end (e.g., getting a base hit). Because there is no empirical connection between the two, rituals are not rational, and sometimes they are actually irrational.

Most rituals in baseball are personal. They are performed by individual players rather than by the team or a group of players. Most are performed in an unemotional manner, in much the same way players apply pine tar to their bats to improve the grip or dab eye black on their upper cheeks to reduce the sun's glare. Baseball rituals are infinitely varied. A player may ritualize any activity—eating, dressing, driving to the ballpark, pregame preparations—that he considers important or somehow linked to good performance. For example, on each pitching day for the first three months of the season, one of my roommates in the Florida State League, Dennis Grossini, set his alarm so that he would awake at exactly 10 A.M. At 1 P.M. he went to the nearest restaurant for two glasses of iced tea and a tuna-fish sandwich. Later, at the ballpark, he changed into the jock and under sleeves he wore during his last winning game, and one hour before the game he chewed a wad of tobacco. During the game, he touched the letters on his uniform and straightened his cap after each ball he pitched. Before the start of each inning he replaced the pitcher's rosin bag to the spot where it was the inning before. And after every inning in which he gave up a run, he washed his hands. When I asked Dennis which part of the ritual was most important, he said, "You can't really tell what's most important so it all becomes important. I'd be afraid to change anything. As long as I'm winning, I do everything the same."

Yankees player Denny Naegle goes to a movie on days he is scheduled to pitch. Jason Bere, while with the Birmingham Barons, listened to the same song on his Walkman on each day he was to pitch. Red Sox Nomar Garciaparra listens to the same music on the way to the ballpark and dresses in the same order—right sock, left sock, right sanitary, left sanitary, right stirrup, and so on.[2] Tigers farmhand Jim Ohms put another penny in the pouch of his supporter after each win. Clanging against the hard plastic genital cup, the pennies made a noise as he ran the bases toward the end of a winning season. The Houston Astros' Glenn Davis would chew the same gum every day during hitting streaks, saving it under his cap. Cardinals infielder Julio Gotay always played with a cheese sandwich in his back pocket (he had a big appetite, so there might also have been a measure of practicality here). Wade Boggs ate chicken before every game, and that was just one of dozens of elements in his pregame and postgame routine, which also included leaving his house for the ballpark at precisely the same time each day (1:47 P.M. for a 7:05 P.M. game). Former Orioles pitcher Dennis Martinez would drink a cup of water after each inning and then place the papercup upside down under the bench. His teammates could always tell what inning it was by counting the cups.

Many hitters go through preparatory rituals before stepping into the batter's box. These include tugging on their caps, touching their uniform letters or medallions, crossing themselves, tapping or bouncing the bat on the plate, or swinging the weighted warm-up bat a prescribed number of times. Consider the Red Sox Nomar Garciaparra. After each pitch, he steps out of the batter's box, kicks the dirt with each toe, adjusts his right batting glove, adjusts his left batting glove, and touches his helmet before getting back into the box. Mike Hargrove, a former Cleveland Indians first baseman, had so many time-consuming elements in his batting ritual that he was known as "the human rain delay." Both players believe their batting rituals helped them regain their concentration before and after each pitch. They consider such routines simply part of the game, a part of hitting and maintaining consistency. But others wonder if they have not crossed the line and become prisoners of superstition.

A player who has too many or particularly bizarre rituals risks being labeled a "flake," and not just by teammates but also by fans and the media. For example, Mets reliever Turk Wendell's eccentric rituals, which included wearing a necklace of teeth from animals he had killed, made him a cover story for the *New York Times Magazine*. Some players, especially Latinos, draw upon rituals from their Roman Catholic religion. Some make the sign of the cross or bless themselves before every at bat, and a few, like the Rangers' Pudge Rodriguez, do so before every pitch. Others, like Detroit Tiger Juan Gonzalez, also visibly wear religious medallions around their necks; others tuck them discretely inside their jerseys.

One ritual associated with hitting is tagging a base when leaving and returning to the dugout between innings. Some players do not "feel right" unless they tag a specific base on each trip to the dugout or field. One of my teammates added some complexity to his ritual by tagging third base on his way to the dugout only after the third, sixth, and ninth innings. Asked if he ever purposely failed to step on the bag, he replied, "Never! I wouldn't dare. It might destroy my confidence to hit." Baseball fans observe a lot of this ritual behavior, such as pitchers tugging on their caps or touching the rosin bag after each bad pitch, or smoothing the dirt on the mound before each new batter or inning, never realizing the importance of these actions to players. One ritual many fans do recognize, largely because it is a favorite of TV cameramen, is the "rally cap"—players sitting in the dugout wearing folded caps, bill up, in hopes of sparking a rally. It seems no other sport produces as many routines, rituals, and superstitions as baseball.

Most rituals grow out of exceptionally good performances. When a player does well, he seldom attributes his success to skill alone, because he knows that his skills were essentially the same the night before. What was different about today that explains his three hits? He decides to repeat what he did today in an attempt to bring more good luck. And so he attributes his success, in part, to an object he found, a food he ate, not having shaved, a new shirt he wore that day, or just about any behavior that was out of the ordinary. By repeating that behavior, he seeks to control his performance. Jamestown Expos outfielder John White explained how one of his rituals started: "I was jogging out to centerfield after the national anthem when I picked up a scrap of paper. I got some good hits that night, and I guess I decided that the paper had something to do with it. The next night I picked up a gum wrapper and had another good night at the plate. . . . I've been picking up paper every night since."

Outfielder Ron Wright of the Calgary Cannons shaves his arms once a week and plans to continue doing so until he has a bad year. It all began two years before, when he shaved his injured arm so it could be taped. He proceeded to hit three homers over the next few games. Now he not only has one of the smoothest swings in the minor leagues, but two of the smoothest forearms.[3] Wade Boggs's routine of eating chicken before every game began as a rookie in 1982, when he noticed a correlation between multiple-hit games and poultry plates (his wife has over forty chicken recipes). One of Jamestown Expos player Mike Saccocio's rituals also concerned food, "I got three hits one night after eating at Long John Silver's. After that, when we'd pull into town, my first question would be, 'Do you have a Long John Silver's?'" Unlike Boggs, Saccocio—and most other players—abandoned his ritual and looked for a new one when he stopped hitting well.

When in a slump, most players change their rituals and routines in an attempt to shake off their bad luck. One player tried taking different routes to the ballpark; several players reported trying different combinations of tagging and not tagging particular bases. I had one manager who would rattle the bat bin when the team was not hitting well, as if the bats were in a stupor and could be aroused by a good shaking. Similarly, I have seen a few hitters rub their hands along the handles of the bats protruding from the bin in hopes of picking up some power or luck from bats that are getting hits for their owners. Some players switch from wearing their contact lenses to glasses. Brett Mandel's Pioneer League team, the Ogden Raptors, tried to break a losing streak by using a new formation for their pregame stretching.[4]

Taboo

Taboos are the opposite of rituals. The word taboo comes from a Polynesian term meaning prohibition. Breaking a taboo, players believe, leads to undesirable consequences or bad luck. Most players observe at least a few taboos, such as never stepping on the chalk foul lines. A few, like Mets Turk Wendell and Red Sox Nomar Garciaparra, leap over the entire basepath. One teammate of mine would never watch a movie on a game day, despite the fact that we played nearly every day from April to September. Another teammate refused to read anything before a game, because he believed it weakened his batting eye. (There may be something to this in that some research suggests that when a person reads for an extended period of time, eye muscles are less able to relax, thereby decreasing visual acuity.)[5]

Many taboos take place off the field, out of public view. On the day a pitcher is scheduled to start, he is likely to avoid activities he believes will sap his strength and detract from his effectiveness. Some pitchers avoid eating certain foods, and others will not shave on the day of a game, sometimes refusing to shave as long as they are winning. Early in the 1989 season Oakland's Dave Stewart had six consecutive victories and a beard by the time he lost.

Taboos usually grow out of exceptionally poor performances, which players, in search of a reason, attribute to a particular event or behavior. During my first season of pro ball, I ate pancakes before a game in which I struck out three times. A few weeks later I had another terrible game, again after eating pancakes. The result was a pancake taboo; I never again ate pancakes during the season. Pitcher Jason Bere has a taboo that makes more sense in dietary terms: after eating a meatball sandwich and not pitching well, he swore off them for the rest of the season.

While most taboos are idiosyncratic, a few are held by all ballplayers. These form part of the culture of baseball and are sometimes learned as early as Little League. Mentioning a no-hitter while one is in progress is a well-known example. It is believed that if a pitcher hears the words "no-hitter," the spell will be broken and the no-hitter lost. This taboo is also observed by many sports broadcasters, who use various linguistic subterfuges to inform their listeners that the pitcher has not given up a hit, while never saying "no-hitter."

Fetishes

Fetishes or charms are objects believed to somehow embody "supernatural" power that will bring the owner luck. Good luck charms are standard equipment for some ballplayers. These include a wide assortment of objects from coins, chains, and crucifixes to a favorite baseball hat. In the words of one pitcher, "When you are going good you take notice of what you are doing. I still use my glove from college. It's kind of beat up, but it's got forty wins in it. I only use my professional glove in practice. I use my college glove in games." The fetishized object may be a new possession or something a player found that happens to coincide with the start of a streak. While playing in the Pacific Coast League, Alan Foster forgot his baseball shoes on a road trip and borrowed a pair. That night he pitched a no-hitter. Afterward he bought the shoes from his teammate, and they then became his personal fetish. Expos farmhand Mark Larosa kept a rock as a lucky charm, and he said, "I found it on the field in Elmira after I had gotten bombed. It's unusual, perfectly round, and it caught my attention. I keep it to remind me of how important it is to concentrate. When I am going well I look at the rock and remember to keep my focus, the rock reminds me of what can happen when I lose my concentration."

For one season Marge Schott, former owner of the Cincinnati Reds, insisted that her field manager rub her Saint Bernard "Schotzie" for good luck before each game. When the Reds were on the road, Schott would sometimes send a bag of the dog's hair to the field manager's hotel room.

During World War II, American soldiers used fetishes in much the same way. Social psychologist Samuel Stouffer and his colleagues found that in the face of great danger and uncertainty, soldiers developed distinct practices, particularly the use of protective amulets and good luck charms (crosses, bibles, rabbits' feet, medals), and jealously guarded articles of clothing they associated with past experiences of escaping from danger.[6] Stouffer also found that soldiers carried out their prebattle preparations in fixed ritualized order, similar to ballplayers preparing for a game.

Uniform numbers have special significance for some players. Since the choice is usually limited, such players try to at least get a uniform that contains their lucky number, such as 14, 24, 34, or 44 if their lucky number is four. When Ricky Henderson came to the Blue Jays in 1993 he paid outfielder Turner Ward $25,000 for the right to wear number 24. Oddly enough, there is no consensus about the effect of wearing number 13. Some players will not wear it, others will, and a few request it. Number preferences emerge in different ways. A young player may request the number of a former star, hoping that—through what anthropologists call *imitative magic*—it will bring him the same success. Or, he may request a number he associates with general good luck. When with the Oakland A's, Vida Blue changed his uniform number from 35 to 14, the number he had worn as a high school quarterback. When 14 did not produce better pitching, he switched back to 35. Former San Diego Padres first baseman Jack Clark changed his uniform from 25 to 00, hoping to break out of a slump. That day he got four hits in a doubleheader, but he also hurt his back. Then, three days later, he was hit in the cheekbone during batting practice.

Colorado Rockies Larry Walker's fixation with the number three has become well known to baseball fans. Besides wearing 33, he takes three practice swings before stepping into the box, he showers under the third showerhead, he sets his alarm for three minutes past the hour, and he was wed on November 3 at 3:33 P.M.[7] Mets reliever Turk Wendell has a strong preference for 99. He wears number 99, and in 1999 he signed a one-year contract for $1,200,000.99 with the chance to earn three bonuses of $4,999. He said, "I want as many 99s in my contract as possible."[8] Fans in ballparks all across America rise from their seats for the seventh-inning stretch before the home club comes to bat because the number seven is lucky, although the origin of this tradition has been lost.[9]

Clothing and the order in which it is put on combines elements of both ritual and fetish. Some players put their uniforms on in a ritualized order. Expos farmhand Jim Austin always puts on his left sleeve, left pants' leg, and left shoe before the right. Most players, however, single out one or two items or quirks of dress to ritualize. After hitting two home runs in one game, ex–San Francisco infielder Jim Davenport discovered that he had missed a buttonhole while dressing for the game. For the remainder of his career he left the same button undone. For outfielder Brian Hunter the focus is shoes, "I have a pair of high tops and a pair of low tops. Whichever shoes don't get a hit that game, I switch to the other pair." At the time of our interview, he was struggling at the plate and switching shoes almost every day. For Birmingham Barons pitcher Bo Kennedy the arrangement of the different pairs of baseball shoes in his locker is critical: "I tell the clubies [clubhouse boys] when you hang stuff in my locker don't touch my shoes. If you bump them move them back. I want the Pony's in front, the turfs to the right, and I want them nice and neat with each pair touching each other. . . . Everyone on the team knows not to mess with my shoes when I pitch."

During streaks—hitting or winning—players may wear the same clothes day after day. Once, I changed sweatshirts midway through the game for seven consecutive nights to keep a hitting streak going. Clothing rituals, however, can become impractical. Jamestown Expos catcher Matt Allen was wearing a long-sleeve turtleneck shirt on a cool evening in the New York–Penn League when he had a three-hit game. "I kept wearing the shirt and had a good week," he explained. "Then the weather got hot as hell, eighty-five degrees and muggy, but I would not take that shirt off. I wore it for another ten days—catching—and people thought I was crazy." Also taking a ritual to the extreme, Leo Durocher, managing the Brooklyn Dodgers to a pennant in 1941, is said to have spent three-and-a-half weeks in the same gray slacks, blue coat, and knit blue tie. During a sixteen-game winning streak, the 1954 New York Giants wore the same clothes in each game and refused to let them be cleaned for fear that their good fortune might be washed away with the dirt. Losing often produces the opposite effect. Several Oakland A's players, for example, went out and bought new street clothes in an attempt to break a fourteen-game losing streak.

Baseball's superstitions, like most everything else, change over time. Many of the rituals and beliefs of early baseball are no longer observed. In the 1920s and 1930s sportswriters reported that a player who tripped en route to the field would often retrace his steps and carefully walk over the stumbling block for "insurance." A century ago players spent time on and off the field intently looking for items that would bring them luck. To find a hairpin on the street, for example, assured a batter of hitting safely in that day's game. Today few women use hairpins—a good reason the belief has died out. To catch sight of a white horse or a wagon-load of barrels were also good omens. In 1904 the manager of the New York Giants, John McGraw, hired a driver with a team of white horses to drive past the Polo Grounds around the time his players were arriving at the ballpark. He knew that if his players saw white horses, they would have more confidence and that could only help them during the game. Belief in the power of white horses survived in a few backwaters until the 1960s. A gray-haired manager of a team I played for in Drummondville, Quebec, would drive around the countryside before important games and during the playoffs, looking for a white horse. When he was successful, he would announce it to everyone in the clubhouse.

One belief that appears to have died out recently is a taboo about crossed bats. Some of my Latino teammates in the 1960s took it seriously. I can still recall one Dominican player becoming agitated when another player tossed a bat from the batting cage and it landed on top of his bat. He believed that the top bat might steal hits from his. In his view, bats contained a finite number of hits. It was once commonly believed that when the hits in a bat were used up, no amount of good hitting would produce any more. Hall of Famer Honus Wagner believed each bat contained only one hundred hits. Regardless of the quality of the bat, he would discard it after its one hundredth hit. This belief would have little relevance today, in the era of light-weight bats with thin handles—so thin that the typical modern bat is lucky to last a dozen hits without breaking. Other superstitions about bats survive, however. Position players on the Class-A Asheville Tourists would not let pitchers swing or touch their bats, not even to warm up. Poor-hitting players, as most pitchers are, were said to pollute or weaken the bats.

Uncertainty and Magic

The best evidence that players turn to rituals, taboos, and fetishes to control chance and uncertainty is found in their uneven application. They are associated mainly with pitching and hitting—the activities with the highest degree of chance. I met only one player who used any ritual in connection with fielding, and he was an error-prone shortstop. Unlike hitters and pitchers, a fielder has almost complete control over the outcome of his performance. Once a ball has been hit in his direction, no one can intervene and ruin his chances of catching it (except in the uncommon event of two fielders colliding). He knows that in better than 9.7 times out of 10 he will execute his task flawlessly. With odds like that there is little need for ritual.

The rituals used by American ballplayers are not unlike those of the Trobriand Islanders studied by anthropologist Bronislaw Malinowski many years ago.[10] His observations of these Melanesian tribal peoples in the early part of this century led to a classic and now widely accepted theory that magic—rituals, taboos, and fetishes—occurs in situations where circumstances are not fully under human control and that it is used to reduce the anxiety uncertainty creates.[11] Malinowski's insight came while watching the islanders fish. In the inner lagoon, where fish were plentiful and there was little risk, the Trobrianders did not use magic. On the open sea, however, where fishing was dangerous and yields unpredictable, they used a great deal of magic to ensure their safety and increase their catch. In professional baseball, fielding is the equivalent of the inner lagoon; hitting and pitching are the open sea.

Obviously the rituals and superstitions of baseball do not make a pitch travel faster or a batted ball find gaps between the fielders, nor do the Trobriand rituals calm the seas or bring fish. What both do, however, is give their practitioners, at no cost, a sense of control and added confidence. And we all know how important that is. If you really believe eating chicken or hopping over the foul lines will make you a better hitter, it probably will.

8. Baseball Wives

The bulk of what has been written on baseball has been written by men, for men, and about men. Even biographies of ballplayers focus mostly on their on-the-field heroics and teammates, with little attention given to life at home or to their wives and families.[1] The fan's image of baseball wives—which comes mostly from televised glimpses of them in the stands—is that they are pretty, wear stylish clothes, and lead a life of privilege. "When people discover that I am married to a ballplayer they are usually impressed," said Heather Gajkowski, wife of the Seattle Mariners' Steve Gajkowski. "They think it's glamorous, and they ask a lot of questions about the life. Even when you tell them how hard it can be, how much your husband is away from home, or how little money you make in the minor leagues, they don't seem to get it."

So what is it like living with a ballplayer? How do the demands of their husbands' all-encompassing occupation shape the lives of the women in the stands?[2]

Mobility

Mobility is the feature of pro ball that exerts the greatest influence on the wives and families of ballplayers. In the minor leagues, the men play in a different town almost every season. If they make it to the major leagues, trades and free agency make them almost as transient there. Because ballplayers rarely play in their hometowns, their wives and children must move every year, not once but several times. In March some wives follow their husbands to Florida or Arizona for spring training; six weeks later, when spring camp breaks, they relocate to the city of their husband's team; and finally when the season ends in September, they return to their hometown. If their husbands play "winter ball," they may move yet again, usually to the Caribbean or Latin America.

Every trade, promotion, or demotion during the season means an additional move. One wife of a ballplayer who had spent ten years in the minor leagues calculated that she had moved twenty-three times and lived in every region of the United States. "We could probably stop in any state in the country and know someone from baseball," she said. Jan Butterfield, wife of Arizona Diamondbacks coach Brian Butterfield, moved a dozen times just in her first four years in pro ball.

When a husband is traded or moved within the organization, he gets a plane ticket and a ride to the airport; his wife is left with the burden of moving—disconnecting the utilities, closing the bank account, removing the kids from school or camp, and then reestablishing the household in a new locality. It is she who packs the household possessions, loads the U-haul, and transports the kids to the new town. In the words of Mary Jane Davis, who has been a baseball wife for thirteen years while her husband, Doug, first played for the Angels and Rangers and now manages in the Mets' organization:

> Moving is probably the toughest part, especially when you have little ones. When we didn't have any children, I made like, "Okay, this is a vacation. Let's go here and let's go there." But when you have children, it's different. They're moving all over, making new friends and then they have to leave them. It gets a little tough on them. I used to be very structured, keeping a schedule book and all, but I've thrown that out the window because there is no way I can be like that anymore. You just go with the flow. There were times that Doug got called up to the majors. He'd have to leave the next morning at six, and here I was stuck with the apartment, the car, the kids, and the dogs. You're excited for him moving up, but you are the one who has to pack everything up and drive down. I've lived or traveled in South America, Canada, and pretty much all of the United States. But you live out of a suitcase, and wherever you end up is usually not where your family is. . . . That's tough on the kids. They want to see Grandma.

Some wives do enjoy the travel, especially before they have children. Mary Jane Davis said, "You get to see a lot of the world. . . . There are only a few states we haven't been in or lived in, and a lot of people can't even say that at the age of fifty or sixty." Yet, however exotic and exciting the travel may be at first, the appeal wears off pretty quickly as the call to move usually comes without warning. Sharon Hargrove wrote about the frustration of a wife she knew who had just paid $67 for a phone jack, had cable TV hooked up, opened a bank account, and ordered checks when, after a mere ten days in town, her husband was reassigned.[3] This instability—reassignments and trades being the main culprits—causes many baseball families to postpone buying homes and possessions. After nine years of marriage, Nancy Marshall, wife of former Dodgers Mike Marshall, said the only furniture she owned was a set of bunk beds, a television, and a rocking chair.[4]

Because every team plays half of its games on the road, husbands are away a good deal during the season. Inevitably baseball wives spend a great deal of time alone; from April through September they are without husbands about half the time.[5] Several of the women I interviewed jokingly referred to themselves not as baseball wives but as baseball widows.[6] While on the road, the men are among teammates and companions; their wives are often home alone. They are friendly with a fellow baseball wife, but otherwise they have no local friendships to depend upon, nor do they typically belong to any groups in town. Even major league wives who have enjoyed a long tenure in one locality often do not have many local friends. "There are so many people out there who want to be around you just because of who you are, who your husband is, that you have to be wary," said Megan Donovan. Not surprisingly, wives frequently find themselves eating out or seeing a movie alone. The young wives in the low minors that I interviewed often admitted to being lonely when their husbands were away.

Chrissy Estrella, twenty, had never been apart from her parents and siblings in Port St. Lucie, Florida, before marrying a ballplayer and moving to Pittsfield, Massachusetts, for her husband, Leo's, first season. Other than the manager's wife, she was the only baseball spouse in town:

> When he is on the road there is nobody, nobody to hang out with. That's the hardest thing. I call my family [in Florida] and I cry to them, you know. When he was on the road this last trip, I found myself sleeping all the time just to pass up the time. I think I gained five pounds, because I didn't do my normal stuff. I don't know the gyms in this area like I do at home. I finally found a job [as a clerk in a Polo outlet store] because I was so bored and lonely.

Toward the end of the season two members of the Pittsfield Mets Booster Club tried to help by telephoning Chrissy when the team was on the road and occasionally inviting her out. Talking to their husbands on the phone, of course, reduces the loneliness, but in the low minors many couples cannot afford the expense of frequent long-distance phone calls. Indeed, some couples run up huge phone bills before they realize it. Many wives listen to their husbands' road games on the radio primarily to make them feel closer to their spouses and lessen the loneliness.

Young wives, who may be only a few years out of high school, are not just lonely but may feel vulnerable and insecure being on their own. "Before the guys leave for a road trip you hear some of the wives talk in the stands about how scared they are to stay by themselves," said a veteran wife of ten seasons. "Some get nervous and will keep the lights on; some of them have alarm systems. Of course, there are others who aren't bothered one bit." Some wives mentioned times when they felt especially defenseless. Fran Kalafatis watched her husband, George, and his teammates board the bus for a road trip in the Southern League as a hurricane approached, leaving her and the children in the parking lot to deal with the approaching storm. As the bus pulled away, the players yelled out warnings and instructions to their wives. In her memoir, Sharon Hargrove recounts two wives who were left alone in Kinston, North Carolina, to cope with a tornado watch. Having come from regions unaccustomed to severe weather, the women were clueless about what to do.[7] Several wives lamented being alone while pregnant and not having their husbands at the hospital when they gave birth.

Even when the team is at home, husbands are not around the house much. Ballplayers may spend late mornings at home, but they typically leave for the ballpark by early afternoon, and by the time the game has ended and they have showered and changed, it is after eleven o'clock. Even then, many players like to go out to eat and unwind before going home. In short, a player's schedule does not mesh well with the needs of a family. Children are in school when he is home in the mornings, and they are asleep by the time he arrives home at night. School summer vacations fall in the middle of the baseball season. Nor do the men have weekends free like most others. In fact, major leaguers have only about three days off per month (minor leaguers even less), and they are often spent traveling. Even when they are home, the physical grind of the baseball schedule can leave husbands with little energy for family life. Referring to the groupies who pursue ballplayers, Waleska Williams, wife of Yankees center fielder Bernie Williams, said, "If the young women that have these fantasies about being with ballplayers really knew what it is like being married to one, they might not be so eager. They don't know that you don't have him around for half of every year, and that there are times you wish he were in some other profession so he would be home at night."

The husband's absence means that his wife cares for the children by herself—supervising homework, preparing meals, setting standards, enforcing discipline—acting as both a father and mother for much of the baseball season. Amused by the irony, Waleska Williams described how in the absence of her husband, it was she who taught their six-year-old son how to play baseball. "It's really like being a single parent," said another wife. Lynn Rigney Schott, the daughter of former player and manager Bill Rigney, recalled her mother's experiences:

> As I look back on what it must have been like for her, I realize it wasn't easy. She struggled with a lot of stuff. Even things like teaching her kids to drive. . . . They want dad, not mom to do it. My mother had to do that with all three of us. My dad should have been the one teaching us to drive. It's a small thing, but it created a lot of tension and stress for her. When we'd get in trouble at school, the things that teenagers do. . . . I came home a couple of times in really deep water, because I had told her a song and dance, and she'd end up calling my dad in Detroit or somewhere, because it's two in the morning and Lynn isn't home yet and she's worried sick. That's pretty crummy. It was hard for her to shoulder all that herself. And we weren't bad—just normal teenage stuff. It was real hard for her. If my dad had been at home, no way would I have stayed out till two in the morning.

Several wives, however, spoke about the benefits of having time to spend with their young children. Lynn Lovullo, who has been married for eleven years to Torey Lovullo while he played the infield for the Detroit Tigers, New York Yankees, Anaheim Angels, Seattle Mariners, Cleveland Indians, Oakland A's, Philadelphia Phillies, and currently for the Yakult Swallows in Japan, said:

> When the kids are still small it can be a great experience. Being away from home, with no other real responsibilities except for caring for your child, and not being able to work, you have quality time to spend with your kids. I loved that part of my life. I remember in 1994, when Torey was playing with the Mariners, our apartment was right near a huge lake with parks and trails. My son, Nicky, was only five months old but we'd go for long walks and stay at the park for hours every day. It was a great bonding time.

The hard part comes when your children go to school, and you can't leave to join your husband until the middle of June when school is over. That makes it tough on both you and the kids. You're torn because you want to be with him and keep the family together, but it means uprooting the kids during the school year, yanking them out school activities, sports teams, special clubs, and away from their friends. So we don't do it. I feel so badly when Nicky tells me he misses his Daddy. You just hope you're doing the right thing.

What wives object to most is being left alone during holidays, birthdays, pregnancies, and special events in their children's lives, such as a toddler taking his or her first steps. "I want a normal life. I want to have cookouts with my kids in the summer and camping trips, do the things that normal people do," said one disgruntled wife. In the words of a mother of three: "My husband has been gone on every one of my kids' first birthdays. My daughter played T-ball for the first time this summer, and he missed that. It's funny, people think that because your husband is a coach that your kid is going to be a talent, but the truth is they aren't ever there to help the kids." Lynn Rigney Schott remembered that the only real family vacation that she ever had as a child was the year her father was fired as the manager of the California Angels. For a few months, he was free to travel with his family.

With husbands away so much and the operation of the household and its decisions left to spouses, it is not surprising that the baseball life requires a wife to be independent. "There are things I never dreamed I would deal with that I have become comfortable with," said Jan Butterfield. Some of the things often reserved for the men in more conventional households, baseball wives learn to do for themselves, such as repairing the car, fixing a leaky faucet, or disciplining the children. Birmingham Barons manager Tony Franklin explained, "It takes a very independent woman to get by in baseball. It takes a woman that does not depend on you to make her life worthwhile. When you are not there, she can't be afraid to do things for herself."

Lynn Lovullo said, "I think of the better baseball wives as being like geraniums. You break off a piece of them, transplant them into a new environment, and they manage to grow, thrive, and even bloom." Former player and coach and now baseball analyst Tom House believed that baseball wives grow up faster than their husbands do, because they have to stay at home to "anchor" the relationship and deal with the real world, while their husbands are off living in a fantasy world.[8] Some older wives said they now enjoy the independence their lifestyle fosters. Fran Kalafatis found that the time her husband was away encouraged her to develop new interests, which she now values. Danielle Gagnon Torrez, wife of journeyman pitcher Mike Torrez (who has played for the Cardinals, Yankees, Red Sox, Expos, Mets, Dodgers, Orioles, and the A's twice), finally came to view the time when her husband was gone as a "minivacation."[9]

Role

Clearly, the baseball wife's primary role is to support her husband and his career. Baseball careers are not only demanding, they are usually short—an average of just four years in the major leagues. Competition from other players, trades, injuries, and prolonged slumps can end a career at any time. Given this uncertainty, husbands and wives want to do everything to maximize his chances of success. To this end, husbands want to be able to focus on baseball, which means wives are expected to shield husbands from distractions. So wives arrange household and children's schedules to suit their husbands, and they screen phone calls and field requests for tickets. Mary Jane Davis tries to get her son involved in new activities to keep him occupied and prevent him from complaining and becoming unhappy, ". . . and that helps him, which helps me, which helps my husband. It's like a chain reaction." "His job is baseball, mine is the home and the kids; I take over all household authority during the season," said Jan Butterfield. "I am both the mother and the father until September," said Megan Donovan.

Most wives said they were expected not to trouble their husbands with domestic problems while the men were at the ballpark. While most wives of businessmen, doctors, and university professors, for example, have no qualms about calling their husbands at the office, it is nearly unthinkable for baseball wives to call their husbands at the clubhouse. The ballpark is sacrosanct. Beverly Crute, who wrote her doctoral dissertation on the wives of professional athletes, quotes one baseball wife, "You just don't call at the ballpark unless they're [the children] on their deathbed or something. I mean, there are girls that have babies while their husbands are at the ballpark, and they don't call them."[10] The enormous financial rewards for those who make it to the major leagues, combined with the brevity of the average career, justify in the minds of most wives the sacrifice required. Not surprisingly, most wives are deeply concerned with their husbands' performance, both for the men's sake and because it affects their joint fortune. "I'm very nervous when he pitches," said Heather Gajkowski, "I can't sit still, I pace the stands or stand on the ramp just out

The wife of Pittsfield Mets' A. J. Burnett watches her husband play. (Photo by William Mesick)

of view so I barely see him. I am especially nervous if he isn't doing well. When he is on the road and I am listening to the game on the radio, I turn the volume down when he isn't pitching well."

When I asked one player how his wife felt about the burdens of being a baseball wife, he replied, "Fine. That's what really attracted me to her, because I knew that she was going to stick by me one hundred percent. She knows I love the game, and she's pretty much in it for me. That's what's great [about our relationship]."

A wife supports her husband not just by listening to him talk about his performance and attending his home games, but sometimes by even participating in his superstitions. Wade Boggs's wife prepared chicken dishes for him everyday for years. Megan Donovan reported that her husband insisted that she wash her hair each day he was to pitch. In her memoir, Danielle Gagnon Torrez reported that one "rule" she learned as a baseball wife was "to support your husband's superstitions, whether you believe in them or not. I joined the player's wives who ate ice cream in the sixth inning, or tacos in the fifth, or who attended games in a pink sweater, a tan scarf, or a floppy hat."

Baseball life is not completely burdensome, of course. Many wives said that despite the hardship, they felt lucky to be in baseball. Reflecting on her eleven years in pro ball, Lynn Lovullo, who has a degree in English from UCLA and writes freelance for magazines, spoke for many wives when she recalled the good times:

> When we were newly married and didn't yet have kids, baseball was such an exciting lifestyle. In the minor leagues, we made really close friends, and we spent the summers like a big family. We usually lived in apartment complexes where several other couples lived. When the guys left for the ballpark or were on a road trip, it was like a big college dormitory. We'd all sleep over at each other's apartments, rent movies, go to dinner, lay out at the pool, hit the malls—whatever. Because we were all in the same boat, living far away from our families and without our husbands much of the time, we forged really good friendships. I think most of us tried to enjoy each others' company for as long as you are able, since nothing in baseball is permanent. I feel lucky to have have gotten to know such a great bunch of really great girls that got along so well. I'll never forget all the sleepovers, therapy sessions, barbecues, and all the camaraderie we enjoyed sitting in ballparks night after night.

Other wives also said they felt fortunate being able to go to the games and watch their husbands at work and that ballgames are usually enjoyable affairs. By providing free tickets, child care, family lounges, and special sections in the stands for wives and children, the teams encourage family attendance. Being at the games can strengthen a wife's identification with her husband's career. As Jan Butterfield said, "You become more involved, and you can talk about it more with him because you are experiencing the moment with him. It creates a bond that might not exist otherwise." At the ballpark, wives also learn a lot about the business of baseball, which enables them to better handle the decisions made by the club about their husband's career. Being at the ballpark also exposes the wife to the fairly unique situation of seeing people cheer or jeer her husband's performance. The wives of teachers, dentists, or stockbrokers never experience anything remotely like it.[11]

Appearance

Baseball wives and girlfriends are expected to look attractive, and most are. "Yes, the wives are usually very striking; you see one and you're like, 'Wow. She must belong to one of the players,'" said one public relations

Lynn Lovullo, wife of infielder Torrey Lovullo, and her son, Nicky, with the Buffalo Bisons' mascot, Buster, North Americare Park, 1997. (Photo by Liz Scott)

director. "They wear no numbers; they are not on any roster. But you can tell they are players' wives," wrote baseball observer Jean Ardell, about wives at spring training games in Arizona.

> It isn't just the jewelry: the golden earrings, rings, and bracelets; a Rolex watch so dazzling with diamonds that you cannot see the time. Nor is it what you might call their daytime evening clothes: backless, strapless, silky numbers that set off their tans and two-carat diamonds. These women are as well kept and sleek as cats. They also possess a feline watchfulness, beyond that of even the most die-hard fan. . . . It is an unlikely sorority. Day after day, the women sit together, their only common interest being their baseball-playing husbands.[12]

In the words of a San Francisco Giants official:

> When you see them all sitting together, it's like a fashion show. They don't come out to the ballpark like other folks, just to have a good time. They are here to watch their husbands play, but they also know they are being looked at and that they have to put their best foot forward. Their appearance is very important to them and to their husbands.

Such comments reveal another aspect of the role of the baseball wife—she is viewed in large measure as a player's property, part of the assets he brings to the game. When I asked team public relations directors about interviewing wives, they invariably said I should first get permission from their husbands. After doing so, I would then approach a wife, saying that I had spoken with her husband and that he said it would be alright to do an interview. Usually, that was good enough for the wife to consent.

When I returned to baseball for this research, I quickly found that the attitudes toward women, the importance of appearance, and the conventions for describing women had not changed much over the years. Today, like thirty years ago, when players show teammates snapshots of girlfriends from home it is standard to praise the pretty and poke fun at the plain. Sometimes I wondered why teammates who did not have photogenic girlfriends, or at least great snapshots, even bothered to show their pictures. It is also routine for players to check out the women in the stands, pointing out the attractive ones and rating their looks on a ten-point scale. Relief pitchers on one Triple-A team rated the women in the stands according to how drunk a player would have to be to sleep with them. A beauty would be no beers, while someone considered ugly might take a dozen. These practices and the focus on the physical attributes of women—face and figure—reflects an obsession with appearance and a tendency to view women as sexual objects, which is especially common to athletes.

At no time is looking good more important than during playoff or World Series games, when television cameras pan the wives' section and zoom in at different moments. Danielle Gagnon Torrez found the attention she received during the World Series, when her husband Mike Torrez was on the mound for the New York Yankees, to be a poignant reminder of the degree to which wives are seen as window dressing. She complained that press photos always showed her and the other wives with "glossy lipstick, white pompons, and continual smiles."[13]

One's looks and behavior, some wives claimed, can even affect a husband's baseball career. "You're part of the package, and if you don't look the part, well, some are going to notice," said Melanie Fox. Fran Kalafatis remembered being told by veteran wives how a baseball wife was to act:

> It was the older wives that taught the new recruits that you were to dress up for the games, and you were to look good. In the 1970s we wore pantyhose in Montgomery, Alabama, when it was ninety-nine degrees. It was insane when you look

Anaheim Angel wives (left to right) Candace Curtis, Lynn Lovullo, Marci Salmon, and Bobbie Frey filming a public service commerical, Anaheim Stadium. (Photo by Liz Scott)

back on it. But you thought it might just make the difference between your husband being called up [to the big leagues] or not if you were presentable. These were the unwritten, unsaid thoughts among the wives.

To capitalize on the fans' fascination with baseball wives—on the wives' public relations value—some major league teams organize public appearances for the wives and involve them in charity work. Baltimore Orioles wives, for example, sponsor an annual canned-food drive for local food banks. Canned goods are collected at the stadium by Orioles wives, each wearing an outsized jersey with her husband's name and number. The charity drive reflects well on the wives and on the team. Fans, of course, are attracted to the promotion by the opportunity to see the wives up close.

Status and Identity

Baseball wives enjoy a measure of status by virtue of being married to professional ballplayers. When they are with their husbands in public, they also receive attention. TV cameras focus on them at games, they are asked to participate in community and charity events, and they may meet celebrities outside baseball. But their identities are always tied to their husbands. Marilyn Monroe aside, the baseball wife's identity is submerged under his. He is seen as the breadwinner, and if he is in the major leagues, he probably earns more in a year than she will in a lifetime. He is in the limelight; he is in demand. As Danielle Gagnon Torrez came to understand, her role outside the home was as an accessory. To the public, baseball wives are not known by their names, rather they are always Mrs. Roger Clemens, Mrs. Bernie Williams, etc. One wife, who is a high school teacher, resented that during the baseball season she simply became an extension of her husband. Others spoke of the irritation they felt when people approached them in public and directed all their conversation and eye contact at their husbands, sometimes never even acknowledging their presence. I came across an ironic illustration of this on the dust jacket of Sharon Hargrove's memoir *Safe at Home*. Despite having written the book, in which she discusses the identities of baseball wives as ancillary to their husbands, the biographical blurb about the author on the dust jacket reads: "Sharon Hargrove is the wife of Mike Hargrove, formerly a big league baseball player and presently a minor league manager. . . ." Nothing else is said about the author, other than her having four children.

Mobility is partially to blame for the wives' dependent identity in that the transient nature of professional baseball makes it next to impossible for spouses to pursue their own careers. Even those who have the credentials or degrees have difficulty finding work. "No one wants to hire you if you are only going to be in town for five months," said one wife with a social-work degree. Several wives talked of being unable to seriously plan careers of their own as long as their husbands were in baseball. The few wives I met who had careers of their own were schoolteachers. They stayed behind when their husbands went to spring training and for the early part of the season, and then joined them during the long school summer vacation. Otherwise, most wives with career ambitions just had to put them on hold until their husbands retired from baseball.[14] As Jessica Stockam, wife of Mets farmhand Travis Stockam, put it, "We will start our life when he gets out of baseball." She meant that she could not begin a normal life until her husband's career was over and they could settle permanently in one place. She did not want him to leave baseball, and she was not unhappy being a baseball wife. She simply recognized that for all its benefits there were certain things baseball did not allow. Above all, it does not offer the kind of stable life most American women expect.

Elinor Nauen, editor of *Diamonds Are a Girl's Best Friend,* an anthology of women writers on baseball, told me of the players' wives she came to know in the Eastern League, "Even the ones who have gone to college and aren't stupid have very much accepted that the important life in the family is his." Danielle Gagnon Torrez, who had to scale back her modeling career when she married Montreal Expos pitcher Mike Torrez, noted that it was unusual to meet a baseball wife who saw the need to have her own achievements apart from her husband's.[15] One wife compared her marriage to a wheel in which her husband was the hub, and she was merely one spoke, with the other spokes being his career, his education, and his other interests. Nancy Marshall wrote to fellow wife Bobbie Bouton in their book *Home Games,* "One of the things I think you and I did wrong from day one was to act like puppy dogs at our husbands' feet. They had all the success, all the glory, and the notoriety. It was only natural that we fell into the trap of idolizing them as much as their fans do."[16]

It would be wrong, however, to claim that all wives feel this way. The discontent that Marshall described was built up over a dozen years of marriage and is uncharacteristic of younger wives. Most of the wives whom I got to know accepted their subservient role as temporary but necessary, and, though they complained about the loneliness and the burdens they shouldered, few were eager to exchange it for a "normal" life.[17]

Another dimension is that a wife's status among the other baseball wives is influenced by her husband's status. "It's amusing," said Lynn Lovullo, "how some wives refer to their husband's stats or performance as 'ours.' You hear things like, 'Our ERA is under 3!' or 'Our agent is negotiating for such and such' or 'Our batting average is second in the league.'" In the major leagues there is usually a loose pecking order among the wives in which their individual standing is swayed by their husband's salary, performance, and standing on the team. The wives of star players bask in the glow of their husbands' fame, while wives of nonstar players, no matter how talented the women themselves may be, enjoy less prestige. As one major league wife explained:

> Somebody who has been in the big leagues for a while might talk about stuff that is out of your range—you know, "Oh, I went to Bloomingdales today, and I bought all this stuff and it's being delivered." Well it's very hard for someone who has just come up from Triple A to relate to spending that much money on

shopping. But a lot depends on the person's personality—it's not just money. Nolan Ryan's wife, Ruth, was the nicest person I ever met, and she would talk to anyone even if they'd only been in the big leagues for two days.

Several wives suggested that the women who had grown up with their ballplayer husbands had a healthier, more realistic perspective on baseball than did the women who had met their men in the big leagues. In the words of one seasoned wife of a dozen years:

> What is really amusing to the veteran wives—those of us who've been with our husbands forever, like since high school or college—are the new wives who've married older established guys who were already in the big leagues. Some of them are really immature, like they gab loudly in the stands about their interior decorators, their new Mercedes, their Nike contracts, their vacation homes, and God knows what else. They've never experienced the lean times in the minor leagues, where you sweat it out for every promotion, living and dying with your husband, practically every pitch. They only know the bright lights and the big money.

Confounding the pecking order a bit, wives caring for young children are often drawn to other wives with young kids, overriding other considerations. On the other hand, spouses of players and the spouses of coaches never mingle much, even when they are of similar age. They may sit together at the ballpark, but rarely do they fraternize on the outside, just as in the business world the wives of management do not socialize with the wives of workers. The anomaly in baseball is that the workers and their wives are usually a whole lot wealthier than the managers and their wives.

Uncertainty

Baseball wives probably contend with more uncertainty than do most American women. In addition to having to move without notice, an injury to a husband can suddenly end his career and a family's livelihood at any time. The vagaries of baseball performance in which bad times or slumps inevitably follow good times can make the baseball life an emotional roller coaster—highs when husband and team are playing well and lows when they are not. And all of it is beyond the wife's control. About the uncertainty big-league wives face, Tom House observed, "One day you're the toast of the town, the next day you're invisible. That's the reality of it. It's an incredibly insecure existence, made tolerable by the false sense of security created by the success and fame. When those start to fade—or, even worse, when they're suddenly yanked away—both husband and wife go down together."[18]

It is not much better for the wives and families of managers and coaches. Most minor league managers are on annual contracts and have little job security. When ownership or general managers change, the new regime usually cleans house and brings in its own people. "It's always in the back of your head," said Mary Jane Davis, married to a Class-A manager. "It takes just one person to buy out the team or come in and take over, and they'll want all their own men. Hopefully another organization will pick you up, but you never know. You try not to look too far into the future with baseball, because it's a crazy situation. You never know what is going to happen."

Wives may also worry about their husbands' faithfulness, especially while they are on the road. Perhaps in all occupations where men travel and are away from home a good deal, there are concerns about infidelity. But many wives say the concerns are greater in baseball, where there is temptation in every town from groupies, those often scantily clad, overly made-up young women who pursue ballplayers. Cyndy Garvey, wife of former Dodgers first baseman Steve Garvey, described her discovery of her husband's "little black book": "I leafed through it. On the back page was a listing of National League cities. New York. Chicago. Cincinnati. St. Louis. And next to each city there was a woman's name and phone number. Some of the names had stars next to them. It was horrible. Too horrible. Too much of a bad cliché to be true."[19]

While many players do not indulge, groupies are successful often enough to make some wives uneasy about what their husbands do while away from home. One major league spouse reported this about wives sitting in the stands together, "You can tell those who have close relationships with their husbands and aren't worrying from those who are paranoid, who aren't sure and are listening to his answering machine, going through his briefcase, and being nosy. Sometimes you just wonder if your own husband has the moral fiber to turn down the easy sex and good times."

Bobbie Bouton and Nancy Marshall devoted an entire section of their memoir, *Home Games,* to the groupie problem. They describe three stages in the evolution of the baseball wife's concern about infidelity. In the first or "True Believer" stage, the wife fully trusts her husband and thinks that he is always faithful. Then, in the "Knock on the Head" stage, the evidence and suspicions of infidelity incrementally mount until finally, in the "Realism" stage, the wife becomes fully aware that her husband sometimes sleeps with other women on the road. She is disillusioned but also realizes—perhaps rationalizes—that it really does not reflect on her, and that it is really "entertainment" for the men while they are away.

Not all wives are so philosophical. Discovery of infidelity does sometimes lead to the break up of the marriage, though probably much less often in baseball than in other professions. Beverly Crute found that some wives coped by excusing their husbands' behavior with the attitude of "boys will be boys" or "what he does on the road is his business, what he does at home is my concern."[20] Pete Rose's wife, Karolyn, declared to some of her husband's teammates, "I know Pete gets fucked on the road all the time: I say as long as he doesn't do it at home, I don't care."[21] Karolyn eventually tired of his extramarital escapades, however, and divorced him.

Many players, of course, do not sleep around, though their wives may still wonder. Some players talked about making an effort to allay their wives' concerns. As one Oakland A's player put it: "We go on a ten-day road trip and there are groupies out there looking for ballplayers in every city. My wife knows that. There's got to be a lot of trust in the marriage. . . . I call home every night and do things that try to make her at ease. Baseball wives should get a lot of respect for what they have to go through." Overall, the wives have little choice but to accept the insecurity, though some said they tried to keep their husbands happy at home in the belief that a contented husband is less tempted to fool around.

Clearly, there are both significant rewards and costs to being the wife of a professional baseball player. Baseball wives are fortunate to have prestige and financial security if their husband reaches the major leagues, but they must also deal with isolation, heavy responsibility in daily life and parenting, and the postponement of their own career plans. It is no wonder that some people refer to the baseball wife as "the fifth base," an anchor point outside of the field, but inextricably bound to the game itself.

In conversations with players, I found that many downplayed the considerable burdens their wives shouldered. Perhaps it was just not macho to show a lot of concern. Nor did I detect much of an effort by the players to lighten their wives' responsibilities, but that may be due to my reliance on interviews. Observation of daily life in baseball households might lead to a different conclusion. Yet there is evidence that players may really be somewhat indifferent. The ready availability of attractive women is clearly a factor. Groupies offering themselves to ballplayers may well increase the player's sense of self-importance (and sense of his attractiveness to women), which can lessen his empathy for a spouse or girlfriend. Also, sociologist Gary Fine reported in his study of Little Leaguers, *With the Boys*, that from an early age the athletes come to see male dominance as the natural order of things. As youths, Fine said, athletes define their masculinity in terms of attributes that females lack, notably competitiveness and aggression, and they learn to avoid displaying feminine qualities, such as emotional expressiveness, nurturance, and compassion. The latter, of course, are the very qualities that would make ballplayers more understanding and compassionate spouses.

Many baseball wives had no idea of what they were getting into when their courtships with ballplayers began, whether it be in school or when he was already in pro ball. In one respect these baseball wives represent a traditional gender role, sacrificing for their husbands' careers, but in another sense, precisely because of this sacrifice, they become far more independent and resourceful than many American women, managing families and households on their own.

9. Groupies

She Hits, She Runs, He Scores: After Hours, Baseball Is Still One Wild, Wild World" was the title of a *Newsweek* feature about women who pursue professional baseball players. Every spring new accounts appear in the press about groupies and ballplayers and the trouble some players get into by consorting with them. Baseball groupies first crept into the American public consciousness in the 1970s through the book *Ball Four* and, later, through popular films like *The Natural* and *Bull Durham*. Who are groupies and what are they looking for? And what do the players make of them?

From Rock Music to Baseball

The word *groupie* first appeared in the rock music scene in the 1960s. In the early years of rock, all young female fans were described as groupies, even though there was a difference between ardent fans who had no contact with the band members, except in fantasy, and those who developed sexual relationships with them. Sometimes groupies of the latter type became celebrities in their own right. In 1969 *Rolling Stone* devoted an entire issue to stories about famous rock groupies.[1] In the article "I'm with the Band," Pamela Des Barres described her lifestyle as a rock groupie in California in the 1960s and early 1970s. She painted an upbeat picture of groupies as integrally involved in the California social and musical scene. Even so, it is clear that groupies were stigmatized and that they were cynically exploited by performers who accepted their adoration and sexual favors as their due. Problems with drug abuse, sexually transmitted diseases, and mental instability were as much a part of the groupie scene as were thrilling encounters with revered rock stars.[2]

By the early 1970s, according to the *Barnhart Dictionary of Etymology,* the term *groupie* had been extended to include any fan or devotee of an activity. By the 1980s groupie was being applied to baseball, replacing "Annie" and "Shirley." Groupies had been on the margins of baseball for at least a generation without much public notice. Before the 1970s sportswriters as a rule did not write about the off-field antics of the players and teams with whom they traveled and covered.[3] Babe Ruth's "stomachache heard around the world," for example, widely reported in the press as being due to overeating hot dogs, was actually venereal disease. Groupies hustled players, and players bedded them, but little was said or written about it. Insider accounts of the lives of professional ballplayers, such as Jim Brosnan's books *The Long Season* (1960) and *The Pennant Race* (1965), made no mention of players' sexual liaisons with Annies. That changed with the publication of Jim Bouton's bestseller *Ball Four* in 1970 in which he revealed the wenching and bawdy behavior of his New York Yankee teammates. For one, Bouton revealed to his readers the players' various techniques for "beaver shooting"—peeping on unsuspecting women—from standing underneath the stands to drilling holes in the adjoining hotel room door.

It was not until the 1988 release of the popular film *Bull Durham,* however, written by former minor leaguer Ron Shelton, that the existence of groupies in baseball became widely known. In Shelton's film, groupie Annie Savoy, played by Susan Sarandon, is a sympathetic character who loves baseball and whose liaison with a young pitcher, Nuke LaLosh, enhances his career. *Bull Durham*'s second groupie, Millie, is closer to the popular conception of groupies with her uncontrolled sexuality and her sleeping with multiple players. We also get a glimpse of groupies of a different kind in Barry Levison's 1984 film *The Natural.* In this adaptation of Bernard Malamud's book, the sinister Memo Paris brings down the hugely talented ballplayer Roy Hobbs. However, Hobbs is saved from disaster and wins the big game for his team after coming under the influence of the virtuous and innocent Iris Lemon.

Some players, most notably Joe Pepitone in *Joe, You Coulda Made Us Proud,* have described liaisons with groupies in their ghostwritten autobiographies.[4] Margo Adams was paid $100,000 to describe her long-term affair with former Red Sox star Wade Boggs in a *Penthouse* article. A mortgage banker, she met Boggs in an Anaheim, California, bar and later accompanied him on sixty-four road trips over several years. In a different vein, the wives of several players have written about the jealousy and strife that groupies create at home—groupie as "homewrecker."[5] Groupies now appear in the sports pages as negative influences on players and their families. Four widely covered incidents in the 1990s were the Mets' Daryl Boston's payment of $600,000 to a groupie to avoid being charged with rape; Yankee Luis Polonia's charge of having sex with an underage girl; Red Sox player Wade Boggs's road trysts with Margo Adams; and the Braves' Chipper Jones's cheating and fathering a child with a Hooters restaurant waitress he met during spring training in West Palm Beach, Florida. Jones admitted to hustling other women at the same time, while his wife was at home in Atlanta. The result of all this attention, both in film and newsprint, is that most Americans today are aware of who groupies are and what they do.[6]

"A groupie," said a Jamestown Expos player, "is any girl who goes to the ballpark who is not there to watch the game." More specifically, other players referred to them as women who, because of low self-esteem, choose to associate themselves with people they consider important or famous. How accurate are these perceptions? What role do stereotypes about women play?

Most of the groupies that ballplayers and ballpark employees pointed out to me were young—late teens to mid-twenties—and single. The vast majority were white. While I was aware of a few African American groupies, I never saw or heard of any Latina groupies. In the minor leagues, most groupies appear to have working- or lower-middle-class backgrounds. Most have not gone to college, and most work in the service sector or in clerical work. In the big leagues, however, where the players earn big money and enjoy some measure of fame, the groupies were of higher social status, including some with careers—travel agents, aspiring models, and actresses—and even a few professionals, including a lawyer and an accountant. Overall, the players' comments about groupies reflected a dichotomization of women into good and bad—good girls versus immoral groupies, safe versus dangerous.

More than Sex

What do groupies hope to attain by pursuing a relationship with a ballplayer? Many appear to just want a good time and have no hopes of developing a serious or long-term relationship with a player. For them, the

Fans Amber Joswick, Age Cuda, Kristy Pulturak, and Gabby Garncarz flirt with Utica Blue Sox catcher Jeff Stevens at Donavan Stadium, Utica, New York. (Photo by Tom Barthel)

ballpark on a warm summer evening, especially in small minor league towns, offers a place to go and something different to do. As two women in their early twenties, who attended all of the Welland Pirates' home games using free tickets provided by players, said: "Here at the ballpark you got something to watch while you have a few beers, it's better than going to a smoky, noisy bar and just drinking beer and trying to get picked up." They had casual relationships with two players, who they went out with after each game. They, like the other casual groupies that I met, said they enjoy hearing players talk about the team and the professional game of baseball. In short, their relationship with the players offered an insider's perspective on pro ball, which in some small-town social circles is valued.

Some groupies said they enjoy getting to know players because they come from afar—notably California, Texas, Florida, and the Caribbean—and that makes them more "exotic" and more interesting than local men whose backgrounds they know all too well. For many, the appeal of going out with ballplayers after the game is simply "partying"—getting something to eat in a cafe and then going back to the players' apartments to hang out. "It's the whole social scene," explained one young woman. For young women of modest means, it is a fun and inexpensive night out—most get free tickets to the games and free beer afterward.

Sex is often part of the relationship, but, not surprisingly, the groupies I interviewed were reluctant to say much about this aspect. For a young groupie in a small town, hooking up with a ballplayer, as long as it is not done too publicly, affords the opportunity to have sex without risking her local reputation. Most ballplayers do not know anyone in the community, and, almost without exception, they leave town at the end of the season. I knew of one groupie in Drummondville, Quebec, for whom part of the appeal of dating ballplayers was the opportunity to act out sexual fantasies in unusual or strange places.[7] A respectable and attractive woman, she could do things with ballplayers that she would not dare do with a local guy.

To many minor leaguers, the primary reasons groupies are interested in them is self-evident: the women want to have a physical relationship with men they think are attractive physical specimens. "They think we're hunks," said one player. Darren Campbell described the several dozen young women who hang around the ballpark in South Bend, Indiana, in hopes of catching the attention of White Sox players, "They're looking for the young stud. A lot of it has to do with us being professional athletes, and they know we are in great shape. You've got to be in shape to do what we do. They are going for a guy who has a nice body, good-looking guy. . . . And, many look great in a baseball uniform." Birmingham Barons broadcaster Curt Bloom, who has spent five years in A ball and three in Double A on the road with teams, said, "Groupies go after players because they are in great shape, they're good looking, and they have a chance to make good money. They get prestige and think they look like queens walking around with a guy who is built like an ox." But the sex may not always be as good as the women expect. As one of Jim Bouton's managers declared, "Baseball players are not, by and large, the best dates. We prefer wham-bam-thank-you-ma'am affairs. In fact, if we're spotted taking a girl out to dinner, we're accused of 'wining and dining,' which is bad form."[8]

Major League and Triple-A players more often emphasize money and celebrity as motives for the groupies interest in them. In the words of a Tacoma Rainers player:

> Some of the guys at this level are making some pretty good money right now, especially guys who have been in the big leagues. Groupies think, why be with some guy from the neighborhood when I can be with a guy who gets his picture in the paper, who you read about every day. They know that the player goes from city to city, that they don't have their wives or girlfriends with them, and that a

lot of them miss the sexual activity. So it might be just a little easier for them to get in.

In the minors, groupies hope that the players they get to know will someday make it to the major leagues and become famous. As one woman usher at the Jamestown Expos ballpark said about groupies, "They're just looking for a brush with something famous, something exciting. Some hope that maybe in five years, when they see one of these players on television, they can say that they knew him." One twenty-three-year-old, slender, red-headed groupie said that having been with a pro ballplayer would be something nice to look back on and tell her kids about. Few groupies understand how slim the chances are of the players they meet in the low minors making it to the big leagues.

Although some groupies hope for a permanent relationship, most are fairly realistic about their chances. They know most players have girlfriends or wives at home and that they are unlikely to leave them. This, however, does not deter them from continuing relationships they find exciting, fun, and often sexual. Sometimes parents encourage their daughters to pursue ballplayers. One family in an Ontario town in the New York–Penn League billeted a player each season in the hope that a relationship might develop between the player and their daughter, hopefully leading to marriage and a more affluent life. She eventually did marry a Dominican player, but the union did not last. At the Jacksonville Suns ballpark one local woman tried to interest players in her comely teenage daughter by asking them to pose for pictures with the girl. Such behavior has its defenders. Carolyn Bushing, a Denver psychotherapist and author of a book about relationships, *The Seven Dumbest Relationship Mistakes Smart People Make,* said women who pursue ballplayers for fame and fortune should not be criticized because they are acting on instinct. Namely, they are looking for good providers.[9] Likewise, Darlene Bordeaux, a Los Angeles–based psychologist and sexual harassment consultant, defended groupies on the grounds that women should have the same rights as men. If men can hit on women, then women should be able to do the same.[10]

Hustling

To attract the attention of ballplayers, groupies go to the places ballplayers congregate and sit where they are most likely to be seen. At the ballpark they sit above the dugout or near the bullpen. "They wear the skimpiest shorts, tightest pants, the brightest blouse, so that they can be picked out of the crowd," said catcher Darren Campbell. "Their heads are always in the dugout. They're making eye contact with you and you with them. Before you know it, a player signals, 'Give me your phone number.' And she'll walk over and give a piece of paper to the bat boy with her phone number on it."

After the game they wait outside the clubhouse or in the parking lot where players will have to pass them. "They yell your name, say 'hi' to you, or just come up and start talking to you," explained one player. Some ask for an autograph and a phone number, adding that they would not mind meeting the player later. One woman somehow managed to get a fresh rose smuggled into the California Angels' clubhouse, in the locker of Doug Davis for several days, hoping to get noticed. In bars after the games, groupies try to catch players' attention. "They sit there and stare at you," explained one player, "they give you the eye and let you know they are interested. I'm looking at you, now you are looking at me kind of thing." To show interest, a groupie may smile, glance, primp, laugh, giggle, toss her head, flip her hair, and maybe even hike her skirt a bit, pat a buttocks, touch a knee.[11] Some groupies are modest and timid, others are bold and aggressive in approaching players. Some go to the hotel of the visiting team and wait in the lobby, call on the house phone, or arrive uninvited at a player's room.

The Players

What do players think of groupies? "That one I couldn't tell you. To be perfectly honest, I don't know where they are, and I don't hang out with them," or similar phrasing, was the typical initial response of players to my query. And it was often followed by something like, "I'm not trying to avoid the question, it's just a scene I never really got involved with." Such denials were especially common among major league players whose experience with reporters has made them cautious, concerned that anything they said might wind up in a newspaper with their name attached. But usually, reminders that I was an anthropologist trying to understand general patterns of behavior, rather than their private lives, resulted in some major leaguers and most minor leaguers opening up. These conversations usually stayed on a level of general patterns, rather than the player revealing his own involvement with groupies. And many players, indeed, had nothing to do with groupies.

Players who have not been in pro ball long are often flattered by the attention they get from the "strange" and "sexy" women who pursue them. The players are not passive in this process. Many routinely scan the stands for pretty women. When one is spotted, she will be pointed out to others on the bench or in the bullpen, and her appearance assessed—face and figure. A lot of the talk about the women reflects a view of them as sexual objects, or at least a fixation on appearance, as the primary reference is usually to their physical attributes and sexiness. Players sometimes relate or joke about what they would like to do with them sexually. Other than mothers, wives, and serious girlfriends, women are seldom talked about openly as thinking, feeling individuals—at least in men's group talk. It has often been suggested that men, whether they are ballplayers or construction workers, bond through such sexist joking.[12] One Tacoma Rainer club official blamed the groupies' pursuit of players for contributing to the athletes lack of respect for women. "The groupies put the athletes up on pedestals and think they can do no wrong, and before long the player himself starts to believe it. He becomes arrogant. He begins to expect women to be hanging all over him. He takes them for granted. If the groupies don't demand the respect they desire, then he's not going to give it." After awhile the player's attitudes toward all women may be colored by his experiences with groupies.

Many young players see groupies as potential sexual partners with no strings attached.[13] In the words of a third-year player:

> They're everywhere. With the snap of a finger you can get laid. They come with professional baseball, you've seen the big ones like the groupies that Wade Boggs and Steve Garvey had around. There are tons of girls that want to be with you—college girls, high school girls, and even some older women. When I played in the Cape Cod League there were even some older divorced women who had a player living with them just so they could get sexual pleasure from them.

Many veteran players, however, who are also more likely to be married, better understand the responsibilities and risks. Many noted that groupies may have communicable diseases—like STDs or HIV—and that they may get pregnant and demand child support, or worse. As Atlanta Braves coach Pat Corrales explained:

A married guy might go out and mess around, have a one-night stand with this girl. Then the next night the girl is knocking at the guy's door saying she is going to go to the newspaper or to the police if he doesn't give her *x* amount of money. Or he gets a phone call from the police saying that they have a girl down there at the station saying that he raped her, and they have a warrant for his arrest. As soon as you go to the police station the press is there, you are a big league ballplayer, you've got a family and kids back home. Then the girl gets on the phone and says that if you don't want to come to the police station, you can send her some money and take care of everything out of court. She walks away with *x* amount of money, like with the Daryl Boston incident. The girl ends up walking away with six hundred thousand dollars for what, for getting laid. She had just as much fun as he did that night, and she is getting six hundred thousand, and he gets taken to the cleaners. She walks away with the money, and you just get screwed over.

Veteran players have become even more cautious after recent incidents in which scam artists have posed as groupies. Many ball clubs now lecture players during spring training about the risks. One scam involves a girl posing as a groupie, then picking up a ballplayer who takes her back to his room. She suggests that he tie her down and do whatever he wants, then it will be her turn. But as soon as he is tied, the groupie's coconspirator walks into the room and takes photographs of both player and groupie in positions no one would ever want to be seen in. In a similar scam, the player's drink is drugged and, when he passes out, his wallet and watch are lifted and pictures taken of him in compromising positions.

Consorting with groupies too frequently, say some players, can damage one's reputation and career by bringing the disapproval of the coaching staff. Players who sleep around excessively are also looked down upon by their more straightlaced teammates. In the words of one player, "There were some guys that were my friends that I lost all respect for. I saw things that you just wouldn't believe. I remember when we played in Orlando, there was this one girl that was waiting for the whole team, and about twelve players took advantage of her. She was a waitress in the hotel where we all ate. I think she entertained every team that came to town. That's going too far."

It is the married player, however, who most risks losing the respect of his teammates. One ball player said, "I've seen married guys with other girls in different cities. . . . You are around each other all the time, and in the locker-room talk you hear, 'This guy did this many girls, and this other guy was with that girl last night, and someone will say what he did to her.' That ain't right." Rod Beaton, who travels with teams while covering the National League for *USA Today,* observed that players who chase women gravitate toward one another: "You'll get single players and the married player who cheats on his wife going out as a group. They bond very closely. It is unfortunate, but chasing women is probably the most solidified bond in the whole clubhouse chemistry."

Many players avoid groupies out of respect or faithfulness to girlfriends or spouses; others do so because they do not want to be distracted from baseball and hurt their performance. In the words of Yankees farmhand Robert Eenhorn:

> I'm so concentrated about making it [to the big leagues] that all that stuff goes by me. If you go out there and want it [women and sex], it's available. But I don't want to think about it. I have no problems with it, it's worldwide. Wherever you have people who are good at what they do, you have others who want to be a part of it. And the more money you have, the more people are going to come to you and want to be a part of it. But it's not for me.

First-round Cardinals draft pick Adam Kennedy said his father and agent warned him about the temptations of groupies before he left home to begin his rookie season. "But I have my head on straight enough to understand what's right and wrong off the field," said Kennedy, after his first month of pro ball.

Players' generally low opinions of groupies can change as they develop relationships. One rookie player talked about a girl who had befriended him at the beginning of the season and whose apartment he was about to move into for the last two weeks:

> She has been real nice. I really don't think of her as a groupie because she doesn't stand out. She doesn't go to bed with everybody. . . . A lot of people might think of her as a groupie just because she is from Jamestown and hangs around us, but I really don't picture her that way, because she really is not in it for the glamour. She just likes to be here because we get along, and she likes to hang around together.

But often, once a woman is identified by players as a groupie, it is difficult to change her status. While traveling with the Jamestown Expos, I listened to players gossip about a teammate who had just become engaged to a groupie. After being dumped by his girlfriend at home, the player had begun dating a local girl who had previously slept with other players on the team. After dating for a month, he proposed and gave her the ring he had intended for his former girlfriend. Although the player was well liked by his teammates, there was much talk about her having slept around and having had an abortion. Even though she was going off to college in the fall, her identity as a former groupie made her, in the eyes of other players, an undesirable bride.

But it is wrong to regard player-groupie relationships as always sexual or exploitative. Both sides may derive other benefits from the relationship. In the all-male world of professional baseball, where players live away from home and away from the coed environment of the high school or college campus, groupies are often the only female companions available, especially in the low minors where most players are single. Some help clean the players' apartments, run errands, and, because most of these players do not have cars and cannot easily get around town, provide transportation. In the minor leagues particularly, women often bring as much to the relationship as the players. And it is there, where player-groupie relationships are more balanced and reciprocal, that women are less likely to be dismissed as mere groupies. In the big leagues, in contrast, players who have money and celebrity have less need for the services groupies can provide, and the relationship between players and groupies becomes more asymmetrical. Hence the groupies' motives are viewed with suspicion. Here, one-night stands are the norm (in fact, rarely is she invited to stay after the sex is over), the women seldom develop friendships with the players they pick up, and the players' attitudes and actions are generally more clearly sexual and narrowly defined.

10. When the Cheering Stops

Parker Brown had just arrived in the clubhouse when Joe Zacek, the Greenville Braves' trainer, gently tapped him on the shoulder, "Don't dress, Brownie, the skipper wants to see you." Brown felt himself blanch. Fixing his eyes on the floor, he walked past the lockers where his teammates were dressing, down the corridor, past the shower and into the cramped, low-ceiling office of his manager, Ed Henley. The expression on Henley's face said it all. "Parker, this is the most difficult thing a manager has to do in life." The rest was a blur. By the time he had returned to the locker room it was empty. His teammates—now former teammates— were on the field. Fighting back tears, he mindlessly stuffed his gear into his canvas travel bag with the Braves' logo emblazoned on each side. Then he went to the front office where the paperwork for his release and a plane ticket home were waiting. Meanwhile, the clubhouse attendant removed the nameplate—Brown—from the front of his locker and tossed it into a wastebasket. His gear and ticket in hand, Brown ascended to the top row of the grandstands, hoping no one would see him, to take a last look around. He stayed only two innings. It was too painful and humiliating.[1]

Although every professional ballplayer knows that one day he, like Parker Brown, will be let go, few are prepared for it. With most jobs, an employee plans for retirement years in advance and may even decide the exact date he will leave work. In baseball only a handful of players, mostly veteran big leaguers, are able to retire in this way—gracefully, choosing when and how they leave. Most players are fired, or in baseball talk "released." They are let go to make room for young and talented players the organization believes have more potential. Veterans are let go as their skills decline. The attrition of skill occurs at a much earlier age in sports than in almost any other profession, and it occurs in public. For big leaguers the decline is chronicled and monitored by millions of fans who study the unsparing statistics that are the measure of accomplishment in pro ball.[2] For many minor leaguers, the end comes when the front office—the player development folks—have seen enough to conclude that the player is unlikely to ever perform at a level that would help their major league team win.

With five or six minor league teams, each organization has room for only about a 125 players on its rosters. Any addition means someone else must go. Thus, the signing of twenty-five or so new players from the annual June draft results in some veteran players being released. When the big club acquires an extra player through a trade or free agency, it is felt down the ladder as rosters are adjusted to make room for the new acquisition. Injuries also end careers, and do so without warning. "The saddest thing in baseball," said Hall of Famer Al Kaline, "are the guys who are cut down in midcareer by freak accidents and injuries."[3]

Being released not only means the end of a ballplayer's career, but the end of boyhood dreams and ambition. There is also the loss of identity. We Americans, perhaps more than most, derive much of our identity from our work. When we meet new acquaintances, for example, one of the first things we are asked is, "What do you do?" Ballplayers have a particularly strong identification with their work. Playing a professional sport confers tremendous prestige, especially given how few openings exist for the millions who aspire to them. Baseball is also an all-encompassing job. Ballplayers are so deeply immersed in their profession that they have little time for other interests. Because a ballplayer's sense of self is so strongly linked to his ability to play the game, telling him that he is no longer good enough or that he does not have the potential to play in the big leagues is a major blow to his self-esteem.[4] And unlike the scientist, professor, musician, or actor, for example, the ballplayer's glory ends early, usually before his thirtieth birthday, and for most minor leaguers earlier still. Baseball, noted George Will in *Men at Work,* "compresses the natural trajectory of human experience—striving, obtaining, declining—into such a short span."[5]

The Unconditional Release

Most players are released during spring training, especially toward the first of April when rosters must be trimmed before camp breaks and the teams head north to begin their seasons. Some organizations post a list of the names of doomed players on a bulletin board, instructing them to report to the front office. Some organizations leave pink slips in the players' lockers. During my time in Tigertown in the 1960s, the players to be released were often called to the front office over the PA system. "Will the following players please report to Mr. Snyder's office. . . ." As soon as the voice began reading the names, nobody moved. Dead silence. Players who were struggling prayed they would not hear their names. One player who had been released by three different organizations said, "The cruelest and most insensitive were the San Francisco Giants, who simply turned the name plate on the player's locker upside down, which was a sign to go to the office and get your plane ticket home. At least the Expos had the decency to call you in and tell you face-to-face, even though the farm director told every player the same story."

When firings take place during the actual season, a player is usually called to the office when he arrives at the ballpark. It begins with a tap on the shoulder before he even starts to get dressed: "Parker, the skipper would like to see you." The manager usually begins by saying how difficult it is for him to tell the player that he is being released. He is probably sincere, since most managers are fond of their players. As veteran minor league manager QV Lowe commented, "It's the single most difficult task in all of pro ball." Most of the nine managers I questioned about releasing players talked about the importance of being honest. "The thing you try to do is make it as delicate as you possibly can, but also be as honest as you possibly can. Tell them exactly why they're being released," said the Indians' Jim Gabella. "You can't paint a rosy picture for them, you can't tell them they might be good enough to play for someone else unless you really believe that, or you'll hurt the kid."

As a rule managers try to keep the meetings short—ten minutes or so—just enough to explain the decision and the procedures. The player must sign a release form that formally terminates his association with the ball club and is then given a plane ticket or the equivalent in cash for the trip home.[6] He is encouraged to leave town as soon as possible. "You do that to keep them from getting into trouble," explained QV Lowe. "Some of them might get into drinking to drown their sorrows. Then something gets torn up, so you try and get him out the same day you release him." By the time the released player returns from the office to the clubhouse to clear out his locker, his teammates are dressed and out on the field. He does not have to face a full clubhouse. He has time and privacy to compose himself and can later say goodbye to his friends.

"This Can't Be Happening to Me"

For most players being released is totally unexpected. Many had no idea their career was in jeopardy. Those who had been slumping or had never put up good numbers might have worried that they were at risk or thought maybe the organization was losing confidence in them, nevertheless their reaction is of disbelief and numbness: "This can't be happening to me."

Sometimes, however, there are clear warning signs, such as being removed from the starting lineup, the arrival of a new player at your position, and, for relief pitchers, infrequent work. Some players talk about how a change in their manager's demeanor or attitude toward them tipped them off. Mike Saccocio's manager for the Gastonia Expos, Junior Minor, usually rode him pretty hard. Then one day, recalled Saccocio:

> I had a lousy batting practice, and as I walked by Junior, waiting for him to get on me, he just looked at me and smiled and very nicely said, "That's all right, Mike, just go grab your glove and take a few flies." I picked up my glove, at first relieved that I didn't get yelled at, and then it hit me, my career was over. I wasn't worth his trouble anymore. Today when I think about it, the saddest words I've ever heard were "It's okay, Mike, you grab your glove and catch a few flies."

Whether or not they had any inkling, most players are devastated. They have lost, in the words of former Braves farmhand and now sportswriter Pat Jordan, "The first, the purest, the most precious dream they would ever have . . . and in their minds no dream would ever equal that." They had invested so much in baseball, devoting most of their lives to perfecting their skills. For many, baseball was the only thing they could do well. Birmingham Barons player Tony Franklin recalled it this way: "When they released me, I didn't know where to go or what to do. How could they tell me that? I was hurt. I cried. I hung around the ballpark for two days not knowing what to do. That's when all of the things that my mother had told me about eggs and baskets hit me. I was twenty-six years old, and I didn't know what I was going to do." "All kids are crushed; they feel like their life is over. I have worried that every kid I've released would run out of the office and commit suicide," said QV Lowe with some hyperbole. After witnessing the release of a better-than-average second baseman, Wayne Ginste, during my first season, I wrote in my journal on June 24, 1965, about my own fear. I was twenty years old:

> I can't believe they let Ginste go, he was hitting .270. I don't know what I'd do if it happened to me. Everybody has an identity, and mine is baseball. That would be the hardest thing about getting released, to lose my identity and respect. Besides, just think of all the people back home that I'd be letting down. I can't bear the thought.

Three years later, a few days after I was released, I wrote this in my journal, "The worst part of it all is being seen as a failure. I miss baseball and all my friends [teammates], but worst of all, I hate having failed." It did not make any difference that my release had less to do with my baseball performance than my off-the-field activities (a newspaper article I had written about the North Carolina town I was playing in and its chief of police, who I believed and alleged in print was a member of the Ku Klux Klan, had resulted in a threatened libel suit).[7] Back home, all that people knew was that I was out of baseball, that I must not have been good enough.

After getting the bad news, most players return briefly to the clubhouse or their living quarters to say goodbye to friends on the team. But a few, whether out of humiliation, embarrassment, or not knowing what to say, simply slip away. In *A False Spring,* Pat Jordan described them returning to the barracks in spring training:

> They moved like sleep walkers back to their cots and sat on them for long moments. Next they looked around the room to see if anyone was watching. . . . They slid their suitcases out from underneath their cots and filled them quickly with their belongings, the small space around their cots suddenly bare, soon to be filled by the belongings of some new players arriving in camp. They moved in quick silence so as not to wake any of the others who would then be witnesses to their humiliation. Finished, they got dressed, glanced around the room and left. And often without saying goodbye to anyone, they would be gone, quickly forgotten.[8]

How do teammates react? The atmosphere in the clubhouse is usually quiet and subdued out of respect for the player. "There isn't any of the usual hootin' and hollerin' and carrying on, because you know it's a serious thing and that he is feeling pretty bad," said one player. Some players try to avoid the victim, often not knowing what to say or because it reminds them of their own vulnerability. Farewell exchanges seem to follow a script in which the player's friends tell him they cannot believe that he has been released, that he was too good, or that it was a "bum deal." Some will say that he is lucky now, that he can go fishing and live a normal life. They do not really mean it, but they say it because they think it will help ease the pain. They tell him to stay in touch, but they know he will not. The goodbyes can be awkward, because everyone knows that they are never going to see the player again. This is especially so in the minor leagues, where there are fewer opportunities for a released player to stay in baseball and remain part of the fraternity. In my own case, it was nearly thirty years before I saw any of the sixty young men whom I had shared my life with on various baseball teams in my early twenties, and the first reunion—with Jim Leyland—happened only as a result of doing the research for this book.

Going home is no less difficult. Adding to the player's pain is the feeling that he has let down his biggest fans and supporters—his parents and friends back home. "My father was clearly very disappointed," lamented Expos farmhand Glenn Kinns. "He subscribed to the local newspaper in every town I played in so that he wouldn't miss a thing, he read *Baseball America* and jotted down the stats of the guys ahead of me to see what my chances were. My career was his dream as much as mine, and now it is over for him too." One player said, "It's sort of like having to tell the folks that your wife has divorced you." From Little League on up the player had always been a star, the pride of the family and hometown. Now he must tell people that he is no longer in baseball, that he will never play in the big leagues, and that he was not good enough. Some players cannot face the truth—they lie, saying they were injured or that they just quit. Many friends and acquaintances do not understand exactly what has happened, and if they do not know baseball well, they will ask, "Who are you going to play for next year?"

The reaction of about half the former players that I interviewed was to look for another job in baseball. Triple-A outfielder Scott Jaster, who was let go in spring training, described his efforts to catch on with another team:

> I got back to the hotel to get my stuff together and realized I had no idea what I was going to do. I called Dad, and I couldn't even talk; I was so upset. It was the first time that I realized I might never play again. When I thought about that, I

couldn't even deal with it. I couldn't function. I couldn't talk to my dad on the phone; I just hung up. . . . I drove around to all the spring training camps that I could—from nine in the morning until dark. I think I went to eight camps . . . and talked to all the minor league directors that I could. They all said, "Sorry, it's too late. Our teams are already set for the season."

Released players who have agents request their help in looking for an organization that might have a spot. When Mike Serbalik was released from the Dodgers' organization after his rookie year playing for the Yakima Bears in the Northwest League, he contacted his agent. The agent called around, making the best possible case for his client (Serbalik was a middle infielder and a third-team Division-I all-American, and he was still young and eager). The Braves and Marlins expressed interest but did not have a roster spot on any of their Class-A teams. They promised to get back to him once the season got under way and things were more settled. Meanwhile, Serbalik's agent got him an offer to play for Godo d'Ange-los in the Italian Baseball League. At $2,500 per month the pay would be three times what Serbalik had earned as a Dodgers rookie farmhand. Yet, he would have happily taken his old salary and signed with the Braves or Marlins if they had only had room for him. But uncertain that they would ever call back, he flew to Italy where at least he was guaranteed to be back in baseball. He played one year, saw some of Europe, hit .350, but then retired once he realized that he was not going to get another shot at pro ball in the United States. Today he teaches hitting in his own indoor baseball facility—The All-Star Academy—in Troy, New York. Occasionally he ponders what might have been had he not signed with the Dodgers and stayed in college for another year. Meanwhile, he still plays in the Albany Twilight League, where he is a three-time MVP.

Some released players ask area scouts back home if they can get them invited to spring training. A few even make the rounds at try-out camps, like Mike Anderson who re-signed with the Seattle Mariners. The trouble was that he did not tell the Mariners that he was the same Mike Anderson who had pitched in the Mets' organization for four years, or that he was really twenty-six, not twenty-one as he had recorded on his tryout form. He might have gotten away with it had he not been arrested in a nearby town for trying to pass a bogus $5,000 check at a car dealership.

For the lucky few who do catch on with another team, the change of scenery and the scare often bring about improved performance. "There is nothing better for some players' motivation," said one coach, "than to be released once, because he'll never take his job lightly again." There are countless examples of re-signed players who went on to have successful major league careers. On the 1999 All-Star team, for example, there were three players who had once been released, the Cardinals' Kent Bottenfield, the Phillies' Paul Byrd, and the Twins' Ron Coomer.

In general, being released and making the transition to a new career is easier for the player who has made it to the major leagues. No matter how brief his stay there, at least he had accomplished what he set out to do. He can say that he fulfilled his dream of being a big leaguer. And, if he still has the skills to play, he has a better chance than the minor leaguer of being re-signed by another organization.

Life after Baseball

Most players do not think much about what they will do when their careers end. Pro ball requires so much of their time and concentration that it is difficult to think about the future. "I feel I need to put all my mental energy into what I'm doing now," said the Braves' Jeff Treadway, a sentiment shared by most. "When it ends, it ends. I'll worry about it then, but right now I don't have the time." Likewise, Birmingham catcher Darren Campbell does not plan for the future because it "scares" him to think about it. "Right now I have a family, I'm playing pro ball, and I'm happy with that. God forbid if something should happen to me, I can't think about it now." Syd Thrift, while serving on a Major League Baseball committee concerned with players' lives, also found that most players do not take the time to learn about things that will affect their lives after baseball, such as how to handle their finances, deal with personal problems, or even how to take better care of their bodies.[9]

It is only when their careers decline—poor numbers, injury, demotion to the bench or a lower league—that ballplayers begin to think of a future outside of the game. When I asked players what they wanted to do, the responses were all over the map, from plumber to astronaut. But many said they hoped to stay in baseball in some capacity—scout, coach, agent, broadcaster, and even front office. "Baseball is what I know best, it's what I've always done, and I like it, so it makes sense to do something in the game if I can," was a typical response.[10] In general, players give the impression of being fairly confident that they will find satisfying second careers.

Starting a new life outside of baseball is often a more difficult adjustment than most expect. "You are so used to being involved with teammates and the team where your whole routine is taken care of," said Birmingham manager Tony Franklin. "All of a sudden you've gone from being a member of a small fraternity, in this highly structured environment, to being outside all on your own. And you ask what happens now?" Released in his fifth year of pro ball, Rich Williams lamented:

> Pro ball is an emotional high. You come out to the ballpark every day . . . four or five thousand people there, you sign autographs, you're with your buddies, there's lots of banter in the clubhouse, lots of laughs. And then all of a sudden you wake up one day, and you're no longer in the game. Then reality sets in. You've lost everything you've ever wanted. That's tough to handle. You're just another individual now. Nothing special. It's like a slap in the face.

Even Frank Robinson, after a long and illustrious career, had great difficulty adjusting to his release as manager of the Cleveland Indians:

> I went through the absolute worst period of my life. . . . I was devastated . . . completely lost, disoriented. For two weeks I never went out of the house. I just sat in front of the television set having no idea what was on the screen. It was only the second time I was ever home in June. I just sat around hardly talking to Barb and the kids; I just listened to my insides trembling. I kept thinking, I was still a young man, forty-one . . . and I don't know what I'm going to do with the rest of my life.[11]

Some never find a satisfying substitute for baseball. "The truth is, no activity, no job, no pastime can ever be as intensely satisfying, fulfilling, and rewarding as an athlete's involvement in a sport," said ex-player and coach Tom House.[12] It has been seven years since Mike Saccocio was released from a Montreal Expos Class-A team:

> Whenever I drive by a park that's lit up at night, I really get a lump. It really hits me. I remember how fun it is, how watching the people filter in, and the kids looking up to you because you have a uniform on, what the field smelled like before the game started. How much fun is it to hit a good pitcher and make a great catch, and then afterward talking about it. I miss sweating hard and having dirt all over me.

What exactly is it about baseball that players miss so much when they leave the game? Two answers came up over and over in the interviews: competition and camaraderie. By competition players mean the excitement

Reunion of former Pittsburgh Pirates (left to right) Bob Purkey, Frank Thomas, Tito Francona, and Jake Thies at a Pirate Alumni Association golf tournament. (Photo by Sally O'Leary)

and thrill that comes from playing the game—pitcher pitted against batter, team against team, fielder trying to get to a ball in time to make a catch. In the words of Orel Hersheiser, "It's that feeling you get when you beat a team or get a guy out with a good pitch. For me, there's nothing like that outside of baseball." Some ex-players referred to those transcendental moments of excellence—the moments of pure joy when they had achieved perfection—such as a diving catch, hitting the ball out of the park, throwing a perfect strike. Few other professions offer the same experience. Many ex-players said their need to compete drew them to golf, hunting, fishing, and other sports after leaving baseball.

The other frequently mentioned loss was camaraderie—the fellowship and friendship of team members. "It's hard not to miss it," rued a former Dodgers farmhand.

> It's a great feeling when you go into the clubhouse and all of a sudden there are all these guys, guys that you play 140 games a season with, guys you joke and work hard with. You have good times that you really can't have in an office. You

go home at night, and the next day comes, and you can't wait to get back together again. That is the best I can explain it.

"In baseball guys can be themselves, they can talk big, they can tell stories, and be a little crazy, whereas when you are back home you have to tone it down," said pitching coach Steve Maddock. Former Giants player Nick Testa explained, "The camaraderie is really big. There are always lots of laughs because everything's a big joke with players. They can find something funny about a broken leg." When Mickey Mantle explained why he became depressed and began to drink heavily after retiring from baseball, he said, "I left all those guys, and I think it left a hole in me. I tried to fill it up by drinking. I still don't feel like I have much in common with a lot of people. But with those guys, I shared life. We still were as close as brothers. I haven't met anybody else I've felt as close to."[13] Ex-players usually lose their circle of baseball friends when they leave baseball and move back to their hometowns. Most admitted that they were not good at maintaining friendships with former teammates from a distance. As seventeen-year veteran Del Crandall noted, "It's amazing how few friends from baseball you carry with you when your days as a player end. . . . All that intimacy of being teammates for years, then suddenly it's gone. What's left is mostly acquaintances and stories of old times."[14]

Some ex-players also said they missed the ballpark environment and the energy and excitement of the crowds. "Big crowds give you a big boost, get you pumped up. You can go home and play semipro ball, but you'd only have twenty people out there, and it ain't anything like pro ball," said Derrick White. For some time after leaving baseball, I got depressed in the early evening about the time I would normally be at the ballpark. I was so used to being on the field at that time, that it did not feel right being at home. Ballparks are magical places—the emerald-green field crisply outlined in chalk, the sweep of the grandstands, the rainbow of the different sections of seating, the silhouette of the light towers and their bright lights against the dark night sky, the sound of metal spikes clacking on a cement runway, and the scents of grass, pine tar, and rosin. Phillip Lowry titled his book on ballparks *Green Cathedrals,* because the more he studied ballparks, the more he thought they resembled mosques, synagogues, churches, and other places of worship. For ex-ballplayers, no workplace can ever match the ballpark.

Largely unsaid, but also a part of what players miss, is their identity as professional athletes, and the social recognition it confers.[15] Listen to Mike Saccocio talk about his separation from baseball: "When I was a player I had my Expos jacket, and I would go to bars with the guys, and I knew I was a professional baseball player. Everywhere I went, everyone knew. That was my identity. When I got released that identity was gone." About the difficulty some players have coping with this loss of status, QV Lowe said:

> It's like total depression. It's like a woman who had six kids, and they all left home. We have created monsters by making players into idols, into gods so they can't let go of the game when they have to leave it. They can't live without their glory, without folks gawking all over them. They don't know how to deal with it. You can't believe what a tragedy it is for some of these guys to be out of baseball.

The loss of status may be acutely felt by older players whose careers are ending right at the age when most men's careers are beginning to take off. Some said they frequently have dreams in which they are still playing. In the video *Boys of Summer*, based on Roger Kahn's book of the same title, one of the long-retired Dodgers poignantly described a recurring dream in which he has been signed to play again and is scheduled to pitch that day, but each time he gets to the ballpark he cannot find an entrance. He circles the stadium, round and round, but can never get in.

That athletes are quickly forgotten once they retire, even by ardent fans and the media, adds to the ex-player's sense of loss. One of my first impressions while doing research in major league ballparks was the lack of fan interest in the coaches. Most were former major leaguers, some had been stars, yet all the adoration and requests for autographs were directed at current players.

Not only do former players lose status, but some find their new lives boring.[16] As much as they may have complained during their careers about the travel, many now miss the stimulation of being in new places; some miss the fans and groupies that once made them feel important. Their new jobs often lack the excitement and adrenaline rushes that playing baseball had given them. About all retired professional athletes, former NBA player Bill Bradley noted, "Athletes must live with never again experiencing the intensity or degree of involvement once a sports career is over."[17] Sportswriter Rod Beaton wondered how today's major leaguers will fare in retirement, having made enough money that they will never have to work, "I think it will be one of the interesting stories of the next decade to see how happy these guys are with nothing to do. I mean how much golf can you play? And what's it going to be like for their wives having these guys at home, not working?"

Few ballplayers have ever worked a nine-to-five job. Some have a difficult time adjusting to life in the "real world," because they have never really grown up, never had full adult responsibilities before. "Terminal adolescence," is how Tom House characterized players who never learned to do things for themselves and whose sense of responsibility began and ended with the competition at the ballpark.[18] As kids, they were star athletes, and other people were usually willing to pick up after them, make excuses for them, and support them in every way. Once in pro ball they were able to get away with things because of who they were. Everyday-practical matters, like making plane reservations and hotel bookings, were arranged by the ball club. Agents negotiated their salary. Wives raised their children, maintained their homes, and moved the household to new cities in their absence. During the baseball strike, when many players had to make their own travel arrangements to get home, sportswriter Rod Beaton observed that some did not even know how to buy an airline ticket, check their luggage, or, in a few cases, understand a baggage carousel. "It's a very strange thing to see these premier athletes who have had everything given to them, people treating them as special, girls throwing themselves at them, and then seeing how helpless some of them are when they have to fend for themselves," said Beaton.

It is not uncommon for marriages to fail within a few years of a player's release or retirement. About the baseball couples she got to know during thirty-five years working in the Pittsburgh Pirates' front office, Sally O'Leary said, "When the woman leaves him, it's usually because the glory days are gone. She thought it was great being married to a ballplayer, but now that he is no longer in uniform, no longer in the limelight, life is a little different." A former all-star pitcher turned sports psychologist and counselor for Major League Baseball, Sam McDowell estimated that about one-third of all player marriages break up in the first few years after the player leaves the game. "And at least 75 percent of the time it's the woman who splits."

Coming Back

After being out of baseball for awhile and not feeling fulfilled in their new careers, many former players attempt to return to the game in some capacity. As Braves manager Bobby Cox said, "The game is an addiction. I've talked to too many guys who have left baseball because they couldn't play anymore, and now they're just dying to get back in. They've discovered how hard it is to make a living outside, how much work they have to do and most of them are not having fun at it. They work just as hard at baseball, but they're having fun doing it." Some call upon former managers or old teammates to help them get back in as a scout or coach. Most of the eight hundred scouting jobs and six hundred minor league managing and coaching jobs in pro ball are filled by former players, many of whom were out of the game for a while.

In returning to pro ball, most go to the bottom of the ladder, usually starting out in Rookie or Short Season A, and then retrace the steps they took as players back up the rungs of the minor league system. Some find it surprising that so many former ballplayers are willing to accept low salaries, bus travel, fast food, half the season spent in hotel rooms and away from home, just to be back in baseball. Atlanta coach Pat Corrales told me that he thinks even more players would like to come back if they could just make a decent living in the minor leagues. If they have not been out of the game long, some even hope to play again. After being released from the Mets' Double-A team, and then quitting baseball on his own accord, Scott Jaster was only out of baseball a few months before he became obsessed with getting back in the game. Jaster and his father, Larry Jaster, a former major leaguer, began making phone calls until finally the White Sox invited him to spring training:

> By then I had been back in school for a month and knew it was going to be a huge risk to go to Florida on a trial basis, but I went for it anyway. The next day I was packed up and gone. I had a month to get back into shape for spring training so I could show them what I could do. My dad was living in West Palm Beach, and the Braves were letting us use their batting cages and facilities. Everyday we were out there—hitting, running, throwing, catching fly balls. We probably only took four days off the whole month. After that I would go lift weights. I was putting in eight or nine hours a day. . . . My attitude was that I was going to work harder than I had ever worked in my life.

Jaster did well in spring training and the White Sox signed him to a Double-A contract with the Birmingham Barons. He played a few more years before a wrist injury led to his release. After a year's rehab he made another comeback. Released again, he is now a scout for the Arizona Diamondbacks.

Thirty-five-year-old rookie pitcher Jim Morris on the mound for the Tampa Bay Devil Rays. (Photo by Robert Rogers, courtesy the Tampa Bay Devil Rays)

Ten years after he had last pitched an inning of pro ball, thirty-five-year-old Jim Morris showed up at a tryout camp in June 1999. Throwing fastballs in the mid-90s, he was signed to a minor league contract by the Tampa Bay Devil Rays. A high school baseball coach and chemistry and physics teacher, he had only attended the tryout to keep his end of a bargain with his high school ballplayers. Impressed with how hard their coach could throw, they negotiated with Morris that if they won their championship that he would attend a tryout camp, that he would give pro ball one last try. Although a high draft pick in 1983, Morris had never pitched above Class A in six seasons before being released by the White Sox with a sore arm. After he was let go, he had surgery on his shoulder and went back to school to earn his degree and begin a teaching career. After the Devil Rays signed him, Morris pitched so well that he was twice promoted, and in August called up to the big leagues and made the national network news.

In 1988, when Jim Morley asked retired players whether they would be interested in playing in the newly created Senior League, more than a quarter said yes. Within weeks of sending out 1,250 inquiry letters to players, 350 had written back to say "Sure, they'd leave their families, their jobs, their lives, whatever they had going and come play baseball again."[19] Injuries—especially pulled hamstrings, the official injury of the Senior League—cut short many hopes for comebacks. A few players, like forty-year-old Vida Blue, were not just hoping to find a new career in the Senior League, but to make it all the way back to the majors.[20]

Jim Bouton, who once wrote, "You spend a good piece of your life gripping a baseball and at the end it turns out that it was the other way round," was so anxious to get back into baseball that, unable to interest any team in signing him, he took a job as a batting-practice pitcher for the Braves' Triple-A team in Richmond, Virginia.[21] At the time, he and his wife were in debt and having difficulty making payments on their house. What he most needed was a decent-paying job. Pitching BP did not solve his financial problems, but at least he was back in baseball. He was happy, but his wife was not. They later divorced.

Pitcher Mitch Williams had retired to his six-hundred-acre ranch in the heart of Texas, looking forward to the solitude. But within a year, he too began to miss the game, especially the adrenaline rush of stalking to the mound in the ninth inning with the game on the line and thousands of people cheering in the stands. But like so many others, his comeback was short-lived. Every time Danny Montgomery, a former Dodgers minor leaguer and now a scout for the Colorado Rockies, watches a major league game on TV or goes to the ballpark, he gets the urge to play again. "It happens every time. I'll be sitting there and it will hit me. I will think that I can play. I'd give up the [radar] gun and the stopwatch and all that stuff to try out for a team again." Common sense usually returns quickly, however, and he realizes that he is just too old for a comeback.

Spring seems to be the toughest time for former players. "You don't miss much in winter," said former Giants player Nick Testa, "but as soon as that first spring training rolls around you do get itchy. You go down in the basement, and you start pounding that ball in your glove. You watch the TV where the guys are taking spring training, and it leaves you with an empty feeling. You feel like you should be there. It's like a void that can't be filled."

Although some former players have made successful comebacks with profitable careers in the big leagues, many more fail. Most, like pitchers Jim Palmer and Steve Carlton, were too far over the hill when they attempted to return and quickly came to their senses, or failed miserably. Some baseball people resent those who had long, successful big league careers trying to come back. "They had their heyday, now get out of the way and let the young kids have the game," said manager QV Lowe. "It's embarrassing to see a Steve Carlton going out there and getting his brains beat out. It's degrading to the game."

New Careers

How well do ex-players fare in their new careers after their playing days are over? I heard many stories about the spectacular successes of some and the equally spectacular failures of others. But the information was all anecdotal until a chance conversation with Pittsburgh's Sally O'Leary. As head of the Pirates' alumni association, O'Leary had tracked down and compiled information on most former Pirates. With the Pirates' data in hand, I was able to categorize 370 former players by occupation (see Table 1). A surprising 40 percent are working at "professional" or "technical" jobs, such as teachers, coaches, stockbrokers, and financial analysts. And the percentage of professionals is even higher among those who left baseball in the past two decades, owing to their having gone to college.[22] Similarly, while 21 percent of the players who left baseball in the 1940s and 1950s worked in blue-collar jobs, only 3 percent of the post-1980 cohort

Table 1

Postbaseball Occupations of Former Pittsburgh Pirates by the Generation in Which They Played (n = 370)

Occupations	1940s–1950s (n = 160)	1960s–1970s (n = 151)	1980s–present (n = 69)
Professional and technical	31% (50)	40% (57)	58% (40)
Managerial and administrative	28% (45)	33% (45)	23% (16)
Clerical	6% (9)	1% (2)	3% (2)
Sales	13% (20)	13% (18)	10% (7)
Craftsmen	8% (12)	1% (2)	1% (1)
Operatives	3% (4)	4% (5)	0
Laborers	3% (5)	0	0
Farmers and farm managers	3% (5)	4% (5)	1% (1)
Farm laborers and farm foremen	1% (2)	0	0
Service workers	5% (8)	4% (6)	3% (2)

Source of job categories: Delbert Charles Miller. *Handbook of Research Design and Social Measurement.* 5th ed. Newbury Park: Calif.: Sage Publications, 1991.

do. The Pirates' data also revealed that over one-third (36 percent) of the former players found jobs elsewhere in baseball. The more recently a player had retired, it seems, the more likely he was to find a job in baseball.[23]

While these former major leaguers have done quite well in their second careers, what about minor leaguers? Unfortunately, no organization tracks their former minor leaguers, so no data exist comparable to the Pirates' alumni register. Instead, I asked four managers, coaches, and scouts to list all their former players who did not make it to the major leagues and of whom they still had knowledge. That yielded information on the occupations of ninety-five minor leaguers.[24] These data suggest that minor leaguers, too, land on their feet, though not to the same degree as major leaguers. Among the former minor leaguers, there were more school coaches, policemen, firemen, realtors, and insurance salesmen, and fewer financial analysts, business managers, and owners of taverns, restaurants, and small businesses than was true of the ex-Pirates. Those who were working in baseball were more likely to be coaching high school or college teams, than pro teams.

Although minor leaguers probably have just as much education, they lack the added prestige of having played in the big leagues, the savings—investment capital—afforded by major league salaries, and the contacts in

Table 2
Baseball versus Nonbaseball Second Careers of Former Pirates

Decade When Ceased Playing	Have Jobs in Baseball
1940s	17% (9)
1950s	31% (22)
1960s	34% (22)
1970s	64% (37)
1980s	71% (36)
1990s	80% (7)
Total	36% (133)

the business community that can provide opportunities and jobs. "Name recognition" was the way one player referred to the latter. Another ex–big leaguer who only had the proverbial cup of coffee in the big leagues, described how he benefits from his baseball past, "When I am out trying to get something done, some people will say, 'Hey, I remember that name. Aren't you the guy . . . dah, dah, dah.' And to this day, probably forever, it has helped me." Nick Testa, who became a college health and P.E. teacher in Queens, New York, said that teaching is easier for him because his students know he once played pro ball—"The guys in particular are more attentive." Testa also believed that his baseball background got him his teaching job.

Favoritism aside, both minor and major leaguers believe they acquired experience and skills in pro ball that carry over and help them in their second careers. Career counselors would refer to these as *transferable skills.* Many ex-players said that they learned how to get along with people. More than in other sports, baseball fosters "people skills"; teammates spend seven hours a day every day of the week together over a very long season. "You're together so much that you have to learn to get along, to give and take," said QV Lowe. Darren Hodges, who grew up in a small Virginia town where there had been little cultural diversity, said:

I just think meeting guys from different parts of the country—at my wedding there was one [teammate] from Sacramento, another from Boston, another from Michigan, another from Tampa—and learning how to get along with everybody you meet in a situation like in pro ball is an education. I even learned a little Spanish from a Columbian and from the Dominican guys. You have a fifteen-day road trip, and you're on the bus with the same guys day in and day out—you'd better learn to get along with other people, people from everywhere. I think that has really helped me in the job I do now [leasing apartments].

Similarly, Danny Montgomery, who became a scout after being released by the Dodgers, explained:

When you throw twenty-four different guys from twenty-four different places in a locker room, it really makes you accept different people and opinions. You learn patience and how to get along with people. You are with guys from Latin countries, too. You get to learn their ways. You get to learn what it's like for them, and how hard and tough it is for some of them to come here and play in the United States. That gives you a better understanding of people.

It is an understanding that Montgomery said made him a better scout, especially at being more adept at projecting the future talent of young men. And, it may help explain why a majority of both the former Pirates and my minor league alumni sample are in jobs, such as sales, teaching, or coaching, that require social skills.

Competitiveness is also a baseball-related attribute that many players use after their ball-playing days are over. According to six-time major league all-star Sam McDowell, now a sports psychologist and counselor:

Competition is how athletes get excitement out of life instead of just looking at flowers and saying, "God, they're beautiful," and enjoying all the wonderment that is out there. . . . Our life is geared toward the adrenaline rush that comes from competition. That serves you well in the business world. To an awful lot of businessmen that intense competition can be very scary, very traumatic. That's why businesses bring in these experts and pay them top dollar to help their employees feel comfortable with competition. To get them not to feel frightened but to focus on their successes. Well, you can see the advantage a guy with background in sports has in this situation.

One ex-player gave much of the credit for his hugely successful real estate business to the competitiveness instilled in him in pro ball.

Closely related to competitiveness, said McDowell and others, is being able to deal with failure. Former athletes, and especially baseball players, they claim, are able to recover quickly from adversity. "If you are a salesperson and you screw up at 9 o'clock," said McDowell, "how long is it going to take you to be yourself again? You'll be a lot better at your work if you can recover quickly, if you are back to being yourself at 9:05 instead of 1:00 P.M. the next day. And that is something that we have learned from sport." Dave Smith, who played in the Mets' farm system and now works

Jerseys in the clubhouse at Hammons Field (Photo courtesy the Springfield Cardinals)

in alumni affairs at Siena College in upstate New York, voiced the same sentiments: "We have projects, and you are involved in situations where the best laid plans just don't work. Some people, even in a minor level, just don't handle it well. . . . They haven't experienced failure. As a baseball player you experience failure everyday. You learn to say, 'Okay, let's pick up the pieces. Let's go on. Let's revamp the plan.'"[25] Jim Bouton said that baseball taught him to take the "long view of things. Baseball players learn that one game doesn't mean anything. . . . What counts is what happens over the course of the season. You have to take a much longer view, which teaches patience . . . and that has been very helpful in every area that I've gone into."[26]

Discipline, good work habits, and the ability to deal with pressure—all essentials in baseball—are also important in many other lines of work. "In baseball you set personal goals and then you go out and you bust your butt trying to achieve them. You learn that hard work pays off. You can see the results plain as day in your batting average or ERA. That's what team sports are all about, and I think you transfer a lot of that to any field you are in," said Sam McDowell. Research also suggests that the ability to concentrate and focus, which players develop in baseball, can carry over to other work settings. Joseph Tractman, who has done experimental research on concentration and biofeedback among ballplayers, has noted that elite athletes are able to generalize their level of concentration to other tasks and often end up being successful in business and in their personal lives because of it.[27] Two ex-players who now teach high school said that their "ability to rise to the occasion," "to focus," and "to get yourself up," which had been fostered in baseball, have helped them overcome fatigue and burnout in teaching.

The picture that emerges is quite positive. Players have some difficulty, at least initially, adjusting to retirement. Many continue to miss aspects of the baseball life, but ultimately most land decent jobs and have successful second careers. This contradicts what many Americans believe about retired athletes,[28] often depicted in fiction as one who stumbles and fumbles his way through adult life and is eventually left by his wife who had out grown him.[29] The failed ex-athlete in John Updike's *Rabbit Run,* said James A. Michener in *Sports in America,* is a significant figure in modern American fiction and someone who has come to symbolize the

American athlete in college English classes.[30] Michener also saw Roger Kahn's renowned *The Boys of Summer,* about the fate of the 1950s Brooklyn Dodgers after they left the glory of the game, as yet another "tragic statement" about the fate of ballplayers in retirement.[31] Although about basketball, Jason Miller's play *Championship Season,* in which five former high school athletes who never achieved much in life and their coach drunkenly reminisce about their former glory, is another well-known example.

Baseball has its share of stories about players who were unable to cope. Former Houston Astros pitcher J. R. Richard, for example, was found broke and homeless, living under a freeway overpass near Sharpestown, Texas. In the early 1980s the six-foot-eight-inch, hard-throwing right-hander had earned $850,000 per season. Bad investments, including $500,000 in a bogus oil venture in California, the failure of his barbecue business, and a costly divorce had forced him to sell his home and take to the streets. He was forty-four years old.

Even worse is Bruce Gardener, who won twenty games in his first year in the minors and then hurt his arm. Out of pro ball, his life-long dream shattered, he was bitter and unable to forgive his mother and his University of Southern California (USC) coach for having talked him into going to college instead of signing out of high school when he had been offered a large bonus by the White Sox. He was just twenty-five when he drove to the USC baseball field, scaled the fence, walked to the scene of his former glory, and laid down half way between the pitcher's mound and second base, cradling his USC diploma and all-American plaque, and shot himself in the temple.

In another highly publicized suicide, Danny Thomas, a talented outfielder who never achieved his potential, hung himself at the age of twenty-nine, three years after leaving baseball. Also well known in baseball circles is the story of Steve Dalkowski, who, signed by the Orioles in 1957 for $40,000 and a Pontiac, was perhaps the hardest thrower of all time. His 100-plus mph fastballs are said to have torn off the earlobe of one unlucky batter, given an umpire a concussion, and broken boards in a wooden backstop. Dalkowski was on the verge of being called to the big leagues when he injured his arm. In 1997, fifty-seven, debilitated by alcoholism and unable to form complex thoughts, he was living in a nursing home in New Britain, Connecticut, near the sandlots, where as a youth he had struck out twenty batters a game and scouts had flocked to see him pitch.[32] Tragic stories, yes, but as the Pirates alumni data clearly show, these cases are not typical.

Certainly, for middle-aged and older former players the allure of baseball never disappears. Even after decades away from the game, memories of their playing days are surprisingly fresh and tinged with nostalgia. Some regret that they did not make more of their opportunity to play pro ball and wish they could have a second chance. "I'd give anything to go back to May 1984," said a former Class-A player about the month he broke into pro ball, as if it were only yesterday. "My biggest regret is that I didn't seize the moment, that I didn't realize that this was my shot. I think back—how dare I have my mind elsewhere, when all I had to do was suck it up and give it my all for a few hours each day? Now, I'll never know how far I could have gone." Some still have dreams in which they are playing. "I don't suppose there will ever again be anything in my life that compares with the thrill I experienced when I was playing baseball, no matter what I do throughout the rest of my life," said Tom House.[33] Perhaps Pat Jordan summarized it best in *A False Spring,* in which ten years after his exit from baseball he still sees himself "not as a writer who once pitched, but as a pitcher who happens to be writing just now."

11. It Ain't the Same Old Ball Game

New in this edition of *Inside Pitch*, this chapter looks at some of the ways baseball culture has changed in the nearly four decades since I was a player. Fans talk about the timelessness of their sport, its respect for tradition. Baseball, they say, doesn't change like football and basketball. To me, after returning to my old ballparks and clubhouses, baseball today looks a lot different. After being absorbed with the game in my youth, I turned completely away from baseball after I was released in 1968. When I finally came back, it was like Rip van Winkle waking up after his twenty-year nap in the Catskills.

Let me remind you of what baseball was like in the 1960s, since that is my baseline for describing change. The season ended with two pennant winners; there were no playoffs. Most World Series games were played during the day. Major League Baseball had just moved west of the Mississippi with the relocation of the Dodgers, A's, Braves, and Giants. There were expansion teams: the Houston Colt 45s and New York Metropolitans came first, followed by the Expos, Padres, and Royals.

In the entire decade there was only one Japanese player in the Major Leagues. He pitched just one season for the Giants and then returned to Japan. It was believed that Japanese players weren't good enough to play pro ball in the United States.

It was the golden age of pitching, with an oversized strike zone and a mound five inches (or one-third) higher than today. The best year for pitchers was 1968, when Bob Gibson's ERA was 1.12 and Denny McClain won thirty-one games. And it was the worst year for hitters: Carl Yastrzemski won the AL batting title with an average of .301, and the entire league batted only .230.

The first indoor stadium opened: the Astrodome, with the first synthetic turf. Old ballparks were replaced by concrete, multipurpose stadiums that served football as well as baseball. Umpires wore coats and ties. There were no sports psychologists, nor agents. Televised baseball was the Saturday "Game of the Week."

While the Vietnam War raged on, people were disenchanted with baseball. Polls showed football fast becoming America's favorite sport, and the NBA was pulling in ever-bigger crowds. The same Denny McClain who'd won thirty-one games and a Cy Young Award proclaimed that he'd rather be a pianist. CBS bought the New York Yankees for $11 million. At the end of the decade, Jim Bouton published *Ball Four*.

That was my era. What follows are the changes that struck me in coming back.

Where Has the Group Gone?

Today's players spend less time in groups than we did. When they go out after a game it's usually in twos or threes. On the road and in their hotel rooms, players spend more time with the TV or their MP3 players and video games than with teammates. Until a few years ago, everyone had a roommate when on the road. In the big leagues, players now room by themselves. A few superstars even stay in separate hotels away from their teams—to avoid groupies and autograph hounds.

This individualism is also evident in the lack of conformity on the field. Although some organizations now have a dress code for their Minor Leaguers, most players have more personal freedom, and there is less of a single-team standard. Some players wear their pants long, right down to their cleats, while some of their teammates wear their pants short, showing their baseball socks. In my day everyone was required to wear the uniform in exactly the same way. We were to be clean-shaven, and no one dreamt of wearing a necklace or an earring. We had a curfew and sometimes a bed check. Facial hair and jewelry are now widespread, and curfews are mostly advisory.

I sense that the bond between players is not as strong as it used to be. Sure, some players hug after a big hit or a win, and certainly players develop strong friendships with some of their teammates, but overall I think there is less sharing of confidences and less genuine camaraderie. This is partially due to free agency, which brings considerable turnover in rosters each new season. No team is going to be as tight or cohesive if its membership changes every year. Another effect of declining intimacy is that fewer players have nicknames (see page 61).

Players no longer chatter in the infield. I developed calluses on my vocal chords from having to keep up the constant talk from first base. On the other hand, in today's dugouts players congratulate one another for the most minor achievements. Everything from a sacrifice bunt to lamely moving a runner over to third with less than two outs elicits high fives. Some say it's a carryover from the celebratory excesses of Little League, where parent-coaches urge their charges to always support their teammates.

Bigger, Faster, Stronger

The belief that today's ballplayers are bigger, faster, and stronger than ever before happens to be true. When I played I was taller (at 6'2") than most of my teammates; today I would be shorter. Over 80 percent of players on opening day rosters in 2006 are over six feet tall. There is hardly a pitcher under six feet, unless he is left-handed.

Better Educated

Players are better educated today. Most have had some college, a rarity in the 1960s. None of my coaches had been to college, and some were disdainful of players who had. It was believed that college kids weren't as hungry to make it in baseball as kids who came right from high school. Now, many organizations prefer to select college players in the annual free agent draft. Nearly 70 percent of North Americans playing in the Major Leagues in 2005 were drafted out of college.[1] Improvement in college baseball programs means that Major League organizations no longer believe they have to sign a kid out of high school in order to mold him into a big leaguer.

Despite being better educated, ballplayers are just as superstitious as ever. The difference today is that players are less willing to admit that they have superstitions. Perhaps it seems pejorative. When I asked today's players directly about their superstitions, most denied having any. However, when I asked what they did mentally to give themselves confidence in playing the game, they often talked about their rituals, taboos, and good luck charms—no different than the players of the 1960s.

Though today's players may have more years of schooling, their coaches and managers say they have less baseball sense. Some Major Leaguers don't run the bases well, and few can drag bunt. Many left-handed pitchers don't have good pick-off moves to first base, and some outfielders don't know how to crow hop to throw out a runner tagging from third. It's partially the result of rushing Minor Leaguers to the big leagues. Another factor is the complete replacement of youth-organized sandlot ball with adult-supervised Little League baseball—athletes raised in the United States today have had a lot less playing time than those in the past.

I realize old-timers often idealize the past, but today's players seem a lot less curious about the history of their sport. Traveling with the very same teams that I had played for thirty years before, I was surprised that players seldom asked me about the old days or how things had changed. You've heard the stories about how today's players don't know much about Jackie Robinson or the contributions of Curt Flood. Baseball clubs might do well to show Ken Burns's documentary *Baseball* to their Minor Leaguers on those idle evenings during spring training when there is little else to do. I also found players less curious about the places they visit; few look out the bus window at the passing scene. In fairness, the country has become somewhat homogenized and less interesting to look at. There is a sameness now to the highways and to the towns they travel to.

Religion

Religion has a presence in baseball that it didn't have in my day. In the 1960s none of us went to church; we played seven days a week, and Sunday was usually a day game. There weren't any Bible studies or Sunday prayer meetings at the ballpark. If there were evangelical Christians in baseball in the '60s, they were invisible. This practice changed in the late 1970s with the dramatic growth of a new organization called Baseball Chapel.[2] Sunday service is now provided in every Major and Minor League clubhouse in the country—one service for the visitors and another for the home team. Attendance at Baseball Chapel varies from a handful to over half the team. I sat in on one service with the Giants, where manager Dusty Baker, two coaches, and nine players listened to a short sermon and some Bible reading, then prayed together for a half hour before the game. I was pleased to learn that the most commonly cited scripture in Baseball Chapel is about it being easier for a camel to pass through the eye of a needle than for a rich man to get into heaven (Luke 18:25).

We also see many expressions of religion on the field, as when players point to the heavens or kneel in prayer after hitting a home run or winning a game. Years ago, a few Latino players crossed themselves before going to the plate, and some wore crucifixes around their necks, but that was it. In postgame interviews today, players even give credit to God for their successes.

Drink, Drugs, and Diet

Today's players drink less, smoke less, and chew tobacco less (it's been banned in the Minor Leagues). The use of recreational drugs has declined after a fling in the late 1970s and early 1980s. But in the 1990s steroids became prevalent, though no one, not even the trainers, know how many players used them. José Canseco claimed 80 percent while hyping his book *Juiced*; Ken Caminitti put the figure at 50 percent; while more credible sources say steroid use never reached those proportions.

Players now eat better—fruit and veggies are now standard fare in postgame spreads, though there are still too many burgers, hot dogs, and pizzas in the diets of Minor Leaguers. In the Arizona Rookie League, one organization actually has its coaches eat breakfast with their players in order to show them what a proper diet is.

The physical training of ballplayers is far ahead of where it was in the 1960s. Every team now has at least one full-time, college-educated trainer; big league teams have three. New medical procedures prolong pitching careers, and new science has put to rest many bad training axioms of my day that may actually have hurt our performance on the field. Unlike in the '60s, players do not eat a large meal with meat before going to the ballpark. Today, they graze at the clubhouse training table on high carb, low fat foods. Players no longer shy away from weight lifting in fear that it will make them tight and mess up their swing; most players now lift weights year round. Pregame stretching is no longer voluntary and casual. We didn't do much more than jumping jacks, toe touches, and windmills. Now, stretching is complex, regimented, done by the whole team, and led by the trainer. It is the first thing players do when they get on the field, and it lasts twenty minutes. Finally, ice is not just something to put in a cooler to keep the drinks cold anymore. It is used on all pitchers' arms after they throw.

Workload

Just as Americans now work a longer day, the workload of players has also increased. We didn't need to be dressed and on the field until 4 P.M. for a 7 P.M. start. Today, players report much earlier, and in the low Minors there may also be extra BP or drills in the morning. Off the field, players are expected to put in appearances at charity and community events.

One thing I enjoyed about playing pro ball was being able to explore new towns and places. Players today don't have time for that. Even in great cities like New York and San Francisco, players seldom go anywhere. As more players have become celebrities, it has become difficult for them to be out in public without being gawked at or hounded for autographs.

Baseball has also become a year-round job. Players are expected to train in the off-season, and some younger players are required to play winter ball in the Caribbean or in the fall instructional leagues. In the old days, when salaries were much less, players held regular jobs during the off-season. Yogi Berra ran a men's clothing store, Jackie Robinson sold appliances, while others worked in sporting goods, on car lots, and so forth.

Vanishing African Americans and the Rise of Latinos

The ethnic and national origins of ballplayers have changed. Thirty percent of Major Leaguers were African American in the mid-1960s; today that figure is only 9 percent and declining. At one point in the 2005 season there were five teams—Red Sox, Orioles, Astros, Braves, and Rockies—without a single African American on their active rosters. In college baseball only 3 percent of Division I players are African American; football and, especially, basketball are becoming the more preferred sports.[3] Just six decades after Jackie Robinson integrated baseball, American-born black baseball players are slowly disappearing from the game. And, not surprisingly, fewer than 5 percent of fans at Major and Minor League games are black.

Taking the place of African Americans are international players: Asians and Australians but especially Latinos, or "Latins" as they are still called in baseball.[4] In the 2005 season 29 percent of all Major Leaguers and 48 percent of all Minor Leaguers were from outside the United States. The Washington Nationals alone had sixteen foreign-born players on their opening day twenty-five-man roster. Nine out of every ten foreign-born players are from the Caribbean or Latin America. The Dominican Republic leads all countries, followed by Venezuela and Puerto Rico.

The presence of so many international athletes is changing the culture of professional baseball. The game is becoming noticeably Latinized. When you walk into a clubhouse today, you are as likely to hear Spanish as English. Clubhouse music is often salsa or meringue. The food on the clubhouse training table and in spring training cafeterias often includes Latin dishes, such as chicken and rice. Some new jargon, like "queso" for fastball and "linea" for line drive, are Spanish.

Latino influence is also evident on the field: Latino players bring a looser, more casual, and sometimes more flamboyant style to the game. Think of Sammy Sosa hopping down the line or Albert Pujols pointing to the heavens after hitting a home run. Think of the elaborate rituals at the plate, such as David Ortiz stepping out of the box after each pitch to tighten his batting gloves, then spitting in each palm and smacking his hands together. Latino players are more likely to be exuberant after making a good play or getting an important hit. Such behavior was called "hot-dogging" in the 1960s when there were fewer Latinos, and it could result in the pitcher knocking the offender down the next time he came to the plate. Latino players and coaches have now reached a prevalence where such behavior is an accepted part of the game.

Latinos, more than Anglos, leave the game on the field. They sulk less in the clubhouse and on the team bus after losses and poor performances. They can laugh after a bad game. My managers expected us to be subdued and would question our devotion to the team if we weren't quiet for a few hours following a loss. I prefer the Latino approach.

Positions are now played differently due to Latino influence. Having grown up playing on rocky fields, where bad hops made it prudent to protect oneself, Latino middle-infielders sometimes field ground balls off to the side instead of getting their bodies directly in front of the ball as American players are taught to do. Latino infielders will often throw off balance or on the run where, in the same situation, Anglo players are likely to plant their feet and then throw. With these changes, I think Latinos have improved the game defensively and made it quicker.

Many Anglo players who never learned Spanish in school now know some of the language, and they've learned something about Latin American geography and customs. International players inevitably also introduce American baseball fans to their countries and cultures. TV color commentators mention foreign customs, and cultural geography is introduced through ESPN specials, such as those that followed Sammy Sosa and Pedro Martinez around their hometowns in the Dominican Republic.

Might Asian players also be agents of change? Because there are far fewer Asians in the sport (twenty-two on 2005 MLB opening day rosters—under one-tenth the number of Latinos), and because they are scattered around the National and American leagues, their influence is bound to be much less than the Latinos'. Some of my baseball contacts did speak of Asian players taking especially good care of their equipment and often having better diets and more disciplined training regimens. When asked about the significance of his accomplishments in the United States, Ichiro Suzuki replied, "I think I have narrowed the gap between America and Japan."[5] He wasn't just referring to baseball.

Women

In the 1960s the only women I saw working in baseball were behind the concession counter preparing and selling food, in the ticket office, or in the front office as secretaries.[6] Since then, several women have served as umpires (Pam Postema reached Triple A and should have been promoted to the Major Leagues), scouts, and supervisors in front offices. One in every five Dodger executives, including the assistant GM, and half of all their supervisors, are women. Over one-third of fans at Major League games are now women. However, only one woman player has broken into pro ball: Ila Borders pitched for several years in the Independent Northern League before retiring at age twenty-six without achieving much success.

Inequality

You don't have to read the sports pages to know what has happened to baseball salaries. The 2005 average Major League salary of $2.6 million was 137 times greater than the $19,000 average in 1967. I assumed Minor Leaguers would also be prospering. Not so. After inflation is considered, most Minor Leaguers are earning less money today than my teammates and I did thirty years ago. The players who were drafted in the spring of 2005 earned just $1,100 per month in their first year of pro ball. In 1965, when I signed, the standard contract was $500 per month—over $3,000 in today's money. Low salaries mean that modern players do not consider a career in the Minor Leagues. Most say they will give themselves four or five years to get to Triple A or the big leagues, and if they don't, they will leave the game. With few players over age thirty playing Double or Triple A, Minor League Baseball has lost many of its crafty, seasoned veterans—the Crash Davises.[7]

When I asked Minor Leaguers if they were unhappy with the enormous disparity between what they and Major League players were paid, most said they hadn't thought about it or weren't concerned because their reward would come when they made it to the big leagues. They seemed to forget that their chances of making it to the big leagues were slim, and of those who would make it, only a handful would stick around more than a few years.

There is also an enormous and growing inequality in the distribution of income within MLB itself. The bottom half of all players took home only 8 percent of the total $2 billion paid in salaries last year. Baseball salary structure is more lopsided than professional football, hockey, or basketball. This unequal distribution of wealth among baseball players (which now mirrors salary distribution in the larger U.S. society) is also true of teams. In the 1960s the highest team payroll was only twice that of the lowest team payroll, while in 2005 the highest payroll (New York Yankees, $208 million) was seven times greater than the lowest (Tampa Bay Devil Rays, $29 million). One Yankee player, Alex Rodriguez, makes more than the entire starting line-up of the Devil Rays, Pittsburgh Pirates, or Milwaukee Brewers.

One unfortunate effect of the larger salaries in MLB has been that money has become a key motivator for players. The old reasons for playing the game—for the pleasure of performing, being a member of a team, and playing before fans—have been diminished by the presence of big money. The status distinctions created by the enormous differences in salaries between players may also be lessening team cohesion. For me, this gross inequality in the distribution of baseball's wealth is the most disturbing of all the changes I have observed.

New Technology

There is a lot of equipment today that did not exist in the 1960s, such as radar guns, body armor, batting gloves, and batting helmets with ear flaps. In the '60s even Major League players had just one cap and two uniforms. Today, players have four caps—BP, home, road, and special occasions or Sundays—and enough different uniform tops and bottoms to make half a dozen distinct combinations. This diversity is mostly done for marketing—each different cap and jersey is another product to be sold to fans in the ever-expanding concession shops or online. To further enhance revenue, teams add to or change their uniforms. Players' lockers are bigger to accommodate all the extra gear.

The new protective equipment, such as body armor and earflaps on batting helmets, helps prevent injury. Yet injury rates are actually up. Some say it's due to better reporting to and by trainers and the effects of bigger muscles (too often produced by steroids). Recovery times, however, are shorter thanks to the use of ultrasound and new physical therapies.

Modern equipment has brought more color to the game. Baseball in the '60s was mostly a black-and-white world. The umps wore black suits and white shirts, home uniforms were always white, road uniforms were always gray, and in many homes the games were still seen on black-and-white television screens. Gloves and bats were natural blonde; now they come in black, brown, and cherry. Shoes were all black; now they come in blue, red, and white. Only the baseball has not changed its color (though for a while Charlie Finley promoted an orange ball).

Today, most equipment is manufactured outside the United States in Japan, Korea, Haiti, and Mexico. Brands like Mizuno, Nokina, and Zett now compete for playing time with Rawlings, Wilson, and Spalding—the staple U.S. baseball labels of my day. The manufacturers' logos are now displayed prominently on all the gear for the TV viewer to see.

Ballparks

Half of the 174 Minor League parks in the United States have been built in the last ten years. Most of them, even in the low minors, have high-quality manicured fields, electronic scoreboards, seating for upwards of four thousand fans, wide concourses, souvenir shops, and often a second tier with skybox suites. There are spacious clubhouses with many creature comforts for the players. It was all made possible by the enormous resurgence in the popularity of Minor League Baseball following the 1994 Major League strike. Many Major League fans tried Minor League Baseball during the strike, liked what they saw, and have stayed on. Teams that I played for that averaged about five hundred fans per game in the 1960s now average five times that.

But the ancillary entertainment is what is really different about Minor League Baseball today: mascots, zany stunts, girls dancing on the dugout roofs, kids racing the mascots around the bases, air guns shooting T-shirts into the crowds, cheer bats, and loud music. The electronic scoreboards entertain with quizzes and video displays, and fans can picnic at the ballpark during the game—and in Colorado Springs even soak in a hot tub while watching the action. The owners seem afraid that their spectators might be bored with baseball alone. One cost of these added features is that ballparks have become less conducive to conversation between friends or between fathers and sons (or mothers and daughters) than they once were. The loud music that has become a constant during the pregame makes it difficult to hear even if you want to converse.

Most Minor League teams, even in A ball, now have identities and names separate from their Major League affiliates. They are no longer called Yankees, Red Sox, or Giants. Rather, they are Alley Cats and Battle Cats, River Dogs and Muck Dogs, Crawdads and Sand Gnats, Renegades and Wranglers, Spinners and Jammers, Volcanoes, Quakes, Storm, and Avalanche. And they have their own uniforms, not last year's recycled Major League uniforms as we did in the 1960s—though I didn't mind wearing Al Kaline's pants one season. I suppose it was the closest I ever got to the big leagues.

For me, another change in going to the ballpark is the prominence of corporate advertising. Sure there was corporate sponsorship and ballpark advertising in the '60s—baseball has always been a business—but nothing like today. Now, the fences, giant scoreboards, programs, and even food containers display the names and logos of hundreds of corporate sponsors. Ballparks themselves are named by corporations—the 2005 World Series was played in Minute Maid Park and U.S. Cellular Field. Every team now has its own official bank, official soft drink, official beer, official airline, and even official hot dog. I still remember when commissioner Bowie Kuhn admonished Atlanta Braves owner Ted Turner for "prostituting" the game by having Burger King sponsor the team's bat day promotion.

Failure

Not all baseball innovations have worked out as expected. For example, in the 1970s the traditional button-down jersey and belted pants gave way to pullover tops and beltless pants. By the late 1990s, however, all teams had returned to the old traditional-style uniforms. The multipurpose stadiums used for both football and baseball that were preferred in the 1970s have been spurned as sterile and soulless and are being replaced by new retro, postmodern ballparks. The love affair with indoor baseball stadiums (e.g., the Astrodome, Metrodome, Kingdome, and Olympic Stadium) is also coming to an end; the same with artificial turf. A few years ago ten stadiums had AstroTurf. Now, it is entirely gone, having been proved to be hard on players, to shorten careers, and to be aesthetically unappealing to fans. Only three teams (Tampa Bay, Minnesota, and Toronto) still play on an artificial surface—called FieldTurf—and all do so because they play in domed or semi-domed stadiums.

Specialization

In all areas of baseball, like in larger society, there is more specialization today. There are players who only hit and do not field (the DH), and among the pitchers there are long relievers, set up men, and closers. Coaching staffs have expanded from four specialties to seven. Trainers now have specialties. And where we once just had batboys, we now also have ballboys and ballgirls. In the front office there are now ten separate departments: six on the business side and four on the baseball side, each with more staff.

Specialization combined with new technology, notably computers and video, has created an explosion of information available to players, such as video coaching and advance scouting reports of pitch patterns, hitting tendencies, and suggested defensive positioning. Much of this data was unavailable just a decade ago. Some players complain, however, about being overwhelmed with too much information and too many meetings; some say they can't remember it all.

Professionalism

Both sides of baseball—the team and the business—seem more professional today. More than ever, baseball organizations are run like other corporations. More front office people have real skills and business degrees, rather than merely being cousins or friends of the owner. There is still cronyism, but it's on the wane. No longer do former players get priority when a new general manager or scouting director is being hired. One current GM didn't even play high school ball.

The players are certainly more professional. They spend more hours each day conditioning and preparing to play—stretching, lifting weights, taking extra BP, getting massaged, reviewing video, having strategy sessions with coaches. Players now train year round.

Overall, I like the look of baseball in the new millennium, but some things are missing from the sport I once knew. Gone are Sunday doubleheaders, two-hour games, heavy bats (every player now understands the benefit of swinging a light bat), hitters choking up on the bat with two strikes, four-man pitching rotations, pitchers that finish what they started, high-cut stirrups, bench banter and ribbing the opposing players, thick-skinned umpires, and live organ music. It's not hard to see that the changes in pro ball—the increased individualism, diversity, internationalism, new technology, specialization, commercialism, professionalism, and the yawning wage gap—parallel changes in U.S. society. Yes, sport, to a large extent, does mirror culture.

Clearly there has been progress in many areas of baseball. The game has become more inclusive, there are more opportunities for minorities, ballparks have vastly improved, careers are longer due to better training, and there is better compensation for Major League players. But there are also areas where baseball has not fared well, notably the growing inequality between the elites and everyone else, the use of steroids, the dominance of big market teams, and the high cost of tickets that prevents most working-class families from ever seeing a live game.

What do these changes mean for the future of baseball? Optimists point out that the crowds are bigger than ever. Average attendance in 2005—over thirty thousand per game—was double the average attendance in the 1960s. In 2005 Minor League Baseball broke its all-time attendance record, which had been set in 1948, when there were over twice as many teams. Pessimists respond that there are fewer kids playing baseball, that television ratings for the World Series have fallen, that baseball players seldom make today's teenagers' lists of most recognizable athletes (today's teens being the paying customers of tomorrow), and that African Americans of all ages are absorbed with basketball and football. In a recent Gallup poll only 10 percent of Americans said baseball was their favorite sport to watch; in 1964 that figure was 48 percent.

Reflections

My initial idea for this book was to relate changes in baseball to changes in American society over the past thirty years. I would use social history as a prism for understanding recent developments in the game. That idea fizzled after I attended the Baseball and American Culture Symposium, held annually at the Baseball Hall of Fame. The Cooperstown symposium draws baseball scholars, particularly historians, from far a field. After listening to them discuss the game and its broader relationship to U.S. society, I quickly concluded that I was out of my league. As an anthropologist devoted to the study of "the Other," I knew far too little about historical trends in my own society.

But the meetings helped me find new direction. During the discussion of a paper on professional baseball in Canada, the author mentioned to the audience that I had once played in Quebec and might be able to shed some light on the issue. Cast in the role of insider, I did have something to say. After the session several participants came up to me with boyish enthusiasm, wanting to know what it had been like to play pro ball. The advantage of once having been a player was now obvious and so to the direction of my research—I would do an ethnography of professional baseball.

I retrieved the journals I had written during my playing days, hoping they might offer insight into what the culture of baseball had been like. More often, though, I discovered how faulty memory can be. I was also stunned to read an entry from July 15, 1967, which declared, "If I play Minor League baseball long enough, I would like to write a book about the rigors of the life." I had no recollection of ever wanting to write a book about baseball. And, I wondered, why had I only mentioned the Minor Leagues? Had I already suspected that I wasn't going to play in the big leagues?

There were times when I had doubts about being able to do the research. I remembered my playing days, when few players had been to college, and there was wariness about things intellectual. When I met Jamestown Expos manager Edie Creech for the first time and used the term "occupational subculture" while explaining my research, he said, "Whoa, slow down with them big words. You're talking to an uneducated Southern boy." Creech turned out to be bright, articulate, and helpful. But his response made me wonder how players would react to my queries and presence. Despite once having been part of their fraternity, I was not confident about being accepted by them now. Not having watched much baseball, I didn't know the names of most big leaguers. After interviewing the broadcaster of the Birmingham Barons, who referred to numerous Barons who had made it to the big leagues, I wrote in my journal: "It must seem curious to him that a former player knows little about the personalities of the game today. Tonight, two fans had to explain to me who the San Diego Chicken is. I've got a lot of catching up to do."

My concerns, though, proved baseless. As I made my way to the back of the bus to use the toilet on the night of my first road trip with the Barons, the players I passed, some half asleep in the darkened bus, briskly moved their outstretched legs from the aisle to let me by. It was a small gesture but done in a thoughtful way that made me feel welcome. Ballplayers, with some exceptions, turned out to be good subjects and were usually agreeable to being interviewed. Baseball needs the media to cover its sport, and therefore management expects its players to cooperate with writers. Sure, players didn't always have a lot to say—some spoke in clichés and, unless prodded, answered questions without giving them fresh thought. In their defense, one manager said, "It is their reaction to being asked so many incredibly stupid questions by people who just don't have a clue." Fortunately, I wasn't asking the usual questions about team performance and player personalities.

Part of the early doubt I experienced was about dealing with celebrities. In my mind, I was not just a professor of anthropology but an ex-Minor League ballplayer hanging out in opulent Major League clubhouses, asking famous athletes to tell me about their lives. As an anthropologist I could do that, but as a former player who had never reached the big time, it was more difficult. That problem lessened as I got to know Major League players better. Nevertheless, I never felt fully relaxed when in confined spaces with groups of players, such as in the clubhouse or around the batting cage where there was a lot of horseplay and joking. I focused instead on talking to players one-on-one.

Oddly, when I began the research I didn't think I was going to enjoy watching baseball, as I had not done so for many years and had come to think of the game as slow. I foolishly admitted this to a sports reporter who was writing about my fieldwork, and it was embarrassing when my comment appeared in the newspaper. As it turned out, being back in the ballpark renewed my interest in the game, and I came to enjoy not just the research but also watching my interviewees perform.

As I learned the ropes, access became easier. Soon, I was granted press credentials at Major League ballparks. My fieldwork usually began three or four hours before game time, when the players and coaches trickled in. During pregame I had access to the field, dugouts, and clubhouses. I conducted interviews and observed the pregame preparations, and once the game started I moved to the press box and occasionally interviewed baseball wives near the family lounge. It wasn't the kind of round-the-clock participant observation I was accustomed to in my former field research, but it would do.

A lot of anthropological research is serendipitous. Such was my decision to include baseball wives and groupies. While interviewing the Yankees' centerfielder Bernie Williams, he kept saying, "Oh, you should really talk to my wife, she would know better than me." After awhile I thought, "Well, why not?" The next day I interviewed Waleska Williams, and she was terrific. She introduced me to other Yankee wives, and I wondered why I had not thought earlier of including them. Speaking to baseball wives led me to an interest in groupies, who became a separate chapter in this book.

Sometimes I sat in stands and took notes, which sparked the curiosity of nearby fans. I'd glimpse them glancing over my shoulder, trying to read what I was writing. They probably assumed I was a scout, although since I didn't have a radar gun they should have known better. It took me a while to get used to middle-aged fans being so obsessed with the doings of ballplayers half their age. The first time I sat in the stands, a man in front of me was wearing a baseball jersey with the name "Jefferies" emblazoned on the back. Greg Jefferies was then playing for the New York Mets. His parents had been good friends of mine, and we had lived next to each other for a baseball season in Canada when Greg was a toddler. It seemed weird to me that he was now idolized.

One of the great pleasures of the research was being in ballparks. These are magical places—emerald green fields crisply outlined in chalk, the sweep of the grand stands, the rainbow of multicolored seating sections, the silhouette of the light towers with their bright lights against the dark night sky. Ballparks are also exciting for their activity—batting practice, infielders taking their positions, outfielders shagging fungoes, fans pleading for autographs, players being interviewed by the media, others playing pepper or sprawled on the grass stretching, groundskeepers watering the infield dirt or rechalking the foul lines. As an ex-ballplayer, no research setting will ever match the ballpark.

A bonus of the research was that it took me back to many of the places I had played a generation before, to towns in Minnesota, North Carolina, and New York, and to Tigertown in Lakeland, Florida, where I went to spring training. Revisiting these towns and ballparks brought back vivid memories: the smells of grass, pine tar, and rosin, the sound of metal spikes clacking on the cement runway. At night I dreamed that

I was playing baseball again and hitting better than ever. Reconnecting with former teammates and old girlfriends I hadn't seen in twenty-five years, I rediscovered who I had been in my youth. Our recollections of one another, though a generation old, were not clouded by new, shared experiences. A chance encounter during spring training with Gail Henley, twice a manager of mine in the Minor Leagues, had a powerful impact.

After chatting about the old times—the crazy pranks and personalities—I asked Gail if he could give me a scouting report on the kind of player I had been. Without skipping a beat, he went through all five tools: speed, arm, hitting power, hitting accuracy, and fielding. "A little slow afoot, average arm, pretty good power, hit to all fields, soft hands." I was stunned. After thirty years it was as though he was talking about one of the players he'd been scouting that very day. Then curiosity got the better of me, and I blurted out the big question that had nagged at me all these years: had I been a real prospect? I'd always wondered if I could have made it to the big leagues. Although I had usually batted cleanup and was twice promoted in midseason, my batting average fluctuated wildly from one season to the next. I had been released from baseball prematurely, my career ended by my writing and a threatened libel suit.

Henley hesitated before answering. "No," he said softly, "you were good but never a real prospect. You weren't the complete package. You were lucky to get out of baseball when you did and go on to graduate school." Now I knew. What did I feel? A pang, disbelief, some defensiveness, but also an odd sense of relief. Henley's assessment put an end to my new fantasies about the life I might have lived and gave me a renewed appreciation for my second chosen career as an anthropologist.[8]

Appendix

Listed below are the players, managers, coaches, and scouts that were interviewed and their team affiliations at the time of the interviews. Some were interviewed more than once. All interviews were conducted between 1991 and 1999.

Players

Matt Allen, Jamestown Expos
Jim Austin, Jamestown Expos
Jason Bere, Birmingham Barons
James Bishop, Birmingham Barons
Bud Black, San Francisco Giants
Adrian Burnside, Yakima Bears
Darren Campell, Birmingham Barons
Will Clark, San Francisco Giants
Craig Colbrunn, Montreal Expos
Scott Cooper, Boston Red Sox
Steve Davis, New York Mets
Joe Deberry, Albany-Colonie Yankees
Andy Dziadkoweic, Binghampton Mets
Robert Eenhorn, Albany-Colonie
  Yankees and New York Yankees
Kevin Elster, New York Yankees
Shawn Estes, San Francisco Giants
Jim Ferguson, Jamestown Expos
Andy Fox, New York Yankees
Ryan Franklin, Tacoma Rainers
Aaron Fultz, San Francisco Giants
Steve Gajkowski, Tacoma Rainers
Brent Gates, Oakland A's
Paul Gibson, New York Yankees

Tom Glavine, Atlanta Braves
Mark Grudzielanek, Jamestown Expos
  and Harrisburg Senators
Heath Haynes, Jamestown Expos
Doug Henry, San Francisco Giants
Orel Hersheiser, San Francisco Giants
Darren Hodges, Albany-Colonie Yankees
Brian Hunter, Pittsburgh Pirates
Scott Jaster, Birmingham Barons
Dave Jaeger, retired
Adam Kennedy, New Jersey Cardinals
Bo Kennedy, Birmingham Barons
Brian Keyser, Birmingham Barons
Glenn Kinns, retired
Mark Larosa, Jamestown Expos
Pat Listach, Milwaukee Brewers
Brian Looney, Jamestown Expos
Matt Luke, Albany-Colonie Yankees
Oreste Marrero, Albany-Colonie Yankees
Sam McDowell, retired
Kevin McGlinchey, Atlanta Braves
Kevin Miller, Niagra Falls Rapids
Kevin Millwood, Atlanta Braves
Tim Naehring, Boston Red Sox

Paul Noce, retired
Mike Oquist, Oakland A's
Russ Ortiz, San Francisco Giants
Bob Padgett, retired
Darren Paxton, Jamestown Expos
Wynter Phoenix, Yakima Bears
Brady Purcell, Watertown Indians
Mike Robertson, Birmingham Barons
Carlos Rodriguez, Albany-Colonie
  Yankees
Mike Saccocio, retired
Kevin Seitzer, Milwaukee Brewers
Mike Serbalik, retired
Paul Smith, Tacoma Rainers
Cory Snyder, San Francisco Giants
Nick Sproviero, Jamestown Expos
Randy St. Claire, Atlanta Braves
Franklin Stubbs, Milwaukee Brewers
Scott Tedder, Birmingham Barons
Nick Testa, retired
Paul Torres, Tacoma Rainers
Jeff Treadway, Atlanta Braves
Anthony Valentine, Pittsfield Mets
Greg Vaughn, Cinncinati Reds
Mo Vaughn, Boston Red Sox
Walt Weiss, Atlanta Braves
John White, Jamestown Expos
Derrick White, Jamestown Expos and
  Harristown Senators
Bernie Williams, New York Yankees
Jerry Wolak, Birmingham Barons

Managers and Coaches

Carlos Alfonso, San Francisco Giants
Carlos Arroyo, Reading Phillies
Dusty Baker, San Francisco Giants

Britt Burns, Florida Marlins
Pat Corrales, Atlanta Braves
Bobby Cox, Atlanta Braves
Roger Craig, San Francisco Giants
Ed Creech, Jamestown Expos
Doug Davis, Pittsfield Mets
Rich Donnelly, Pittsburgh Pirates
Tony Franklin, Birmingham Barons
Jim Flemming, Jamestown Expos
Jim Gabella, Canton Indians
Art Howe, Milwaukee Brewers
Bruce Kimm, Colorado Rockies
Jim Leyland, Pittsburgh Pirates and
  Colorado Rockies
Bob Lillis, San Francisco Giants
QV Lowe, Jamestown Expos
Steve Maddock, Albany Colonie
  Diamond Dogs
Rick Peterson, Birmingham Barons
Gene Roof, London Tigers
Joe Vavra, Yakima Bears
Bill Virdon, Pittsburgh Pirates
Mookie Wilson, New York Mets
Don Zimmer, Boston Red Sox and
  New York Yankees

Scouts and Player Development

Hep Cronin, Atlanta Braves
Jim Howard, Baltimore Orioles
Scott Jaster, Arizona Diamondbacks
Bill Livesey, New York Yankees
Dan Montgomery, Colorado Rockies
Rich Schlenker, Anaheim Angels
John Stokoe, Baltimore Orioles

Notes

Chapter 1. Talent for the Game

1. Sports-socialization research suggests that the kids most inclined to go into sports are those who receive more favorable feedback from significant others about their sports participation and have positive peer interaction and peer acceptance (see Nixon, *A Sociology of Sport,* 86).
2. See Hall, *Fathers Playing Catch with Sons;* and Messner, *Power at Play.*
3. Messner, *Power at Play,* 28.
4. Philosopher Jack Doody argued that baseball does not create an exceptional relationship; the same bond can be created among fathers and sons who play golf, football, soccer, or basketball together. But has Doody overlooked the importance of season? Baseball is a summer game, played in good weather when children are out of school and are on vacation. There are simply more opportunities for fathers and sons to play catch or watch baseball games together than is true of other sports. Baseball is also an easier game to talk about while watching than the faster-paced clock sports of football and basketball. The leisurely pace, the long periods of inaction between pitches and between innings, and the lower noise level of outdoor baseball stadiums are clearly more conducive to conversation (another reason domed stadiums are not good for baseball). Doody, "Baseball in America: A Sociological Perspective," 13.
5. Morris, "An Enduring Game of Catch," 10.
6. Williams and Patterson, "In His Father's Spike Marks: Parental Influences on the Choice of Baseball as a Career," 8.
7. Laband and Lentz, "The Natural Choice," 43.
8. Ibid., 38. Laband and Lentz also suggest that it is a natural tendency of children to want to earn approval from their parents and that most young boys want to grow up to be like their fathers. However, Williams and Patterson found that sons often play different positions than their fathers, the exception being pitchers. They report, for example, that the sons of major league catchers are twice as

likely to be outfielders than catchers. They speculate that sons feel less pressure to live up to their fathers' reputations if they play a different position.

9. There are also the "special-assignment scouts" who are at the beck and call of the organization and sent wherever there is a need for information, whether it be to look at an outstanding prospect in Venezuela, to check the Dominican winter league, or to scout a major league player who might be involved in a trade.

10. Schwarz, "Radar Love."

11. For years there have been two basic types of radar guns: the "slow gun," which measures the speed of a pitched ball about 10 feet from home plate, at which point it has lost about 4 mph, and the "fast gun," which measures the speed of the ball shortly after it leaves the pitcher's hand. Since 1992 a third type, the Stalker, has been capable of giving both readings (velocity out of the hand and velocity at the plate). Now the model of choice, or top gun, the Stalker can be hooked up to a laptop computer and the data printed out. Kurkjian, "Inside Baseball," 70.

12. Critics also say that radar guns can give faulty readings. When several scouts sit near one another using different models of guns, the frequency bands can tangle up and produce erratic readings, like fastballs of 140–150 mph. Schwarz, "Radar Love."

13. Although it is a physical impossibility for a baseball to rise on its trajectory to home plate without defying gravity, some pitchers throw fastballs that appear to rise.

14. In the major leagues, pitching coaches often have a radar gun set up behind the plate with a face reading in the dugout so that they can monitor their pitcher's velocity throughout the game. When the pitcher begins to lose a little speed, the coach then knows it may be time to get a relief pitcher warmed up.

15. Major league average from the left side of the batter's box is 4.2 seconds, and 4.3 seconds from the right side (personal communication, Jim Howard).

16. For a catcher to prevent an average base runner from stealing second base he needs to be able to release the ball after catching the pitch in under 2 seconds. Any longer than that, even with a strong arm, he's not going to be able to throw out the runner.

17. According to Kevin Kerrane, the numerical system was developed by Al Campanis, the Dodgers' executive who lost his job in baseball over a remark he made on television about the inability of blacks to enter baseball management. Campanis explained how he chose to replace the old letter-grade systems with numerical ratings: "I needed something more refined, so I went to numbers, I thought like a school teacher: 70 is a passing grade, so that can represent the major league average on arm or speed or whatever, and 60 and 80 can be the extremes." See Kerrane, *Dollar Sign on the Muscle*.

18. Quoted in Zack, "The Scout," 9.

19. Only amateur players residing in the United States, Canada, and Puerto Rico are eligible to be drafted, and only after their high school class graduates. Players enrolled in four-year colleges may be selected only after their junior or senior years, unless they are twenty-one or older. These rules, which offer some encouragement to the player to stay in school, do not apply to youth in other countries, where major league organizations are able to sign amateur players to professional contracts, no matter whether they graduated from high school or not, once they turn sixteen.

20. Kerrane, *Dollar Sign on the Muscle,* 20.

21. Many of the college players signed with several more years to go before earning their degrees. Many will eventually graduate thanks to their receiving money, which as part of their signing bonus, earmarked for tuition and expenses.

22. Quoted in Zack, "The Scout," 8.

23. Felson, "Self and Reflected Appraisal among Football Players."

24. Generally, the lower-round picks are quicker to sign than higher-round athletes, who are looking for large signing bonuses and who want to see what the market is like before they commit themselves.

25. Schwarz, "Drafts Inexact Science Misses All Future All-Stars."

26. Ibid.

Chapter 2. Breaking In

1. Some clubs arrange for their players to stay with local families. This practice was common in the 1950s and is now slowly returning to popularity.

2. Curry, "Fraternal Bonding in the Locker room," 274.

3. Glenn Kinns was a student of mine in the early 1980s at Union College. He signed as a free agent with the Montreal Expos; before going off to begin his first season, I urged him to keep a journal and read Jim Bouton's *Ball Four* and especially Jim Brosnan's *The Long Season* as models. Once he left campus I did not hear from him again. When I began this research I called him to arrange an interview and learned that he had indeed kept a journal during his three years in the minor leagues.

4. Gammons, "End of an Era," 18.

5. Manuel, "Bat Wars," 29.

6. Ibid.

7. Cook and Mravic, "Back to the Crack of the Bat," 32.

8. Ibid.

9. This compares with an average of 77.5 percent for the entire country. The U.S. Census Bureau defines a metropolitan area as a city with more than 50,000 inhabitants or an "urbanized area" of at least 50,000 inhabitants in a total Metropolitan Statistical Area population of at least 100,000 (75,000 in

New England). See *Statistical Abstracts of the United States.* Supt of Docs, U.S., GPO, 1995, 896.

10. In *A False Spring,* an autobiographical account of his minor league career, Pat Jordan described the boredom he experienced playing in McCook, Nebraska. "There was nothing else there, nothing beyond the limits of their town, nothing to do, no place to go except after a two-hour drive across the plains, another town exactly like the one they'd left."

11. One player who did have a car rarely drove it because, on a rookie's salary, he could not afford the gas.

12. Even in the large cities of the high minors, it is uncommon for players to use public transportation.

13. Milton Jamail, personal communication.

14. House, *The Jock's Itch,* 82, describes a similar experience.

15. Samuel Regaldo, in an article about the experience of Latinos playing in the minor leagues, notes that as far back as the 1960s some clubs, notably the Giants, recognized the difficulties that the Latino had understanding American racism. "They reasoned that not only might the player's performance and progress be hampered but, it 'might sour a foreign Negro on the United States as a whole.' Hence, the Giants began to designate Latinos, white and black, to minor league clubs in regions other than the Deep South." Regalado, "The Minor League Experience of Latin American Baseball Players in Western Communities, 1950–1970," 66.

16. Ibid.

17. Complaints about long bus rides are more frequent in Double-A baseball where the teams are more geographically dispersed, requiring longer trips. Also, by Double A most players have been in pro ball for four years and have become weary of the travel.

Chapter 3. Learning the Culture

1. Another reason for spelling out the organization's rules in a handbook is to ensure that everyone in the system, from top to bottom, does everything the same way.

2. It is the degree of control that has caused some observers to liken baseball organizations to the "greedy" institutions that sociologist Lewis Coser writes about—institutions that seek and exercise considerable control over their employees and demand their undivided loyalty. See Coser, *Greedy Institutions.*

3. For a list of all the Tigertown rules in the mid-1970s, see Rick Wolff's memoir *What's a Nice Harvard Boy Like You Doing in the Bushes?* 13–15. For example, all of the following were prohibited in one's dorm room: eating, gambling, smoking, food of any kind, and women; even wives were not allowed.

4. Mandel, *Minor Players, Major Dreams,* 188.

5. Ballplayers have an advantage over newcomers in many occupations, however, in that they have already learned some of the vocabulary as amateurs. They also learn from watching major league games on television (or, better, listening to them on the radio) as the broadcasters, especially the color commentators who are ex-ballplayers, often use jargon.

6. Mandel, *Minor Players, Major Dreams,* 188.

7. Trice, *Occupational Subcultures,* 101.

8. Mandel, *Minor Players, Major Dreams,* 157.

9. Pilcher, *The Portland Longshoreman,* 102.

10. Kurkjian, "Inside Baseball," 18.

11. Wickensham, *ESPN Magazine,* 101.

12. Phillips and Homes, *Yogi, Babe, Magic: The Book of Sports Nicknames,* discusses the origins of some well-known nicknames.

13. Quoted in Horn, "Jolting Joe Has Left and Gone Away," 70.

14. *The Baseball Encyclopedia* lists the names, nicknames, and records of more than 11,000 men who played in the major leagues since 1871.

15. By 1979 there was just one nickname for every fourteen that existed fifty years before (Horn, "Jolting Joe Has Left and Gone Away," 70). However, one wonders how often players had nicknames that for one reason or another were not recorded in the encyclopedia. According to the encyclopedia listings, only an average of three nicknames per team were listed during the peak years, 1910–29.

16. The demise of nicknames is not restricted to baseball, said Skipper, but is probably also true of politicians, military personnel, entertainers, and even members of organized crime.

17. Former Pittsburgh Pirates broadcaster Bob Prince, for example, gave some players nicknames that stuck, and by which they are still known today in retirement.

18. Quoted in Trice, *Occupational Subcultures,* 124.

19. Miriam Lee Kaprow, personal communication.

20. Minor league cards have made local fans more interested in the players, perhaps because they make the players look more like major leaguers. Some fans specifically collect minor league cards; and serious collectors want to own the first or rookie card of a player who eventually becomes a popular star.

21. From Topps Co., for example, the player only receives a check for five dollars and some complimentary cards. Only if he makes it to the major leagues does he receive royalties or a percentage of the sales of his card.

Chapter 4. Moving Up the Ranks

1. In an evaluation of position players who appeared in at least one hundred major league games last year, Rob Neyer determined that their average age when they

became regulars in the big leagues was 24.3 years and that they spent an average of 461 games in the minor leagues. *Baseball America,* May 25–June 7, 1998.

2. Each Rookie League team is permitted to use a few veteran players as long as they have had no more than two years of pro experience, otherwise all players are new draft picks.

3. Baseball's National Association further divides the rookie leagues into "advanced" (the Appalachian and Pioneer Leagues) and just "Rookie" (the Arizona and Gulf Coast Leagues). Each summer, major league organizations also run a rookie league in the Dominican Republic for Caribbean recruits.

4. T. Ringolsby, *Baseball America,* April 14–27, 1997, 8. During the negotiations leading up to the 1990 professional baseball agreement, the majors threatened to dissolve dozens of minor league affiliations and simply transform the minors into "complex ball," like the two rookie leagues mentioned in note 3. Panek, *Waterloo Diamonds,* 81.

5. Baseball's National Association has labeled them simply "Class A" and "Class A Advanced."

6. Figures taken from Blahnik and Schulz, *Mudhens and Mavericks.*

7. Although Buffalo's attendance has declined since then, the team still leads all minor league baseball with more than 700,000 fans per season.

8. Bere had 12 wins and 5 losses in 1993, and went 12 and 2 in the following year. Since then he has bounced around the major leagues, playing for four different teams, with a few stints in Triple A.

Chapter 5. Making It

1. Verducci, "Staff Infection," 84–86.
2. Ibid.
3. Salisbury, *The Answer Is Baseball,* 59.
4. Ibid.
5. Gmelch and Weiner, *In the Ballpark,* 88.
6. The free continental breakfast that many hotels put out until 10 A.M. induced the minor leaguers I traveled with to get out of bed early, but most returned for more rest after eating.
7. Koppett, *The New Thinking Fan's Guide,* 212.
8. After September 1, when the team rosters expand to forty players, the visitors usually get a full hour of BP.
9. Gordon, *Foul Ball,* 15.
10. In soft toss one player kneels to the side and softly tosses a ball underhand into the batters strike zone. The batter hits the ball into the net a few feet away.
11. Bowman and Zoss, *Diamonds in the Rough,* 242.
12. The etiquette for signing a baseball is for the players to put their names one

under another in the horseshoe, leaving the narrow band of space opposite the trademark for the manager.

13. At sports card shows professional traders set up booths and tables to display their stock. Often a ballplayer is contracted to sign autographs for a fee; big-name players sometimes fetch as much as $15 per autograph.

14. Bob Rose and Kerry Marr, personal communication.

15. The major league minimum salary in 2000 was $200,000.

16. Mike Royko, "Baseball Can Be Barry, Barry Good For You," *Times Union,* 4 May 1992.

17. The average major league player's salary of $19,000 in 1967 had risen to $402,094 by 1987. In the next five years it more than doubled to $1,028,667 in 1992. In 2000 the average salary was $1,572,329.

Chapter 6. The Mental Game

1. Dorfman and Kuehl, *The Mental Game,* xi.

2. Schwarz, "Gwynn Staves Off Old Age with Video," 8.

3. Wann, *Sports Psychology,* 235.

4. Dorfman and Kuehl, *The Mental Game,* 139.

5. While the terms *visualization* and *imagery* have only been around the baseball scene for a few decades, the practice of mentally reviewing images of one's hitting or pitching as a way of preparing to play and of enhancing one's performance has probably been around as long as the game itself.

6. Murphy and Jowdy, "Imagery and Mental Practice," 20.

7. Ibid., 25.

8. Ibid.

9. *Buffalo News,* 17 August 1991.

10. Although maintaining an even keel is relatively rare among the youth players that I have coached, there is an awareness that a nonemotional, almost stoical attitude toward success and failure, is the preferred mode.

11. Mantle, "Time in a Bottle," 6.

12. Dorfman and Kuehl argued in *The Mental Game,* a how-to book written for players, that the player who lets his mistakes or failures affect his emotions will "make faulty judgments—he'll perceive situations emotionally, rather than rationally." In short, emotions, whether they be elation or depression, get in the way of peak performance.

13. Thrift, *The Game According to Syd,* 149.

14. Dorfman and Kuehl, *The Mental Game,* x.

15. Sports sociologist Ellen Staurowsky suggested several reasons why even many college coaches have been slow to teach visualization: 1) too little time—they already have too many things to do in practice; 2) they are more comfortable

with drills and techniques, which they can control; 3) visualization is internal, controlled by the athlete; and 4) few coaches were introduced to visualization during their own training (personal communication).

Chapter 7. Rituals of Uncertainty

1. See Gmelch, "Baseball Magic."
2. I. J. Rosenberg, "This Is Nomar's World," *The Atlanta Constitution,* 8 June 1998, D-01.
3. Gyle Konotopetz, "Superstitions: Wright Plans to Keep Shaving His Forearms until He Has a Bad Season," *Calgary Herald,* 1 June 1997, B5.
4. Mandel, *Minor Players, Major Dreams,* 156.
5. Thrift, *The Game According to Syd,* 151.
6. Stouffer, *The American Soldier.*
7. Seligman, "By the Numbers," 205.
8. Ibid.
9. Allen, "The Superstitions of Baseball Players," 104.
10. Malinowski, *Magic, Science, and Religion and Other Essays.*
11. See Gmelch, "Baseball Magic," 237; and Felson and Gmelch, "Uncertainty and the Use of Magic," 587.
12. Skinner, *Behavior of Organisms.*

Chapter 8. Baseball Wives

1. Several wives (e.g., Torrez, *High Inside,* Garvey, *The Secret Life of Cyndy Garvey,* and Hargrove, *Safe at Home*) have published memoirs about their experiences being married to ballplayers, and two graduate students (Crute, "Wives of Professional Athletes," and Powers, "Psychological and Sociological Effects of Professional Sports on the Wives and Families of Athletes") have produced dissertations about the role of wives among professional athletes generally.
2. Tape-recorded interviews were conducted with twenty-five wives from all levels of pro ball—rookie league through the major leagues. Most of the interviews were done at the ballpark, and all were done while their husbands were absent, which served to minimize the men's influence over what their wives might say. Some follow-up interviews were done over the telephone. I also interviewed the adult children of several baseball families about their experiences growing up in a baseball household, and their perceptions of the roles of their mothers and the relationship they had with their baseball husbands. Overall, the wives and children were cooperative and open.
3. Hargrove, *Safe at Home,* 48.

4. Bouton and Marshall, *Home Games,* 85.

5. The time varies depending on whether they accompany their husbands to spring training (most minor league wives do not) and winter ball. The geography of the league also influences how long their husbands are away. Long road trips are less frequent in the low minors, where teams are less spread out.

6. Beverly Crute also likened professional baseball to L. Coser's concept of the "greedy institution"—that is, institutions that consume all the time and energy of their employees. See Crute, "Wives of Professional Athletes."

7. Hargrove, *Safe at Home,* 89.

8. House, *The Jock's Itch,* 55.

9. Torrez, *High Inside,* 225.

10. Crute, "Wives of Professional Athletes," 142.

11. Danielle Gagnon Torrez (1983) described feeling insulted by fans yelling at her husband, pitcher Mike Torrez, but being careful not to get involved and further enrage them. In order to protect the wives from abusive and gawking fans, major league teams are increasingly sitting the wives and children in a special section, with security, shielded from the other patrons.

12. Ardell, "Letter from Spring Training in the Cactus League," 365–66.

13. Torrez, *High Inside,* 163.

14. Crute, in "Wives of Professional Athletes," 12, noted the same pattern among the wives of professional athletes in other sports.

15. Torrez, *High Inside,* 59.

16. Bouton and Marshall, *Home Games,* 170.

17. Ibid.

18. House, *The Jock's Itch,* 59.

19. Garvey, *The Secret Life of Cyndy Garvey,* 20.

20. Crute, "Wives of Professional Athletes," 124.

21. Quoted in Altherr, "Eros at Bat," 7.

Chapter 9. Groupies

1. See several articles in *Rolling Stone* 27 (1969).

2. In the rock music business, the word "groupie" often is applied not only to fans, but to women who work in the business. Sheryl Garratt noted that if a woman wishes to be involved in any way in the music business, it is often assumed that she is only there because she is attracted to the men (See Garratt, "All of Us Love All of You," 149).

3. Those who followed baseball closely, as noted in Bowman and Zoss, *Diamonds in the Rough,* took it for granted that a lot of ballplayers "drank, and brawled, and wenched."

4. For other examples, see Bryan, *Pure Baseball,* and Winfield and Parker, *Winfield: A Player's Life.*

5. See Hargrove, *Safe at Home;* Bouton and Marshall, *Home Games;* and Torrez, *High Inside.*

6. In a brief survey of college students (N = 136) on two campuses, Patricia San Antonio and I found that nearly all had a basic knowledge of the groupie phenomenon in professional sports. A brief questionnaire was administered in three different anthropology classes in which students were asked: Define the term groupie? Who are groupies? and What do groupies do? There was no prior discussion of or reference to entertainment or sports or the subject of groupies in the classes. See Gmelch and San Antonio, "Groupies and American Baseball," 190.

7. Los Angeles Laker Magic Johnson discussed the sexual motives of groupies in some detail in his book *My Life.*

8. Bouton, *Ball Four,* 218.

9. John Henderson, "Players, Groupies Follow Age Old Storyline," *Denver Post,* 7 September 1998, E-05.

10. Ibid.

11. Such flirting skills, noted Monica Moore in a study of the gestures that women use to signal their interest in men, are as important in attracting a man as her physical attractiveness.

12. Curry, "Fraternal Bonding in the Locker Room," 130.

13. Former player and coach Tom House (in *The Jock's Itch,* 39–40) described the attitudes of some of his teammates in the 1970s and 1980s: "There's a time-honored ritual that says if you have a roommate and you bring a girl back to your room, you either share or let him watch. . . . Sometimes a 'show' is set up ahead of time: a player knows he will be bringing someone to his room and the closet will be full of four or five guys peeking through the slats or around corners while the player and his unsuspecting friend do whatever. And there's no question that the sexual thrill derived from this is nothing compared to the exhilaration of being able to say that they pulled it off."

Chapter 10. When the Cheering Stops

1. Names and places have been changed in this paragraph.

2. Will, *Men at Work,* 320.

3. Bowman and Zoss, *Diamonds in the Rough,* 358.

4. As research by Peter Warr and others has shown, those who identify themselves with their work strongly link how they feel about themselves to how they feel about their work. See Warr, *Work, Unemployment, and Mental Health,* 338.

5. Will, *Men at Work,* 320.

6. All releases, like free-agent signings and trades, are public. The baseball week-

lies publish the names of all released players. And for big leaguers, even local newspapers list releases in their sports sections.

7. After a complaint and threat of a libel suit against me were made to the Detroit Tigers by the police chief, I was dismissed from the road trip we were on and sent back to Rocky Mount, North Carolina. When I was finally, a week or so later, reactivated I was moved down in the lineup from fourth to eighth, and the next day released.

8. Jordan, *A False Spring,* 134.

9. Thrift, *The Game According to Syd,* 160.

10. About half of those who wanted to stay in baseball, however, wanted to do it outside of the pro ranks, such as coaching at the high school or college level. Often the reason was a desire to stay close to home. Coaching in pro ball involves living away from home and spending half the season on the road, and many were tired of that. Some also said that they wanted to stay close to home to make up for lost time with their children.

11. Robinson, *Extra Innings,* 155.

12. House, *The Jock's Itch,* 124.

13. Mantle, "Time in a Bottle," 74.

14. Quoted in Lamb, *Stolen Season,* 104.

15. Tharenou, *Work-Derived Self-Esteem,* 316, 339.

16. The literature on job satisfaction offers other clues to why many retired players miss baseball and find their new jobs less satisfying. Some researchers have, for example, found job satisfaction and motivation strongly linked to "skill use"— workers being able to employ their skills in the jobs they do. Presumably ballplayers, like other professional athletes, rank at or near the top on this variable. Peter Warr, in *Work, Unemployment, and Mental Health,* reported that concrete measures of performance (or, in the jargon, "environmental clarity") is also strongly related to job satisfaction. Again, baseball gets high marks: ballplayers know exactly how well they are doing because almost every aspect of their play is measured by one statistic or another. The other variables that researchers find strongly correlated with job satisfaction, notably "valued social position" and work with high levels of "social interaction" (i.e., closely working with other people), are also evident in baseball. Indeed, these two variables underlay the players' comments about the loss of prestige and camaraderie.

17. House, *The Jock's Itch,* 126.

18. Ibid.

19. Whitford, *Extra Innings,* 11.

20. Ibid., 41.

21. Wolff, "Triumphant Return," 7.

22. As noted in Chapter 3, about half of all players drafted each year are taken from the college ranks. Many of those who have not yet graduated, along with many

players who signed out of high school, attend college in the off-season. By the time their baseball careers are over, perhaps as much as 60 percent have either a two- or four-year degree.

23. Most of them (57 percent) work in professional baseball, while 11 percent coach or manage in high schools and colleges.

24. The data may be skewed a bit toward ex-players who went on to college and who have fared well.

25. Dave Smith, interview with Ryan Almstead, July 10, 1998.

26. Jim Bouton, interview with Ryan Almstead, July 18, 1998.

27. See Thrift, *The Game According to Syd*, 150–54.

28. Informally, I asked about twenty friends and students—all people out of baseball—for their perceptions of how well baseball players fared after leaving the game. Slightly over half thought they did not do well, especially the minor leaguers who did not have the enormous savings that most major league veterans were believed to have. Many thought the ex-players would always miss the "excitement" or "thrill" of playing a professional sport.

29. Bowman and Zoss, *Diamonds in the Rough*, 346.

30. Michener, *Sports in America*, 225.

31. Ibid., 227. Roger Kahn (Kahn, *Good Enough to Dream*), however, did not see it quite the same way. He came away from his visits to his former Dodgers heroes not full of sorrow but rather with the belief that most of the players had "aged with dignity, courage, and with hope." Kahn did recognize, however, that it was difficult for athletes to grow old.

32. Mangolick, "The Boys of Spring," 112.

33. House, *The Jock's Itch*.

Chapter 11. It Ain't the Same Old Ball Game

1. International players are not drafted and were not counted in the percentage of players who had some college education.

2. W. C. Kaskhatus, "The Origins of Baseball Chapel and the Era of the Christian Athlete, 1973–1990," *Nine* 7, no. 2 (1999): 75–90.

3. For a discussion of why many young black athletes have turned to basketball, see D. C. Ogden and M. L. Hilt, "Collective Identity and Basketball: An Explanation for the Decreasing Number of African-Americans on America's Baseball Diamonds," *Journal of Leisure Research* 35, no. 2 (2003): 213–27. Also, D. C. Ogden and R. A. Rose, "Using Giddens' Structuration Theory to Examine the Waning Participation of African Americans in Baseball," *Journal of Black Studies* 35, no. 4 (2005): 225–45.

4. The major causes of the international labor migration to U.S. baseball are the following: (1) the availability of highly skilled players in other parts of the world,

along with a shortage of talented U.S. players, due to the growing popularity of other sports and activities (e.g., computer games) that have diverted many U.S. youth away from baseball; (2) Major League expansion, which began in the 1960s, resulted in a shortage of qualified players in North America; (3) salary arbitration and the escalation in the salaries of U.S. players after the introduction of free agency in 1976 made cheaper foreign talent especially attractive; (4) the introduction of free agency in Japanese baseball allowed the likes of Hideki Matsui, Ichiro Suzuki, and others to come to the United States.

5. Robert Whiting, *The Meaning of Ichiro* (New York: Warner Books, 2004), 30.

6. For an excellent account of women in baseball, see Jean Ardell, *Breaking into the Game* (University of Southern Illinois Press, 2005).

7. One exception are the older "organization" players, such as Pat Borders, who stay on because they are being groomed for a possible coaching position once their playing days are over.

8. Some people have asked why I didn't study baseball earlier in my career. Perhaps it was too risky. Warren Goldstein, a professor of American studies and the author of *Playing for Keeps: A History of Early Baseball*, recalls the reaction of his would-be dissertation advisor, who, upon receiving Goldstein's prospectus to study baseball history, stormed into the department office and slammed the proposal on the secretary's desk, loudly announcing that he would have nothing further to do with this "ridiculous" project. Years later, when his academic credentials were secure, Goldstein finally turned his pen to baseball. Only recently have universities reached the maturity where studying sport is seen as legitimate, and endeavors like this book are acceptable scholarship.

Bibliography

Alexander, Charles C. *Our Game: An American Baseball History.* New York: Henry
Holt and Company, 1991.

Allen, Lee. "The Superstitions of Baseball Players." *New York Folklore Quarterly*
20, no. 2 (1964): 98–109.

Altherr, Thomas. "Eros at Bat, on the Bases, and on the Mound." Manuscript. 1999.

Angell, Roger. *The Summer Game.* New York: Viking, 1972.

Ardell, Jean. "Letter from Spring Training in the Cactus League." *Nine: A Journal of
Baseball History and Social Policy Perspectives* 2, no. 2 (1995): 365–66.

Ball, D. W. "Failure in Sport." *American Sociological Review* 41 (1976): 726–39.

Ballew, Bill. *Brave Dreams: A Season in the Atlanta Braves Farm System.* Indi-
anapolis: Howard W. Sams and Co., 1996.

Barrett, Richard. *Culture and Conduct: An Excursion in Anthropology.* Belmont,
Calif.: Wadsworth Publishing Co., 1984.

Blahnik, Judith, and Phillip S. Schulz. *Mudhens and Mavericks: The New Illustrated
Travel Guide to Minor League Baseball.* New York: Viking Studio Books, 1995.

Blake, Mike. *The Minor Leagues.* New York: Winwood Press, 1991.

Blanchard, Kendall. *The Anthropology of Sport: An Introduction.* Westport, Conn.:
Bergin and Garvey, 1995.

Bosco, Joesph. *The Boys Who Would Be Called Cubs.* New York: William Morrow,
1990.

Bouton, Bobbie, and Nancy Marshall. *Home Games: Two Baseball Wives Speak
Out.* New York: St. Martin's Press, 1983.

Bouton, Jim. *Ball Four.* New York: World, 1970.

Bowman, John, and Joel Zoss. *Diamonds in the Rough: The Untold History of Baseball.* New York: Macmillan, 1989.

Cline, Cheryl. "Essays from *Bitch:* The Women's Rock Newsletter with Bite." In
The Adoring Audience: Fan Culture and Popular Media, edited by Lisa A. Lewis.
New York: Routledge, 1992.

Coakley, Jay J. *Sport in Society: Issues and Controversies.* St. Louis: Mosby, 1978.

Connor, Anthony J., ed. *Baseball for the Love of It: Hall-of-Famers Tell It Like It Was.* New York: Macmillan, 1982.

Cook, Kevin, and Mark Mravic. "Back to the Crack of the Bat." *Sports Illustrated,* August 9, 1999, 32.

Coser, Lewis. *Greedy Institutions: Patterns of Undivided Commitment.* New York: Free Press, 1974.

Crute, B. "Wives of Professional Athletes: An Inquiry into the Impact of Professional Sport on the Home and Family." Ph.D. diss., Boston College, 1981.

Curry, T. J. "Fraternal Bonding in the Locker Room." *Sociology of Sport Journal* 8 (1991): 119–35.

Doody, J. "Baseball in America: A Sociological Perspective." Manuscript. 1995.

Dorfman, H., and Karl Kuehl. *The Mental Game of Baseball: A Guide to Peak Performance.* South Bend, Ind.: Diamond Communications, 1995.

Ehrenreich, Barbara, et al. "Beatlemania: Girls Just Want to Have Fun." In *The Adoring Audience: Fan Culture and Popular Media,* edited by Lisa A. Lewis. New York: Routledge, 1992.

Eitzen, D. Stanley, and George H. Sage. *Sociology of American Sport.* Dubuque, Iowa: W. C. Brown Co., 1978.

Felson, Richard. "Self and Reflected Appraisal among Football Players." *Social Psychology Quarterly* 44 (1981): 116–26.

Felson, Richard, and George Gmelch. "Uncertainty and the Use of Magic." *Current Anthropology* 20 (1980): 587–89.

Fine, Gary Alan. *With the Boys: Little League Baseball and Preadolescent Culture.* Chicago: University of Chicago Press, 1987.

Fornoff, Susan. *Lady in the Locker Room.* Champaign, Ill.: Sagamore Publishing, 1993.

Gammons, Peter. "End of an Era." *Sports Illustrated,* July 24, 1989, 16–23.

Garratt, S. "All of Us Love All of You." In *Signed, Sealed, and Delivered: True Life Stories of Women in Pop,* edited by S. Steward and S. Garratt. Boston: South End, 1984.

Garvey, Cynthia. *The Secret Life of Cyndy Garvey.* New York: Doubleday, 1989.

Gaston, Paul L. "Resurgence of Minor League Baseball." In *Cooperstown Symposium on Baseball and the American Culture,* edited by Alvin L. Hall. Westport, Conn.: Meckler in association with the State University of New York College at Oneonta, 1991.

Gay, Douglas, and Kathlyn Gay. *The Not-So-Minor Leagues.* Brookfield, Conn.: Millbrook Press, 1996.

Gerlach, Larry. *The Men in Blue: Conversations with Umpires.* New York: Viking, 1980.

Giamatti, Bartlett. *Take Time for Paradise: Americans in Their Games.* New York: Summit Books, 1991.

Gmelch, George. "Baseball Magic." *Human Nature* 1 (1978): 32–50.

Gmelch, George, and J. J. Weiner. *In the Ballpark: The Working Lives of Baseball People.* Washington, D.C.: Smithsonian Institution Press, 1998.

Gmelch, George, and Patricia San Antonio. "Groupies and American Baseball." *Journal of Sport and Social Issues* 22 (1998): 32–45.

Golenbock, Peter. *The Forever Boys: The Bittersweet World of Major League Baseball as Seen through the Eyes of the Men Who Played One More Time.* New York: Carol Publishing Group, 1991.

Gooden, Dwight, with Richard Woodley. *Rookie.* Garden City, N.Y.: Doubleday, 1985.

Gordon, Alison. *Foul Ball! Five Years in the American League.* New York: Dodd, Mead, 1985.

Gregorich, Barbara. *Women at Play: The Story of Women in Baseball.* San Diego: Harcourt Brace, 1993.

Hall, Alvin L., ed. *Cooperstown Symposium on Baseball and the American Culture.* Westport, Conn.: Meckler in association with the State University of New York College at Oneonta, 1991.

Hall, Donald. *Dock Ellis in the Country of Baseball.* New York: Coward, McCann, and Geoghegan, 1976.

———. *Fathers Playing Catch with Sons: Essays on Sport, Mostly Baseball.* San Francisco: North Point Press, 1985.

Hargrove, Sharon. *Safe at Home: A Baseball Wife's Story.* College Station: Texas A&M University Press, 1989.

Harris, D. S., and D. Stanley Eitzen. "The Consequences of Failure in Sport." *Urban Life* 8 (1978): 177–88.

Hernandez, Keith, and Mike Bryan. *Pure Baseball: Pitch by Pitch for the Advanced Fan.* New York: Harper Collins, 1994.

Hersch, Hank. "The Good Wood." *Sports Illustrated,* April 14, 1986, 66–80.

Hill, P., and B. Lowe. "The Inevitable Metathesis of the Retiring Athlete." *International Review of Sport Sociology* (1979): 5–32.

Higgins, George V. "Fields of Broken Dreams." *The American Scholar* 59 (Spring 1990): 199–210.

Horn, J. "Jolting Joe Has Left and Gone Away." *Psychology Today* 19 (June 1985): 70.

House, Tom. *The Jock's Itch: The Fast-Track Private World of the Professional Ballplayer.* Chicago: Contemporary Books, 1989.

Jenson, Joli. "Fandom as Pathology: The Consequences of Characterization." In *The Adoring Audience: Fan Culure and Popular Media,* edited by Lisa A. Lewis. New York: Routledge, 1992.

Johnson, Earvin "Magic," with William Novak. *My Life.* New York: Random House, 1992.

Jordan, Pat. *A False Spring.* New York: Dodd, Mead, 1975.

Kahn, Roger. *Boys of Summer.* New York: Harper and Row, 1972.

———. *Good Enough to Dream.* Garden City, N.Y.: Doubleday, 1985.

Kerrane, Kevin. *Dollar Sign on the Muscle: The World of Baseball Scouting.* New York: Beaufort Books, 1984.

Klein, Alan. *Baseball on the Border: A Tale of Two Laredos.* New Jersey: Princeton University Press, 1997.

Klinkowitz, Jerry, ed. *Writing Baseball.* Urbana: University of Illinios Press, 1991.

Koppett, Leonard. *The New Thinking Fan's Guide to Baseball.* New York: Simon and Schuster, 1991.

Kurkjian, T. "Inside Baseball." *Sports Illustrated,* May 5, 1997, 18.

Laband, David N., and Bernard F. Lentz. "The Natural Choice." *Psychology Today* 30 (1985): 36–39.

Laband, David N., and Bernard F. Lentz. *The Roots of Success: Why Children Follow in Their Parents' Career Footsteps.* New York: Praeger, 1985.

Lackritz, James R. "Salary Evaluation for Professional Baseball Players." *The American Statistician* 16 (1990): 4–8.

Lamb, David. *Stolen Season: A Journey through American and Baseball's Minor Leagues.* New York: Warner Books, 1991.

Lazzaro, Sam. *More Than a Ballgame: An Inside Look at Minor League Baseball.* Blacksburg, Va.: Pocahontas Press, 1997.

Levine, Peter, ed. *Baseball History.* College Station, Pa.: Cyberbooks, 1990.

Lewis, Lisa A., ed. *The Adoring Audience: Fan Culture and Popular Media.* New York: Routledge, 1992.

Lingo, Will. "At Long Last, Fresno Gets Its PCL Franchise," *Baseball America,* 27 October 1997.

Lowry, Philip J. *Green Cathedrals: The Ultimate Celebration of All 271 Major League and Negro League Ballparks, Past and Present.* Reading, Mass.: Addison-Wesley, 1992.

Malinowski, Bronislaw. *Magic, Science, and Religion and Other Essays.* Garden City, N.Y.: Doubleday, 1954.

Mandel, Brett. *Minor Players, Major Dreams.* Lincoln: University of Nebraska Press, 1997.

Mangolick, D. "The Boys of Spring." *Vanity Fair,* May 1997.

Mantle, Mickey. "Time in a Bottle." *Sports Illustrated,* April 18, 1994, 66.

Manuel, John. "Bat Wars." *Baseball America,* January 18–31, 1999, 26.

Messner, Michael. *Power at Play: Sports and the Problem of Masculinity.* Boston: Beacon Press, 1992.

Michener, James A. *Sports in America.* New York: Random House, 1976.

Miller, Delbert Charles. *Handbook of Research Design and Social Measurement.* 5th ed. Newbury Park, Calif.: Sage Publications, 1991.

Minor Leagues, Major Dreams. Directed by Nathan Kaufman. Cameron Park, Calif., 1992. Videocassette.

Modica, Andrea. *Minor League*. Washington, D.C.: Smithsonian Institution Press, 1993.

Moore, Monica. *Nonverbal Behavior in Women as a Function of Situation and Sex Partner(s)*. Columbia: University of Missouri Press, 1981.

Morris, Bob. "An Enduring Game of Catch." *Orlando Sentinel Florida Magazine,* April 5, 1992, 83–84.

Murphy, S. M., and D. P. Jowdy. "Imagery and Mental Practice." In *Advances in Sport Psychology,* edited by Thema S. Horn, 221–50. Champaign, Ill.: Human Kinetics Publishers, 1992.

Nauen, Elinor. *Diamonds Are a Girl's Best Friend: Women Writers on Baseball.* Boston: Faber and Faber, 1994.

Nixon, Howard, and James Frey. *A Sociology of Sport.* Belmont, Calif.: Wadsworth, 1996.

Ojala, Carl F., and Micheal T. Gadwood. "The Geography of Major League Baseball Player Production, 1876–1988." In *Cooperstown Symposium on Baseball and the American Culture,* edited by Alvin L. Hall. Westport, Conn.: Meckler, 1991.

Panek, Richard. *Waterloo Diamonds.* New York: St. Martin's Press, 1995.

Patton, Phil. "Wooden Bats Still Reign Supreme at the Old Ball Game." *Smithsonian,* October 1984, 152–76.

Pepitone, Joe, with Berry Stainback. *Joe, You Coulda Made Us Proud.* New York: Dell Publishing, 1975.

Phillips, Louis, and Burnham Holmes. *Yogi, Babe, and Magic: The Complete Book of Sports Nicknames.* Englewood Cliffs, N.J.: Prentice Hall, 1993.

Pilcher, William W. *The Portland Longshoremen: A Dispersed Urban Community.* New York: Holt, Rhinehart, and Winston, 1972.

Powers, Anne. "Psychological and Sociological Effects of Professional Sports on the Wives and Families of Athletes." Ph.D. diss., Ohio State University, 1990.

Pronger, B. "Gay Jocks: A Phenomenology of Gay Men in Athletics." In *Sport, Men, and the Gender Order: Critical Feminist Perspectives,* edited by M. A. Messener and D. S. Sabo. Champaign, Ill.: Human Kinetics Publishers, 1990.

Radar, Ben, and Randy Roberts. *Baseball: A History of America's Game.* Urbana: University of Illinois Press, 1992.

Regalado, Samuel. "The Minor League Experience of Latin American Baseball Players in Western Communities, 1950–1970." *Journal of the West* 16 (January 1987): 65–70.

Ringolsby, T. "Later Rounds Determine Draft Success," *Baseball America,* April 14–27, 1997, 8.

Robinson, Frank. *Extra Innings.* New York: McGraw-Hill, 1988.

Rubin, John, and Paul McCarthy. "Keep Your Eye on the Ball." *Psychology Today* 20 (April 1988): 11.

Salisbury, Luke. *The Answer Is Baseball.* New York: Vintage Books, 1990.

Schwarz, A. "Drafts Inexact Science Misses All Future All-Stars," *Baseball America,* June 10, 1992.

———. "Radar Love." *Baseball America,* November 25–December 8, 1996, 14–15.

———. "Gwynn Staves Off Old Age with Video." *Baseball America,* May 31–June 13, 1999, 8.

Seigel, Barry, ed. *The Sporting News Baseball Register.* St. Louis: Sporting News Publishing Company, 1991.

Seligman, Miles. "By the Numbers." *The Village Voice,* 44, no. 31 (1999): 205.

Seymour, Harold. *Baseball: The People's Game.* New York: Oxford University Press, 1990.

Shlain, Bruce. *Baseball Inside Out: Winning the Games within the Games.* New York: Viking, 1992.

Sommers, Paul M. "An Empirical Note on Salaries in Major League Baseball." *Social Science Quarterly* 71 (1990): 861–67.

Stouffer, Samuel Andrew, et al. *The American Soldier.* Princeton, N.J.: Princeton University Press, 1949.

Sullivan, William M. *Work and Intergrity: The Crisis and Promise of Professionalism in America.* New York: HarperCollins, 1995.

Tharenou, Phyllis. *Work-Derived Self Esteem.* Brisbane: University of Queensland Press, 1977.

Thrift, Syd, and Barry Shapiro. *The Game According to Syd: The Theories and Teachings of Baseball's Leading Innovator.* New York: Simon and Schuster, 1990.

Torrez, Danielle Gagnon. *High Inside: Memoirs of a Baseball Wife.* New York: G. P. Putnam's Sons, 1983.

Trice, Harrison Miller. *Occupational Subcultures in the Workplace.* Ithaca, N.Y.: ILR Press, 1993.

Trice, Harrison, and Janice Beyer. *The Cultures of Work Organizations.* Englewood Cliffs, N.J.: Prentice Hall, 1993.

Verducci, Tom. "Staff Infection." *Sports Illustrated,* May 19, 1997, 84–89.

Wann, Daniel L. *Sport Psychology.* Englewood Cliffs, N.J.: Prentice Hall, 1997.

Warr, Peter. *Work, Unemployment, and Mental Health.* Oxford: Oxford University Press, 1987.

Warshay, Leon H. "Baseball in Its Social Context." In *Social Approaches to Sport,* edited by Robert M. Pankin. Rutherford, N.J.: Fairleigh Dickinson University Press, 1982.

Weinstein, L., G. A. Prather, and Anton F. DeMan. "College Baseball Pitchers' Throwing Velocities as a Function of Awareness of Being Clocked." *Perceptual and Motor Skills* (1987): 1185–86.

White, G. Edward. *Creating the National Pastime: Baseball Transforms Itself, 1903–1953.* Princeton, N.J.: Princeton University Press, 1997.

Whitford, David. *Extra Innings: A Season in the Senior League.* New York: Harper Collins, 1991.

Wickersham, Seth. "Great Unknown." *ESPN Magazine,* July 24, 2000, 101.

Will, George. *Men at Work: The Craft of Baseball.* New York: Macmillan, 1990.

Williams, Peter. "You Can Blame the Media: The Role of the Press in Creating Baseball Villains." In *Cooperstown Symposium on Baseball and the American Culture,* edited by Alvin L. Hall. Westport, Conn.: Meckler in association with the State University of New York College at Oneonta, 1991.

Williams, Savannah, and Wayne Patterson. "In His Father's Spike Marks: Parental Influence on the Choice of Baseball as a Career." In *Cooperstown Symposium on Baseball and the American Culture,* edited by Alvin L. Hall. Westport, Conn.: Meckler in association with the State University of New York College at Oneonta, 1991.

Winfield, David, and Tom Parker. *Winfield: A Player's Life.* New York: W.W. Norton, 1988.

Wolff, Rick. "Triumphant Return." *Sports Illustrated,* August 21, 1989, 6–9.

———. *What's a Nice Harvard Boy Like You Doing in the Bushes?* Englewood Cliffs, N.J.: Prentice Hall, 1975.

Wulf, Steve. "Minor League Baseball: A Staple of Americana for Many Years, Is Now in the Midst of a Sensational Comeback." *Sports Illustrated,* July 23, 1990, 26–29.

Zack, William. "The Scout." *Choptalk,* June 1994.

Index